CAMBRIDGE LANGUAGE EDUCATION
Series Editor: Jack C. Richards

This new series draws on the best available research, theory, and educational practice to help clarify issues and resolve problems in language teaching, language teacher education, and related areas. Books in the series focus on a wide range of issues and are written in a style that is accessible to classroom teachers, teachers-in-training, and teacher educators.

In this series:

Agendas for Second Language Literacy *by Sandra Lee McKay*

Reflective Teaching in Second Language Classrooms *by Jack C. Richards and Charles Lockhart*

Educating Second Language Children: The whole child, the whole curriculum, the whole community *edited by Fred Genesee*

Understanding Communication in Second Language Classrooms *by Karen E. Johnson*

The Self-directed Teacher: Managing the learning process *by David Nunan and Clarice Lamb*

Functional English Grammar: An introduction for second language teachers *by Graham Lock*

Teachers as Course Developers *edited by Kathleen Graves*

Classroom-based Evaluation in Second Language Education *by Fred Genesee and John A. Upshur*

From Reader to Reading Teacher: Issues and strategies for second language classrooms *by Jo Ann Aebersold and Mary Lee Field*

Functional English Grammar

An introduction for second language teachers

Graham Lock

City University of Hong Kong

CAMBRIDGE
UNIVERSITY PRESS

PUBLISHED BY THE PRESS SYNDICATE OF THE UNIVERSITY OF CAMBRIDGE
The Pitt Building, Trumpington Street, Cambridge CB2 1RP, United Kingdom

CAMBRIDGE UNIVERSITY PRESS
The Edinburgh Building, Cambridge CB2 2RU, United Kingdom
40 West 20th Street, New York, NY 10011–4211, USA
10 Stamford Road, Oakleigh, Melbourne 3166, Australia

© Cambridge University Press 1996

First published 1996
Third printing 1997

Printed in the United States of America

Typeset in Sabon

Library of Congress Cataloging-in-Publication Data

Lock, Graham
Functional English grammar : an introduction for second language
teachers / Graham Lock.
p. cm. – (Cambridge language education)
Includes bibliographical references and index.
ISBN 0-521-45305-4. – ISBN 0-521-45922-2 (pbk.)
1. English language – Study and teaching – Foreign speakers.
2. English language – Grammar. 3. Functionalism (Linguistics)
I. Title. II. Series.
PE1128.A2L54 1996
428'.007–dc20   95-1743
                                                                           CIP

A catalog record for this book is available from the British Library

ISBN 0-521-45305-4 hardback
ISBN 0-521-45922-2 paperback

Contents

Series editor's preface

Although there are numerous works that provide grammatical descriptions of English, as well as many reference grammars of English intended for use by language teachers, this book offers a different treatment of pedagogical grammar, for it approaches the subject from a functional perspective. The term *functional* has a number of meanings in linguistics, but in Lock's book it refers to an approach to understanding grammar that focuses on how language works to achieve a variety of different functional and communicative purposes. The emphasis is thus on how the purpose for which language is used and the contexts in which it appears affect the choices speakers and writers make. Lock draws, in particular, on the work of M. A. K. Halliday, which has been used in a wide range of applied linguistics contexts but is not well known among ESL teachers, particularly in North America. The book is hence a welcome introduction to a functional perspective on English grammar.

Readers who are acquainted with other approaches to grammar will find some material that is familiar in Lock's functional description of English, as well as much that is different. The differences are prompted by the need to explain the relationships between different elements of grammar and how they interact to create meanings in context. Drawing on a wide range of authentic examples to illustrate how form and function are interrelated in language use, the book will be of particular interest to language teachers. The analysis of key grammatical categories and components in English and the explanations of typical problems second language learners have in acquiring various aspects of grammar will provide teachers not only with a clearer understanding of the nature of grammar but also with many ideas on how teaching can address typical learning problems.

Jack C. Richards

Preface

This book presents a functional approach to grammar – that is, grammar is viewed as a resource for creating meaning in spoken and written discourse. This is very different from the view of grammar as a set of rules, rules that are to be applied even when they seem arbitrary. By taking a functional perspective, this book is able to provide teachers with ways of thinking about English grammar in use that they will be able to draw on in various aspects of their work, including:

- Integrating a functional perspective on grammar into English language teaching programs and materials
- Understanding the kinds of problems learners may have with grammar
- Evaluating coursebooks and grammar reference materials
- Helping learners develop a better understanding of the functional resources of grammar

The first chapter provides an orientation to functional grammar and introduces a number of basic concepts. Subsequent chapters explore the resources of the grammar for doing a number of things, including:

- Representing *things* (Chapters 2 and 3)
- Representing various kinds of *processes,* such as doing, happening, thinking, perceiving, liking, wanting, being, and having (Chapters 4 through 7)
- Representing time (Chapter 8)
- Interacting (Chapter 9)
- Expressing attitudes and judgments (Chapter 10)
- Organizing messages so that they are coherent and relevant to context (Chapter 11)
- Creating complex sentences (Chapter 12)

Functional English Grammar is designed so that it can be used either as a text for preservice and in-service teacher education programs or for self-study. No previous study of English grammar or linguistics is assumed. Each chapter contains numerous examples, tasks that enable the reader to apply concepts introduced in the text, and discussion questions that encourage the reader to explore teaching applications. In addition, the final chapter explores issues in the learning and teaching of grammar and reviews methodological options for teaching grammar in the classroom.

The examples used for analysis are for the most part authentic and are drawn from a range of contemporary spoken and written sources. In addition, longer extracts from eight different texts are included in the Appendix and are referred to throughout the book so that the reader can gradually develop an understanding of how selections from the different grammatical resources of English together contribute to the meaning of a text. A number of examples are also given from languages other than English. These are intended to indicate some of the ways in which other languages differ from English and some of the problems learners of English may consequently face.

The use of some technical terms is inevitable in the systematic description of any phenomenon as complex as language. However, an effort has been made to keep terminology to the minimum and where possible to use terms which may be familiar to readers or whose meanings are fairly transparent. At the end of each chapter is a list of the main terms introduced in the chapter. Equivalent (or nearly equivalent) terms used by other grammarians are listed where appropriate.

Symbols and abbreviations used with the examples in this book warrant explanation:

An asterisk is used preceding an example to indicate that it represents a form which would normally be unacceptable in any context, for example, *he may went there before.* In some cases, these may be errors produced by learners; in other cases, they may be examples invented to illustrate an ungrammatical form.

A question mark is used preceding an example to indicate that it represents a form which would be unacceptable to most people, or would be acceptable only in very rare contexts, for example, *?I want that you should remember this.*

In addition, numbered examples are frequently authentic samples of spoken or written English. Those followed by *[inv.]* were invented by the author. When the number of an example is followed by the letter *a* or *b* or *c,* etc., the example is a variant of an earlier example with the same number and is not an authentic sample.

Acknowledgments

The approach to the analysis of English grammar adopted in this book is essentially that developed by M. A. K. Halliday and his colleagues. My copy of Halliday's *An Introduction to Functional Grammar* (London: Edward Arnold, 2d ed., 1994) has become very well worn. I have also drawn valuable insights from Christian Matthiessen's *Lexicogrammatical Cartography: English Systems* (Tokyo, Taipei, and Dallas: International Sciences Publishers, in press), which he generously made available to me before it went to press, and from J. R. Martin's *English Texts: System and Structure* (Amsterdam and Philadelphia: Benjamins, 1992). However, because this book is intended for teachers rather than for linguists or text analysts, I have felt free to adapt, reinterpret, and use selectively the insights provided by the above-mentioned works, and there may be some material in this book that these authors would not agree with.

Other works that I have frequently consulted with profit are *Syntax: A Functional-Typological Introduction* by Talmy Givon (Amsterdam and Philadelphia: Benjamins, vol. 1 1984, and vol. 2 1990); *Collins COBUILD English Grammar* (London and Glasgow: Collins, 1990); and the indispensable *A Comprehensive Grammar of the English Language* by Randolph Quirk, Sidney Greenbaum, Geoffrey Leech, and Jan Svartvik (London and New York: Longman, 1985).

I have benefited enormously from feedback given by the following colleagues, who took the time to read and comment on drafts of chapters or, in some cases, of the whole book: Jackie Greenwood, Lawrence Lau, Marilyn Lewis, David Li Chor Shing, Charles Lockhart, Lindsay Miller, Martha C. Pennington, Gillian Perrett, and Amy B. M. Tsui. I am also indebted to two outstanding functional linguists, Christopher Nesbitt and Guenter Plum, for answering (electronically and face-to-face) my many queries. Thanks also to the MATESL students of the City University of Hong Kong for pointing out inconsistencies and ambiguities in early drafts of this book.

Finally, I should like to express my gratitude to the series editor, Jack C. Richards, for his encouragement and advice at all stages in the preparation of this book.

Graham Lock

1 *Some basic concepts*

This chapter will consider the nature of functional grammar and its relevance to language learning and teaching. It will then begin to explore some basic organizational principles of grammar and the relationship between grammar and meaning. Finally, a number of grammatical functions will be introduced and illustrated.

1.1   Formal and functional grammar

There are many ways of describing the grammar of a language. One approach sees grammar as a set of *rules* which specify all the possible grammatical structures of the language. In this approach, a clear distinction is usually made between grammatical (sometimes called *well-formed*) sentences and ungrammatical sentences. The primary concern is with the *forms* of grammatical structures and their relationship to one another, rather than with their meanings or their uses in different contexts. A grammarian interested in this kind of description will often use for analysis sentences that have been made up to illustrate different grammatical rules rather than sentences drawn from real world sources.

Another approach sees language first and foremost as a system of communication and analyzes grammar to discover how it is organized to allow speakers and writers to make and exchange meanings. Rather than insisting on a clear distinction between grammatical and ungrammatical forms, the focus is usually on the appropriateness of a form for a particular communicative purpose in a particular context. The primary concern is with the *functions* of structures and their constituents and with their meanings in context. A grammarian interested in this kind of description is likely to use data from authentic texts (the term *text* is used here for both spoken and written language) in specific contexts.

The former approach to grammatical analysis is often called **formal,** while the latter approach is normally called **functional.** The two approaches are not, of course, mutually exclusive. Formal analyses must at some stage take account of meaning and function, and functional analyses must at some stage take account of form. However, most descriptions of grammar can be located primarily within one or the other of these two approaches.

The difference between formal and functional approaches can be briefly and simply illustrated with the following sentence:

(1)   I had also been rejected by the law faculty.

In analyzing the *voice* of this sentence, both formal and functional grammarians would agree in calling it a *passive voice* sentence. However, a formal grammarian would be primarily interested in finding the best abstract representation of the structure of the sentence and in how it might be related to the structure of the *active voice* sentence:

(1) a. The law faculty had also rejected me.

For example, rules can be set out to show how sentence 1 may be derived from sentence 1a. These would specify (1) the movement of the constituent *the law faculty* to a position at the end of the sentence following the preposition *by;* (2) the movement of the constituent *me* to the front of the sentence and its change in form to *I;* and (3) the change from *had . . . rejected* (an active form of the verb) to *had . . . been rejected* (a passive form of the verb).

A functional grammarian would also take note of such formal differences between the active and passive structures. However, he or she would be more concerned with questions such as (1) how the communicative effect of the message in the sentence is different when it begins with *I* rather than with *the law faculty,* (2) what the effect is of putting *the law faculty* at the end of the sentence, and (3) what features of the context may have led the writer to select passive rather than active voice. These kinds of questions would lead the linguist to consider the role of the *voice* system in organizing information within sentences and texts, and in contributing to coherent communication (questions that will be considered in Chapter 11 of this book).

1.2   Functional grammar and language teaching

Learning a second language is hard work and for most people involves a considerable commitment of time and effort. The work may sometimes be enjoyable, but learners do not usually undertake such a task without the expectation of a payoff. A few people, academic linguists perhaps, may embark upon the study of a language for the intellectual satisfaction of acquaintance with unfamiliar grammatical patterns and elegant paradigms of forms, but for most learners the payoff will be the ability to communicate with other speakers or writers of the language. To be of real use to language learners and teachers, therefore, a description of the grammar of a language needs to do more than simply lay out the forms and structures of the language. It needs to show what they are for and how they are used. As already noted, the primary aim of a functional grammatical analysis is to understand how the grammar of a language serves as a resource for making and exchanging meanings. A functional grammar is therefore the kind of grammar most likely to have useful things to say to language learners and teachers. (Issues in grammar and language teaching are explored more fully in Chapter 13.)

A number of "brands" of functional grammar have appeared within the last twenty years or so. As this is not a textbook in linguistics, the author has felt free to select and adapt insights from a number of sources. However, a good deal of the theoretical and analytical framework adopted in the book, as well as much of the terminology, is drawn from the work of systemic-functional linguists, in particular M. A. K. Halliday (e.g., Halliday 1978, 1994). Over the years, Halliday has had a great influence on both mother tongue and second language education, and systemic-functional analyses of English grammar have already proved themselves very useful in a number of applications, ranging from multilingual text generation by computer (e.g., Bateman et al. 1991) to the development of first language literacy (e.g., Martin 1993; Christie et al. 1992; Rothery 1984 and 1993). It seems likely that work coming from this tradition will have an increasing role in all areas of applied linguistics.

1.3   Levels of analysis

In studying how language works, linguists of all schools recognize several different levels of analysis. The following four levels are those usually identified:

Phonology
Lexis
Grammar
Semantics

Phonology refers to the sound system of a particular language, roughly corresponding to the more familiar term pronunciation. In this book, phonology will be touched upon only briefly.

Lexis refers to the words of a language, roughly corresponding to the more familiar term vocabulary.

Grammar includes two aspects: (1) the arrangement of words and (2) the internal structure of words. For example, in a sentence such as

(2) He kicked the ball out of the court.

we may be interested in how the words combine to form a meaningful sentence. This aspect of grammar is usually called **syntax.** However, we may also be interested in the fact that the word *kicked* can be divided into two parts – *kick + ed.* The first part represents an action and the second marks past tense. This aspect of grammar is called **morphology.** The focus of this book will be primarily on syntax rather than morphology.

Semantics refers to the systems of meaning in a language, for example, how sentences relate to the real world of people, actions, places, and so on.

There are no clear-cut dividing lines between the four levels of phonology, lexis, grammar, and semantics: different analyses will make the divisions in different ways. Taking a functional approach to grammar, this book is concerned with meaning to a much greater extent than a formal approach might be. In other words, this book examines areas which some grammarians might prefer to deal with separately under the rubric *semantics.* And since this book focuses on how grammar can express meaning, it also sometimes becomes difficult to draw a clear line between grammar and lexis (the two are in fact sometimes put on the same level and referred to as *lexico-grammar*).

1.4   The organization of grammar

The organization of grammar itself can now be considered. Two important concepts are needed for this, rank and class.

1.4.1 Rank

Rank refers to different levels of organization *within* grammar. Consider the following example:

(3) People throw stones.   [*inv.*]

This stretch of language consists of one sentence and three words. **Sentence** and **word** are two ranks of grammatical organization, which in English are recognized in the writing system, the former by an initial capital letter and final full stop (or other final punctuation mark) and the latter by spaces between the units. As will be seen later, identification of sentences in speech is not so straightforward. However, it is useful to retain the term *sentence* for the highest rank of grammatical organization in both spoken and written English.

Speakers of English generally agree over boundaries between words. However, there may be some variation or indeterminacy about where some words begin and end. For example, should we write: *non standard, non-standard,* or *nonstandard*? Linguists also sometimes recognize a single unit (technically *lexical item*) where the writing system has two or more words. For example, *brought up* as in *she brought up the question first* can be analyzed as one lexical item (compare: *she raised the question first*). However, for present purposes the term *word* as it is usually understood will be adequate.

It is also necessary to recognize ranks between sentence and word. For example, compare the following sentence with sentence 3.

(4)   People who live in glass houses shouldn't throw stones.

Like number 3 (*People throw stones*), this sentence can be analyzed into three **units.** Two of these units can be regarded as expansions of single words in number 3.

(i)   People who live in glass houses (expansion of *people*)
(ii)   shouldn't throw (expansion of *throw*)
(iii)   stones

These units are called **groups.** Note that one of the groups (iii) contains only one word, but it is still referred to as a group. Thus, this sentence consists of three groups, each of which consists of a number of words. Another way of saying this is that the words are units which are **constituents** of the groups and the three groups are units which are **constituents** of the sentence. This is set out in Figure 1.1.

Further patterns of organization can be recognized within the groups. These will be dealt with when the internal structures of the various types of groups are examined. It is not necessary to recognize any rank between group and word.

It is necessary, however, to recognize an additional rank between group and sentence. Take, for example, the following sentence.

(5) She's great fun but her husband's rather dull.

The two underlined units are called **clauses.** This sentence consists of two clauses, each of which consists of a number of groups, which themselves consist of a number of words, as shown in Figure 1.2. The word *but,* which is a **conjunction** and joins the two clauses, does not really belong to either clause, although it is conventionally analyzed as belonging to the second clause.

Thus, the analyses in this book will take into account four ranks within grammar: **word, group, clause,** and **sentence.**

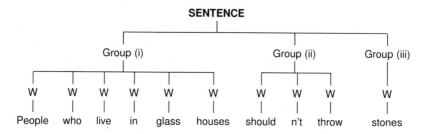

Figure 1.1   Sentence, group, and word.

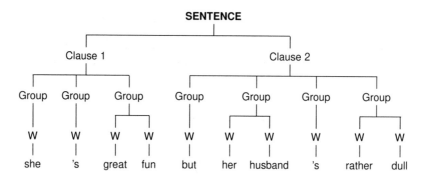

Figure 1.2   Sentence, clause, group, and word.

1.4.2   Class

Terms like **noun** (N) and **verb** (V) are names of *word classes* (traditionally known as *parts of speech*). The words in sentence 3 can be labeled according to their class.

```
     N      V       N
People  throw  stones
```

The same class labels are also used to label the groups. Thus, in number 4 *People who live in glass houses* is a *noun group* (NG) and *shouldn't throw* is a *verb group* (VG).

Two other major word classes are **adjective** (Adj) and **adverb** (Adv) and the same class labels are also used to label the groups, for example:

```
              Adj
```
(6)   That's good!

```
                 Adj
```
(7)   We remained firm friends

Adj G
(8) . . . a letter from a very angry parent . . .

Adj G
(9) . . . we were both good enough, . . .

Adv
(10) Some of my white friends abruptly changed schools.

Adv
(11) Fortunately, the situation has changed for the better.

Adv G
(12) It is very deeply rooted in the American psyche.

Adv G
(13) Almost inevitably, the swelling of the ranks has brought with it . . .

Note that *pronouns,* such as *he, she,* and *it,* are regarded as a subcategory of noun.

1.4.3 Phrases

Where the term *group* has been used here, some grammars use the term **phrase,** for example, *noun phrase* and *adverb(ial) phrase* for noun group and adverb group. However, in this book the only kind of phrase which is recognized is the **prepositional phrase.**

A clear distinction can be made between groups and phrases. As all the previous examples of groups show, a group can be thought of as an expanded word. A phrase, however, is more like a miniclause. For example, the following clauses contain a verb group followed by a noun group. The noun group functions as what later will be called the *object.*

Clauses

VG   NG/OBJECT
She slowly approached the two frightened boys . . .

VG   NG/OBJECT
The expedition had crossed the bridge that morning.

A prepositional phrase has a comparable structure, with a **preposition** (a word like *to, from, behind, in, on, with, through,* and *about,* or a complex preposition such as *in front of, in spite of,* and *by means of*) followed by a **prepositional object.** For example:

Prepositional phrases

PREP   NG/PREP Obj
toward the two frightened boys

PREP   NG/PREP Obj
across the bridge

In other words, the words following prepositions in prepositional phrases are not *expansions* of the prepositions but *objects* of prepositions. Prepositional phrases are therefore quite different kinds of structures from groups.[1] Note, however, that prepositional phrases normally operate at the same rank as groups. We should, strictly speaking, therefore refer to group/phrase rank, rather than just group rank.

1.4.4   Embedding

One of the noun groups in number 4 – *people who live in glass houses* – contains within it a clause – *who live in glass houses.* Cases of this kind, where one unit is used as a constituent of another unit at the same or a lower rank, are known as **embedding.** The clause *who live in glass houses* is therefore said to be *embedded* within the noun group *people who live in glass houses.* Embedding will be considered in more detail in Section 3.4.2.

Task 1a

1. Analyze the following sentences by identifying clauses, groups, and phrases, ignoring cases of embedding.
2. Label the word class of each group. (You may find it useful to look back at the examples given in Section 1.4.2.)
   a. Most probably the students will be producing some very good work.
   b. In my opinion the changes were made too quickly.
   c. He opened the door and strode into the hall.
   d. Columbus may not have discovered America, but his accomplishments brought the medieval world into a new era.
   e. At the start of the week, hopes for a peaceful conclusion to the dispute were quite high.

All tasks are discussed or answered at the end of each chapter. The reader is advised to do the tasks and read the discussions before continuing.

1.5   Meaning in grammar

In order to think about grammar as a resource for making and exchanging meanings, it is necessary to explore what might be meant by *meaning.* Three types of meaning within grammatical structures can be identified: **experiential meaning, interpersonal meaning,** and **textual meaning.**

---

1 Note, however, that there are such things as prepositional groups. For example, the underlined constituents in the following prepositional phrases are all prepositional *groups* (expansions of prepositions): *all along the watchtower; right behind the main quadrangle; directly in front of the theater.*

1.5.1   Experiential meaning

Consider the following example:

(14) Peggy arrived at 8.30.

The question *What does this sentence mean?* might be answered by explaining what it is about. It is about one person (*Peggy*) performing an action in the past (*arrived*) at a certain time (*at 8.30*). Meaning in this sense is known as **experiential** meaning. Experiential meaning has to do with the ways language represents our experience (actual and vicarious) of the world as well as the inner world of our thoughts and feelings. In other words, it is concerned with how we talk about actions, happenings, feelings, beliefs, situations, states, and so on, the people and things involved in them, and the relevant circumstances of time, place, manner, and so on.

1.5.2   Interpersonal meaning

The following sentences are also possible:

(14) a. Did Peggy arrive at 8.30?
(14) b. Peggy might have arrived at 8.30.

Sentences 14a and 14b are still about the same things as number 14 – one person performing an action at a certain time in the past. So they both have the same *experiential* meaning as number 14. However, they differ in other aspects of meaning.

Sentence 14 informs the listener that the event took place, whereas number 14a calls on the listener to confirm or deny that the event took place. The term *statement* is used to refer to sentences like number 14, and the term *question* is used to refer to sentences like number 14a. (These terms are further considered in Section 9.1.)

Sentence 14b is still a statement, but it introduces into the sentence an assessment by the speaker of the likelihood of the event actually having taken place.

Numbers 14a and 14b differ from number 14 (and from each other) in terms of their interpersonal meaning. **Interpersonal meaning** has to do with the ways in which we act upon one another through language – giving and requesting information, getting people to do things, and offering to do things ourselves – and the ways in which we express our judgments and attitudes – about such things as likelihood, necessity, and desirability.

1.5.3   Textual meaning

There are still other ways in which the experiential meaning of number 14 could be expressed, for example:

(14) c. She arrived at 8.30.
(14) d. It was Peggy who arrived at 8.30.

In number 14c the name of the performer of the action has been replaced by the pronoun *she*. The listener would need to refer to something in the context (e.g., a preceding sentence such as *Peggy left for the office at about 8*) to know who *she* refers to.

In number 14d, the experiential content has been reorganized so that there is a strong focus on *Peggy*. Again, the listener would need to refer to some aspect of the context to understand why this structure has been used. For example, another speaker might have just said *I hear that Kitty came in at 8.30 this morning* and 14d is being used to deny that it was Kitty and affirm that it was Peggy who arrived at 8.30.

Numbers 14c and 14d differ from number 14 (and from each other) in their *textual meaning*. **Textual meaning** has to do with the ways in which a stretch of language is organized in relation to its context. Textual meaning is important in the creation of coherence in spoken and written text.

Nearly every clause of English simultaneously expresses these three aspects of meaning. Subsequent chapters of this book will explore the grammatical resources of English for the expression of such meanings.

1.6   Grammatical functions

In order to explore the contribution to meaning of any unit of grammatical structure, it is necessary to consider its function in context. However, the word **function** has been used in a variety of ways in linguistics and in language teaching and it is necessary to clarify how the term is being used in this book.

In the approach to language teaching usually called *functional language teaching,* functions usually refer to things such as asking for directions, describing people and places, talking about the past, and so on. In other words, functions refer to possible *uses* of language.

Function in this sense is not a very useful starting point for the investigation of grammar. First, there is no agreed-upon list of the total number of such functions in English nor is there an agreed-upon classification of them. Second, it is not helpful to assign just one function to each sentence or each utterance. As we have seen, each clause simultaneously embodies three kinds of meaning – experiential, interpersonal, and textual – and they all need to be taken into account to understand how the clause functions in context.

Finally, such lists of the functional uses of language are external to language, in the sense that they are arrived at by observing (or introspecting about) the different things people do with language and then trying to match these with different linguistic expressions. However, in order to explore grammar as a communicative resource, it is more useful to start from the other end, in other words to investigate how language itself is organized to enable speakers (and writers) to express different kinds of meaning – experiential, interpersonal, and textual. The first step is to try to interpret the functions of grammatical structures and their constituents. Functions in this sense are sometimes called *grammatical functions.* These are the kinds of functions that this book is mainly concerned with.

1.6.1 Two grammatical functions: Subject and Finite

It was noted in Section 1.4.2 that words and groups can be labeled according to class. For example, the constituents of the following clause (from Extract 4) can be labeled in this way.

	PP	NG	VG

(15) With a quick movement of its tail, the sea-serpent would overturn

	NG

fishing boats . . .

However, this does not identify the functions of the constituents, that is, what the different classes of phrases and groups are doing in this particular clause. One function that may be familiar is that of **Subject.** (From now on the first letter of *functions* will always be uppercase.) In this clause, the noun group *the sea-serpent* is functioning as the Subject. Another way of putting it is to say that the Subject function in this clause is *realized* (i.e., *expressed*) by the noun group *the sea-serpent.*

A function closely associated with Subject is that of **Finite.** In this clause, the *auxiliary* (a subclass of verb) *would* is functioning as Finite. The functions Subject and Finite are crucial to the realization of *mood,* which is a system of the grammar centrally concerned with the expression of interpersonal meaning. Mood will be explored in some detail in Chapter 9. This chapter is concerned just with the identification and some of the formal characteristics of Subjects and Finites.

1.6.1.1 IDENTIFYING SUBJECTS

The most straightforward way to identify the Subject of a clause is to add to the clause what is called a *tag.* The pronoun in the tag refers back to the Subject of the clause, as illustrated in the following examples.

	SUBJECT		Tag

(15) a. . . . the sea-serpent would overturn fishing boats, wouldn't it?

(16)   SUBJECT
         It   attacked wood-cutters and travellers through the mountains,

         Tag
         didn't it?

                                              Tag
         SUBJECT
(17)   The third evil was a man named Zhou Chu, wasn't it?

                                           Tag
                           SUBJECT
(18)   Your electronic gizmo,   you   've still got it, haven't you?

Subjects can be identified by other formal characteristics:

1. Subjects are typically noun groups, as in all the preceding examples (note that pronouns also count as noun groups). Less typically, certain kinds of clauses can also function as Subjects. These include *that* clauses, *wh-* clauses, *to* + V[2] (often called *infinitive*) clauses, and V*ing* clauses. For example:

    (19) That they would succeed in overcoming the difficulties of a multitude of languages, currencies, legal systems, and countless clashes of culture is a formidable demonstration of European willpower.   (*that* clause)
    (20) How he did it is obvious; why he did it is less clear.   (These are both *wh*-clauses — note that *how* is classified as a *wh-* word, along with *who, when, where, why, what,* and *which.*)
    (21) . . . but to finish the whole lot will take a week at least.   (*to* + V clause)
    (22) Really understanding this aspect of grammar needs a fair bit of work.   (V*ing* clause) [*inv.*]

    As well as functioning as Subjects, the five underlined clauses in numbers 19 through 22 share the characteristic that they are not operating at clause rank. Like the embedded clause in *People who live in glass houses,* they have, in a sense, been shifted down to group rank. Unlike *who live in glass houses,* however, they are not embedded within noun groups but function on their own as if they were noun groups. Because of this, such clauses are called **nominal clauses.**

2. Five pronouns have special subject forms – *I, he, she, we,* and *they* (as opposed to *me, him, her, us,* and *them*), for example:

    (23)   They didn't really believe her. [*inv.*]
    (23) a. She didn't really believe them.

3. In *declarative mood clauses* (clauses that make statements, considered in detail in Chapter 9), the Subject is normally the noun group (or nominal clause) which immediately precedes the Finite, as in all the previous examples.

2 V is used to symbolize the base form of the verb (i.e., the form with no inflections such as *-s, -ed,* or *-ing* added).

1.6.1.2 IDENTIFYING FINITES

Finites can similarly be identified by the addition of a tag, which picks up not only the Subject but also the Finite of the preceding clause, as in numbers 15a to 18 above, in which the Finites are *would, did, was,* and *have.* In addition, Finites have the following characteristics:

1. If a verb group contains a Finite, the Finite will always be the first constituent of the verb group, for example, *did* in number 23 and *have* in the following:

   (24)   Philosophers have latterly been explaining . . .

   Note that if the verb group contains only one word, that word may function as Finite. For example, *is* and *needs* in numbers 19 and 22 are both functioning as Finites, as is *appeared* in this example:

   (25)   At about the same time, a huge sea-serpent appeared at the bridge across the river.

2. Only Finites are marked for *tense.*[3] For example, compare number 23 with:

   (23) b. They don't really believe her

   and compare number 25 with:

   (25) a. Every day, a huge sea-serpent appears at the bridge across the river.

3. Only Finites are marked for **number agreement,** that is, their form changes according to the number and person of the Subject. This is seen most clearly with the verb *be,* for example:

   (26)   The clown was very funny
   (26) a. The clowns were very funny.
   (27)   They are measured in the same amount . . .
   (27) a. It is measured in the same amount . . .
   (28)   We are going to do an art activity.
   (28) a. I am going to do an art activity.

   However, with other Finites, number distinctions are neutralized in the past tenses and there is no unique form to agree with *I.* There are also some Finites which show no agreement at all, the *modal* auxiliaries (see Section 4.1.2).

1.6.1.3 CLAUSES WITHOUT FINITES

In traditional grammar, every clause was said to contain a Finite. However, most grammarians nowadays also recognize **nonfinite clauses,** that is,

---

3 Strictly speaking, this should read *absolute tense.* The difference between absolute tense and relative tense will be explained in Chapter 8.

clauses which lack the function Finite. Note that the verb form Vs – the base form of the verb plus s (e.g., *kicks* and irregular forms like *is* and *has*) – is always Finite. A clause containing a Vs form will therefore always be a finite clause, for example:

       Finite clause   Finite clause
(29) Bob never *barks* when he *is* working sheep.

On the other hand, the verb forms V*ing* (e.g., *being, having,* and *kicking*) and *to* + V (the *infinitive,* e.g., *to be, to have, to kick*), are always nonfinite. Therefore clauses containing verb groups beginning with these forms will be nonfinite clauses, for example:

      Nonfinite clause
(30) When *working* on taps, insert the plug and . . .

             Nonfinite clause
(31) It goes upstairs *to be* crushed between rollers . . .

The form V (e.g., *have* and *kick*), and, for many verbs, the form V*ed* (e.g., *had* and *kicked*), may be finite or nonfinite.[4] For example:

          Finite clause
(32)   They *pass* all queries on to the course coordinator. [*inv.*]

            Nonfinite clause
(32) a. What they do is *pass* all queries on to the course coordinator.[5]

         Nonfinite clause
(33)   *Eulogised* in a Western constituency for probity and veracity, he is more

      often . . .

          Finite clause
(33) a. They *eulogised* him for his probity and veracity.

However, some verbs with irregular finite V*ed* forms, such as *broke, wrote, ate, was,* and *were,* also have separate nonfinite forms (symbolized V*en*), such as *broken, written, eaten,* and *been.* For example:

       Finite clause
(34) Mr. Kohl *wrote* to Jacques Delors . . .

       Nonfinite clause
(35) *Written* on bamboo tablets, the texts are mainly lists of . . .

Task 1b

Identify the Subject and the Finite of each finite clause in the following sentences.

---

4 An exception is the V form *be,* which is always nonfinite. The finite V forms of the verb *be* are *am* and *are.* Finite and nonfinite forms of the verb group are set out fully in Figure 4.1.

5 Note that this nonfinite clause is also a nominal clause.

1. I don't know why he always gets so angry about a few students talking in class.
2. The answers given by the students have on the whole been very good.
3. Despite all our hard work, the project will not be finished on time.
4. The territory in order to survive and prosper will need political stability.
5. To err is human, to forgive is – out of the question.
6. The slide-lathe enabled machines of precision to be made.
7. Only Princess Diana's wedding dress was awaited more impatiently, greeted more enthusiastically, and copied more slavishly than are new ideas in psychology.
8. There are problems with the identification of the Subject in existential clauses. [*inv.*]

1.6.1.4 LEARNING AND TEACHING SUBJECT AND FINITE

Many languages, particularly non-Indo-European languages, do not have a regular distinction between finite and nonfinite verb forms in the way English does. However, mastering the functions of Subject and Finite from the beginning is important for second language learners. Without such mastery, they are likely to have many problems with basic sentence structure, with the formation of questions and negatives, and with the marking of tense and of number agreement.

Even fairly advanced learners sometimes use a nonfinite verb group where a finite verb group is required, for example:

(36) *I have little exercise except sometimes I swimming with my brother.

Note that in this example, the presence of the Subject *I* in the second clause requires the presence of a Finite. In other words, a nonfinite clause with neither Subject nor Finite would be possible (*except sometimes swimming with my brother*), or a finite clause with both functions (*except I sometimes go swimming with my brother*).

Problems with number agreement can be particularly persistent, as in the following from an advanced learner:

(37) ?The level of imports during the last quarter of the year have begun to decline.

In this example, the problem no doubt lies in the identification of *imports* rather than *level* as the *head* (i.e., the part of the noun group which determines the number agreement; see Section 2.2.1) of the noun group which is functioning as Subject. Such lack of Subject-Finite agreement is quite common in native speaker speech and in many cases would hardly be noticed. However, in formal written English such lack of agreement is regarded as unacceptable.

Questions for discussion

- How useful do you think it is for learners of English to have some *explicit* knowledge of the functions of Subject and Finite? How might this knowledge be developed?
- How can intermediate or advanced learners who still make frequent agreement errors in their written work be helped to develop self-editing skills in this area?

1.6.2 More functions: Object, Complement, Adjunct, and Predicator

Subject and Finite are just two functions that can be identified in clauses. In number 15 (*With a quick movement of its tail, the sea-serpent would overturn fishing boats*), *the sea-serpent* was identified as Subject and *would* as Finite. Two other functional constituents can be identified in this clause – an **Object** *fishing boats* and an **Adjunct** *with a quick movement of its tail.*

Objects normally follow the Finite and the rest of the verb group. Like Subjects, they are typically realized by noun groups. A characteristic of Objects is that they can normally become the Subjects of related passive voice clauses, as in the passive voice version of number 15.

```
          SUBJECT
(15) a. Fishing boats would be overturned by the sea-serpent . . .
```

Some clauses may have two Objects – an **Indirect Object** (IO) and a **Direct Object** (DO). The Indirect Object precedes the Direct Object. Both Objects can usually become Subjects of related passive voice clauses, for example:

```
              IO      DO
(38)    I'll give you your paper
```

(38) a. You will be given your paper . . .

(38) b. Your paper will be given to you . . .

However, clauses which have *linking* verbs, like *be, look,* and *have,* do not have Objects. They have what are called **Complements.**

```
          SUBJECT              COMPLEMENT
(39) Most of the trees were    eucalypts
```

	SUBJECT		COMPLEMENT
(40)	You	look	very pale.

	SUBJECT	COMPLEMENT
(41)	The town	has a fine Norman church.

Complements can be realized by noun groups, nominal clauses, adjective groups, and prepositional phrases. The various kinds of Complement will be explored in Chapter 7.

Adjuncts are typically realized by prepositional phrases or adverb groups. They cannot function as Subjects and it is often possible to omit them without making the clause ungrammatical (as *with a quick movement of its tail* could be omitted from number 15).

The only constituent of the clause in number 15 for which a function has not yet been identified is the word *overturn*. The label for this constituent is **Predicator.** The Predicator is everything in the verb group *except* the Finite. In other words, a nonfinite verb group such as *having been examined* consists only of a Predicator, whereas a finite verb group such as *has been examined* consists of a Finite (*has*) and a Predicator (*been examined*). Sometimes a Finite verb group consists of only one word, as in *they* examined *the object carefully.* In this case, the single word *examined* realizes both Finite and Predicator functions.

Task 1c

1. Identify all the Adjuncts in this sentence from Extract 3.[6]

After a wild youth, he embraced the way of asceticism, became a begging monk called Bodhi Dharma and went to China as a Buddhist missionary, vowing never to sleep in penance for his wild night of debauchery.

2. What kinds of experiential meanings are expressed by the Adjuncts in this sentence?
3. Which verb groups in the sentence consist only of a Predicator?

Summary

1. Formal and functional grammatical analyses differ in their approaches and assumptions. Formal analysis tends to be primarily interested in abstract representations and relationships between structures and less interested in meaning and context. Functional analysis tends to view language as a communicative resource and to be primarily interested in how linguistic structures express meaning.

6 All references to numbered extracts refer to the extracts found at the end of the book, in the Appendix.

2. Four levels of linguistic analysis can be identified: semantics (meaning), grammar (the arrangement of words and word shape), lexis (vocabulary), and phonology (pronunciation).
3. Within grammar itself, four ranks of organization can be recognized: sentence, clause, group/phrase, and word.
4. A group can be thought of as an expanded word. A phrase has a structure which makes it more like a miniclause.
5. Embedding takes place when a unit of one rank is used as a constituent within another unit at the same or at a lower rank.
6. The major word classes are nouns, verbs, adjectives, and adverbs.
7. Nearly every clause expresses three kinds of meaning: experiential meaning, which is concerned with the representation of our experience of the world and of the inner world of our thoughts and feelings; interpersonal meaning, which is concerned with language as interaction and the expression of judgments and attitudes; and textual meaning, which organizes the former two kinds of meaning into coherent text relevant to its context.
8. Five clause-rank grammatical functions are Subject, Finite, Predicator, Object, and Adjunct.
9. Subjects normally precede the Finite in declarative clauses and determine the person and number of the Finite (if marked). Subjects are typically realized by noun groups.
10. Finites are normally marked for tense and may be marked for number agreement (i.e., agreeing with the person and number of the Subject).
11. Predicator function is realized by everything in the verb group *except* the Finite.
12. Objects typically follow the Finite and Predicator in declarative clauses. A constituent functioning as Object in an active clause can normally become the Subject of a related passive clause. Objects are typically realized by noun groups.
13. Adjuncts are additional constituents that cannot become Subjects of related clauses and can often be omitted. Adjuncts are typically realized by adverb groups and prepositional phrases.

Key terms introduced

This text	*Alternative(s) used in the field*
adjective	
Adjunct	sometimes divided into Adjunct, Conjunct, and Disjunct; adverbial
adverb	
class	parts of speeech

clause

Complement   (This term sometimes covers Direct Object,
                                 Indirect Object, and Complement)

conjunction

constituent

Direct Object   complement

embedding   relativization (for embedding of finite clauses
                                 only)

experiential meaning   propositional, ideational (this latter term in-
                                 cludes logical meaning as well as experien-
                                 tial meaning)

Finite   finite verb; finite auxiliary

formal grammar

function

functional grammar

grammar

group   phrase (used for both group and phrase)

Indirect Object   complement

interpersonal meaning   interactional

lexis

morphology

nominal clauses   noun clauses

nonfinite clause   participial phrase, infinitive phrase

noun

number agreement

Object   Complement

phonology

phrase

Predicator   Predicator sometimes refers to the function of
                                 the whole verb group, including the Finite

preposition

Prepositional Object   prepositional complement

prepositional phrase

rank

semantics

sentence   clause complex

Subject

syntax

textual meaning   pragmatic function (this term is sometimes
                                 extended to cover interpersonal meanings)

unit

verb

word

Discussion of tasks

Task 1a

NG = noun group ; VG = verb group; AdjG = adjective group; AdvG = adverb group; PP = prepositional phrase; Conj = conjunction.

```
       AdvG              NG            VG                    NG
a. Most probably the students will be producing some very good work
```

```
       PP              NG          VG        AdvG
b. In my opinion the changes were made too quickly.
```

```
        CLAUSE                      CLAUSE
  NG   VG    NG       Conj    VG         PP
c. He opened the door  and  strode into the hall.
```

```
                        CLAUSE
     NG              VG                  NG
d. Columbus may not have discovered America,
```

```
                             CLAUSE
  Conj        NG             VG              NG              PP
   but  his accomplishments brought the medieval world into a new era.
```

```
           PP                              NG              VG
e. At the start of the week, hopes for a peaceful conclusion to the dispute were
```

```
   AdjG
quite high.
```
Note that the noun group *hopes . . .* has a prepositional phrase (*for a peaceful conclusion to the dispute*) embedded within it.

Task 1b

1. Subject: *I*, Finite: *do*
   (b) Subject: *he*, Finite: *gets*
2. Subject: *The answers given by the students*, Finite: *have*
3. Subject: *the project*, Finite: *will*
4. Subject: *The territory*, Finite: *will*
5. Subject: *To err*, Finite: *is*
   (b) Subject: *to forgive*, Finite: *is*
6. Subject: *The slide-rule*, Finite: *enabled*
7. Subject: *Princess Diana's wedding dress*, Finite: *was*. The Subject and Finite of the second and third finite clauses in this sentence have been omitted and are *understood* to be the same as in the first clause (i.e., [*Princess Diana's wedding dress was*] *greeted more enthusiastically* and [*Princess Diana's wedding dress was*] *copied . . .*)
   Subject: *new ideas in psychology*, Finite: *are*. Note that the usual order of Subject followed by Finite is reversed here.
8. Subject: *There*, Finite: *are*. Note that in *there is* and *there are* structures such as this (technically known as *existential clauses*), *there* occurs in

front of the Finite and is picked up by the tag (*there are . . . aren't there?*) and can therefore be identified as the Subject. However, the Finite is marked for number agreement with the following noun group (at least in formal written English).

Task 1c

1. The adjuncts are all underlined.

   <u>After a wild youth</u>, he embraced the way of asceticism, became a begging monk called Bodhi Dharma and went <u>to China</u> <u>as a Buddhist missionary</u>, vowing <u>never</u> to sleep <u>in penance for his wild nights of debauchery</u>.

2. In this sentence, the Adjuncts add information about time (*after a wild youth*), place (*to China*), role (*as a Buddhist missionary*), frequency (*never*) and reason (*in penance for his wild nights of debauchery*). These are all kinds of *circumstances.* Circumstances are typically expressed by Adjuncts in this way. However, there are other kinds of Adjuncts, including some which express interpersonal meaning (e.g., *unfortunately, luckily, probably*) and some which express textual meaning (e.g., *however, on the other hand, similarly*).[7] See Sections 9.5.4, 10.1.6, and 11.6.

3. The verb groups *called, vowing,* and *to sleep* consist only of a Predicator, and are therefore nonfinite verb groups.

---

7 In Halliday (1994) Adjuncts of frequency or usuality such as *never* are treated as modal (i.e., interpersonal) Adjuncts. In this book, they are treated as Circumstantial Adjuncts of time (see Section 8.5.3).

2 Representing things I: Nouns and noun groups

This chapter will explore some of the resources of English grammar for representing what can be called *things* or *entities.* The key word class for performing this function is the class of nouns, traditionally defined as the names of persons, places, or things. This definition distinguished nouns from verbs, which were defined as the word class used to express doing, happening, or being. Such definitions are not really adequate. For example, words such as *action, evaporation,* and *laughter* clearly express doing or happening, yet they are nouns not verbs. However, there is an element of truth in the traditional definitions. Everyday nouns, such as *table, cat, person, book,* or *chair,* do represent things that we can see or touch, and everyday verbs such as *walks, breaks,* and *is* do represent doing, happening, and being. When speakers or writers express certain kinds of doing, happening, and being by nouns rather than by verbs, they are, in a sense, choosing to treat them as if they were things. There may be a number of reasons for doing this, some of which will be explored in Section 3.5.

Task 2a

Decide which of the following words are *not* nouns, and state, as explicitly as you can, how you reached your decision in each case: reference, hear, life, kick, kicked, lived, sunshine, often, activity, on, act, talk, living, loneliness.

2.1 Countability

A major source of problems for learners is the area of *countability* in English nouns.

2.1.1 *Mass and count nouns*

Nouns in English can be classified as **count nouns,** which have both singular and plural forms, or **mass nouns,** which have only one form. In the following list, the nouns in column 1 are classified as mass nouns and those in column 2 are classified as count nouns.

1	*2*
rubbish (*rubbishes)	a book, books
advice (*advices)	an idea, ideas
electricity (*electricities)	an inch, inches
bravery (*braveries)	a month, months

Like any other grammatical distinction, the distinction between mass noun and count noun is based on meaning. When we use a count noun we are representing something as occurring in the form of discrete entities which can be counted (*one book, two books,* and so on), whereas when we use a mass noun we are representing something as an undifferentiated whole which cannot be counted. Names of materials and substances (e.g., *wood, oil, grass*) and names of abstract entities (e.g., *love, intelligence, power*) are all typically mass nouns, whereas names of things which occur in individual units (e.g., *cat, tree, box*) and names of parts of a whole (e.g., *bit, slice, inch*) are all typically count nouns.

Although the distinction between mass and count nouns in English is not an arbitrary one, it is often hard for a learner of English to see why certain nouns should be mass rather than count, or vice versa. For example, the following nouns are often used as count nouns by learners; that is, they are either used in the plural (as in the examples given) or they are used in the singular preceded by *a* or *an*. It is interesting to consider why these nouns should be mass rather than count (or indeed whether there are any contexts in which it might be acceptable to use them as count nouns).

furnitures	traffics	informations
luggages	sceneries	advices
equipments	homeworks	machineries
punctuations		

2.1.2   Nouns which are both count and mass

A further complicating factor for learners is that many nouns can be used both as count nouns and as mass nouns. However, there is normally a clear difference in meaning between a noun used as a count noun and the same noun used as a mass noun.

Task 2b

The following nouns are often used both as count nouns and as mass nouns. In each case think of a context in which the noun could be used as a count noun and a context in which it could be used as a mass noun (e.g., *Chocolate is very fattening* — mass; *Help yourself to a couple of chocolates* – count). What generalizations can you make about the differences in meaning between the count and mass uses of these nouns?

cheese	chocolate	experience
wine	life	kindness
metal	noise	business
cake	war	work
egg	time	

Many nouns which we think of as typically count or as typically mass *can* be used as nouns in the opposite category in certain, often somewhat unusual, contexts. For example, it is not very difficult to think of contexts in which a noun like *cat,* which is normally count, could be used as a mass noun. For example:

(1) After the accident, there was cat all over the windscreen.   [*inv.*]
(2) Last night we had roast cat for dinner.   [*inv.*]

Because of this, it is sometimes argued that we should not classify nouns into count and mass. Instead we should classify the *uses* of nouns into count or mass. However, most nouns are clearly either count or mass in the contexts in which they are most frequently used; and from the learner's point of view, it is worth first learning the countability status of a noun in the meaning and context most likely to be encountered. Later, learners may learn to manipulate countability for particular effects. For this, learners need to have access to a good dictionary in which the different uses of nouns associated with any differences in their countability status are clearly marked.[1]

2.1.3   *Invariable plural nouns and collective nouns*

A small class of nouns have only plural forms. The most common of these are nouns which refer to tools and clothes which have symmetrical parts, such as *scissors, pliers, trousers,* and *glasses.*

There is also a subclass of count nouns which when singular may nevertheless be referred to by plural pronouns such as *they* and which as Subjects may take a plural Finite. These nouns refer to a group of things (e.g., *committee, family,* and *staff*) and are normally called **collective nouns.** The choice of whether to use a plural or a singular pronoun or Finite usually depends on whether the speaker or writer is thinking of the group as a whole or of the group as composed of individual members. For example:

1 For example, *Collins COBUILD English Language Dictionary* (Collins 1987) and *Longman Dictionary of Contemporary English* (Longman 1978) are both dictionaries suitable for learners which clearly mark count and mass usages of nouns.

(3) The committee has tried to strike a balance . . .
(4) The committee have found it hard to reach a consensus.
(5) My family is living in Kuala Lumpur . . .
(6) My family are now all living overseas.   [*inv.*]
(7) Our staff is growing very fast.   [*inv.*]
(8) Our staff are all highly qualified.

There is some difference between U.S. and British usage with collective nouns. In formal American English, particularly written English, the use of plural pronouns and plural Finites with such nouns is generally avoided.

Students may confuse collective nouns with count nouns which refer to individuals, for example:

(9) *We have recruited many new staffs recently.   (compare: *many new workers*)

Words such as *people, cattle,* and *police,* which, when functioning as Subjects, always require plural Finites, are sometimes also regarded as collective nouns. However, for the learner, they are probably best treated as irregular plural forms.

Questions for discussion

- Think of a context in which all or most of the nouns used would be count nouns and a context in which all or most of the nouns would be mass nouns. How can these contexts be exploited for teaching purposes?
- Suggest some activities for advanced learners to sensitize them to differences in meaning between the same nouns treated as mass and treated as count.

2.2   Noun groups

As noted in Chapter 1, noun groups can be regarded as expanded nouns, as in the following example:

N
<u>Water</u> is cold.

NG
<u>The water in the bath</u> is cold.

Note that *water* in the first sentence and *the water in the bath* in the second sentence are both operating at the same rank, and it is conventional to refer to both of them as noun groups, despite the fact that *water* is one word.

2.2.1   The structure of noun groups

The structure of a noun group such as *the water in the bath* may be represented as:

PREMODIFIER HEAD POSTMODIFIER
The   water   in the bath.

The **head** of the group is the noun whose experiential function is to represent the *thing,* where *thing* covers both inanimate and animate – including human – entities. The term **Thing** is used to refer to this function. A noun group may include other groups, phrases, or even clauses embedded within it (see Section 1.4.4). Thus the noun group *the water in the bath* contains within its postmodifier a prepositional phrase (*in the bath*), a constituent of which (*the bath* – the Prepositional Object) is itself a noun group with its own premodifier + head structure.

Task 2c

1. Decide which of the following units are *not* noun groups.
2. Be as explicit as you can about how you made your decisions.
3. Identify the head of each noun group.

the continual heavy rain
because of the large number of applicants
the poor
are being subject to attack
fast food
information display
the ghost in the machine
the lowering of the entire drainage basin by about a foot every
    4,000 years
about yesterday's meeting
a user's guide
the one you told me about last night

2.2.2   Functions within noun groups

A noun group such as:

(10) the two slightly nervous assistant lecturers from the English department
    who taught grammar last year   [*inv.*]

contains a large number of constituents performing a number of different functions. The head noun *lecturers* functions as Thing. We can gloss the various functions of the premodifiers and postmodifiers as follows:

The	referring
two	quantifying
slightly nervous	describing
assistant	classifying
who taught grammar last year	qualifying

The rest of this chapter will be concerned with the referring function. The other functions will be looked at in Chapter 3.

2.3   Referrers

Words which perform the function of referring normally come first in the noun group. They provide information about the scope of reference of the Thing (represented by the head). The term **Referrer** will be used for this functional constituent of the noun group.

2.3.1   *Generic, indefinite, and definite reference*

Referrers may signal whether a whole *class* of things is being referred to or just a *subset* of a class. For example, *teachers* in *teachers are odd* refers to teachers as a class – all teachers are considered by the speaker to be odd. In this case ZERO (i.e., the *lack* of an explicit Referrer before the head), together with the plural form of the noun, signals that the reference is to a class of things (although this interpretation depends also on context, as will become clear later).

However, *a teacher* in *a teacher got drunk last night* does not refer to all teachers but to a subset, in this case a subset of one teacher. Here the Referrer is *a.*

The Referrers may also signal whether a subset is *unidentified* or *identified.* For example, *a teacher* in the above example is not identified – the reader or listener is not expected to know exactly which teacher got drunk. However, in *the teachers who taught us English literature last year* the reader or listener is expected to know exactly which teachers are being referred to (the ones who taught us English literature last year and no others). The reference is identified.

The usual term used for reference to a whole class of things is **generic reference,** the usual term for reference to an unidentified subset is **indefinite reference,** and the usual term for reference to an identified subset is **definite reference.** These are the terms that will be used in the rest of this chapter. The things being referred to are called the *referents.*

There are four main kinds of Referrers:

Articles:	*a(n), the,* ZERO (i.e., no expressed Referrer)
Demonstratives:	*this, that, these, those*
Possessives:	*my, her, his, your, our, their, Peter's, Rosina's,* etc.
Inclusives:	*all, either, both, each, every, neither, no*

The rest of this chapter will explore the use of articles, demonstratives, and possessives. The inclusive Referrers will be further considered in the next chapter (Section 3.1).

The words *some* and *any* are also often included among the articles. However, they are used in ways different from the other Referrers and could equally well be classified as Quantifiers. For convenience, their various uses will all be dealt with in Section 3.2, on Quantifiers.

Articles, demonstratives, and possessives are mutually exclusive. In other words, they cannot be used to produce sequences like *the my, your those, Rosina's the,* and so on.

There is no simple, one-to-one relationship between the selection of Referrer and the three reference categories generic, indefinite, and definite. For a start, the choice of Referrer depends upon whether the head is a singular noun, a plural noun, or a mass noun, as Figure 2.1 shows. A further complication is that there is no form *dedicated* to the expression of generic reference. Generic reference is expressed by extending the uses of both definite and indefinite articles. Thus, generic reference may be expressed by more than one form, and the same form may be interpreted in one context as generic reference and in another as definite or indefinite reference. For example, the underlined noun groups in numbers 11 and 12 both refer in general to the class of things *computers,* despite the fact that in 11 the article is *the* and in 12 it is ZERO.

(11) The computer has revolutionized the distribution of information.   [*inv.*]
(12) Computers have revolutionized the distribution of information.

On the other hand, the same article (ZERO) is used in examples 13 and 14, although in 13 the reference is indefinite and in 14 it is generic.

(13) Would you like chips or peanuts with your drinks?   [*inv.*]
(14) I hate chips.   [*inv.*]

	Singular	**Plural**	**Mass**
Definite	*the* cat, *this* cat, *that* cat, *our* cat,	*the* cats, *these* cats, *those* cat, *our* cat	*the* water, *this* water, *that* water, *our* water
Indefinite	*a* cat	cats	water

Figure 2.1   Referrers (excluding inclusives).

Task 2d

Which of the following noun groups (taken from Extracts 1, 2, 4, 5, 6, and 7) would you consider to have generic reference, which indefinite, and which definite? (You will need to refer to the extracts.) The first example in each extract has already been done.

Extract 1   *the kiwi* (line 1) = generic reference. (The reference is to all kiwis – kiwis as a class.)

Kiwis (line 3)
Australia's equally cute national symbol (line 6)
the nostrils on the end of their long bill (line 11)

Extract 2   *those countries which are affected by the MONSOON RAINS* (line 1) = definite reference. (The reference is to the subclass of countries affected by the monsoon rains, and no other countries.)

The population of Monsoon Asia (line 9)
ECOLOGICAL NICHES (line 9)
these ecological niches (line 12)
densities (line 14)
a DEMOGRAPHIC TRANSITION (line 18)

Extract 4   *a small town in Jiangnan* (line 1) = indefinite reference. (The fact that the town is named in the first part of the sentence does not make the reference definite; note the difference if the reference were definite: *Yixing is the small town in Jiangnan –* "you know, the one I mentioned just now.")

the Yangzi River (line 1)
The town (line 1)
the green hills which ring the town (line 3)
colorful flowers (line 4)
This story (line 5)
the first evil (line 12)
a man-eating tiger (line 12)
the small children (line 16)

Extract 5   *a river* (line 1) = generic reference. [The reference is to the whole class of rivers, that is, rivers in general (see Section 2.3.2).]

The constant rubbing and bumping of these materials on the river bed (line 2)
the walls (line 4)
the action (line 5)

the result (line 7)
the earth (line 8)

Extract 6   *the person* (line 3) = definite. (The reference is to an identified person in the student's picture.)

this one (line 4)
your piece of paper (line 7)
the special plastic stuff (line 11)
a lovely picture (line 13)

Extract 7   *reality* (line 2) = generic. (The reference is to reality in general.)

measurement (line 2)
phenomena (line 3)
the power to manipulate them (line 4)
scientists (line 5)
their thinking (line 6)
doubt (line 7)

2.3.2   More on generic reference

Three forms of generic reference can be found in the above examples:

1. *the* + singular count noun (e.g., *the kiwi*)
2. ZERO + plural noun or mass noun (e.g., *kiwis; reality*)
3. *a* + singular count noun (e.g., *a river*)

The form *a* + singular count noun is identified as having generic reference on the grounds that the information in the text applies to *all* rivers, not just one – unidentified – river. Here one example of a class has, in a sense, been picked out to represent the whole class. The same phenomenon is perhaps clearer in the following sentence:

(15) A mammal is an animal which suckles its young.

The definition is here clearly meant to apply to *all* mammals.

Task 2e

From the point of view of the learner (and the teacher), it is not very helpful to be told that there are three ways in which count nouns can have generic reference. The three forms are not, in fact, freely interchangeable. Below are some additional examples of the three different forms of generic reference with count nouns.

1. Try substituting the different forms for one another (e.g., *A tarsier monkey* or *tarsier monkeys [come]* for *The tarsier monkey [comes]*) and decide which are acceptable and which not.
2. What generalizations can you make about (i) the restrictions on the use of the different forms and (ii) the contexts in which you would expect to find one form more commonly used than another?
   a. *The tarsier monkey* comes from the tertiary era and stands at the crossroads on the evolutionary chart where man and ape branch off from one another.
   b. *The sociologist* moves in the common world of men, close to what most of them would call real.
   c. *Gibbons* keep together in families and line up in trees.
   d. *Dialect divisions* must be seen as a product of the universal tendency of speech habits to vary.
   e. *Boys* have low voices and they always wear baggies[2] and jeans and T-shirts.
   f. *A file* is a collection of related information.
   g. The front of *a floppy disk* is smooth, while the back has visible seams.

The form ZERO + plural count noun can sometimes be interpreted as generic reference (as in *kiwis* in Extract 1) and sometimes as indefinite reference (as in *colorful flowers* in Extract 4). There is, in fact, a somewhat fuzzy line between the generic and indefinite interpretations. What can be said is that the generic is the default interpretation. That is, unless there is anything in the context to suggest otherwise, a plural noun with the ZERO article will be interpreted as referring to all members of a class of things. A test one can use is to try putting Quantifiers (see Section 3.1.2) such as *some* or *many* into such a noun group. If it is possible to do this without too great a change in meaning, the reference is indefinite, not generic. For example:

(16) the green hills which ring the town are covered with <u>many</u> colorful flowers
    . . . [*inv.*]

is not very different in meaning from the original, which lacks the word *many* (Extract 4, line 3), but

(17) <u>Many</u> kiwis have no wings, feathers . . . [*inv.*]

would greatly change the meaning of the original (Extract 1, line 3); that is, it would suggest that there are some kiwis who do have wings.

A mistake common to many learners with different language backgrounds is the use of a singular count noun with no article, where generic

2 *Baggies* are loosely cut pants.

reference is intended (i.e., treating it as if it were a mass noun). For example:

(18) *Computer has brought many advantages to business.

A useful rule of thumb for students is that singular count nouns can never be used without an article or other Referrer, except when they appear in one of a number of idiomatic prepositional phrases, such as *on foot.*

Sometimes, however, it is possible that the learner simply does not know that a particular noun is a count noun. For example,

(19) *Traffic jam is very serious in the city.

(Compare example 19 with *Traffic congestion is very serious in the city* and *Blackcurrant jam is delicious.*)

Other learners use *the* for generic reference with mass nouns, particularly those referring to abstract entities, for example:

(20) *The love is the most important thing in the world.

Carryover from the learner's native language may contribute to such errors. Many European languages use a form comparable to English *the* for the kind of generic reference in number 20, as in the French *vive l'amour* ("long live (the) love").

Questions for discussion

- Which form of generic reference would it be most useful for learners to learn first? Why?
- Suggest contexts that would be appropriate for introducing the other forms of generic reference.

2.3.3   More on definite reference

Definite Referrers signal that the referent is identified in some way. Possessives and demonstratives themselves provide some information for the identification of the referent. Possessives do this by referring to a possessor. Demonstratives in general indicate the proximity of the referent – either near the speaker or writer (*this/these*) or farther away from the speaker or writer (*that/those*). The proximity can be in terms of space (including space within the text) or of time. For example:

(21) Look at this one. It's much nicer than that one.   (space)   [*inv.*]
(22) These days nobody worries much about it, but in those days it was regarded as a serious offense.   (time)
(23) This view of language acquisition may be compared to *that* presented in the previous chapter.   (text space)

However, *the* provides no such information. It merely signals to the listeners or readers that they *ought* to be able to identify the referent because the information needed is available somewhere in the context. For example, in the noun group *The town* in line 1 in Extract 4, the Referrer *The* tells us that the town in question is identified somewhere. So the question is *which town?* The answer is, of course, that it is the same town first referred to as *a small town* in the previous sentence, where it had the label *Yixing* attached to it. So the definite Referrer *the* can be said to *point* back to the noun group *a small town.*

Task 2f

Look back at the noun groups you identified in Task 2d as having definite reference. State where the information can be found that would allow the listener or reader to identify the referent, that is, what the Referrer points to.

In doing Task 2f, you will have found that the information needed to identify referents is located in a number of different places. Sometimes, such information is in the preceding text, as in the example from Extract 4 already cited:

(24) . . . a small town . . .   <u>The</u> town   (line 1)

This is called **backward-pointing reference.** Example 24 is the most straightforward kind of backward-pointing reference – a reference back to an earlier noun group with the same noun as head (*town*).

The reference can often be more indirect. For example, to identify *the walls* (Extract 5, line 4) as referring to the walls of *its* (a river's) *valleys,* the reader has to refer back to that earlier noun group *and* draw upon a knowledge of the world that includes the fact that valleys may have walls. Similarly, *the small children* (Extract 4, line 16) has definite backward-pointing reference. Our knowledge of the world tells us that towns contain houses, families live in houses, and families often contain small children. Thus although no children have previously been mentioned in the story, the reference can reasonably be supposed to be to the children who live in the houses (*every house,* line 16) which are part of the town of Yixing (*the town,* line 3).

In some cases, the reference may not be to a previous noun group at all, but to a larger portion of text; for example, *The action* (Extract 5, line 5) refers back to the whole of the previous sentence.

Sometimes it is necessary to look forward for the information necessary to identify the referent. For example:

(25) . . . those countries which are affected by the MONSOON
     RAINS   (Extract 2)
(26) The population of Monsoon Asia   (Extract 2)
(27) The tools with which a river excavates its valleys   (Extract 5)

A reference which points forward in the text in this way is called
forward-pointing reference.

In examples 25 through 27, it is postmodifiers in the same noun group
that indicate which population or tools or countries are being referred to. It
is very common for definite Referrers to point in this way to identifying
constituents in the same noun group. In fact, in many written texts this
usage is the most common type of pointing associated with the definite
article *the,* although this usage sometimes tends to be ignored in teaching.

The two categories backward-pointing and forward-pointing are not mutually exclusive. Sometimes the information needed to identify a referent
may be found both earlier and later. For example, in *The first evil* (Extract 4,
line 12), *The* requires us to look back to *three evils* (line 11) as well as
forward to the word *first* in the same noun group.

Backward-pointing and forward-pointing reference both point to information somewhere within the text. However, the information needed for
identification is sometimes outside the text. For example, with *this one*
(Extract 6, lines 4 and 6) we would have to be present in the classroom to
know precisely which person was being referred to in each case. A transcript containing only the words spoken does not provide sufficient
information.

Reference which points beyond the text in this way can be called
outward-pointing reference.

With outward-pointing reference, the reference may be not to something
in the immediate situation, but to something in a wider context, knowledge
of which is assumed to be shared by speaker or writer and hearer or reader.
For example, we might be in California and hear the following sentence at
the beginning of the news broadcast on a local radio station.

(28) Last night the governor announced his intention to resign.   [*inv.*]

To interpret this as referring to the one human being who at the time of
the news broadcast occupies the post as governor of California, the listeners
must share with the newsreader (1) the assumption that references within a
local broadcast in California are to be interpreted within the context of
California unless some other context is invoked and (2) the knowledge that
the political system of California includes such a post as governor and that
California has only one governor at a time.

This kind of outward-pointing is often called *unique reference,* as the
reference is to something of which there is only one example in the relevant
context. This category also includes the definite reference in noun groups

such as *the sun, the moon,* and *the earth* (Extract 5, line 8). In the vast majority of contexts, *the sun* and *the moon* refer to the medium-sized star orbited by the planet on which all human beings live and the single natural satellite which orbits this planet. However, if these noun groups were within, say, a science fiction story, the reference could well be to a sun and a moon within a different solar system. The point to note here is that the distinction between outward-pointing reference and internal backward-pointing and forward-pointing reference is something of a simplification, as the text itself can invoke or construct the context within which the reference is to be interpreted.

2.3.4   More on indefinite reference

Two forms of indefinite reference can be found in the examples given in Task 2d:

1. a + singular noun (e.g., *a man-eating tiger*)
2. ZERO + plural and mass nouns (e.g., *colorful flowers, doubt*)

The use of the ZERO article for indefinite reference shades into its use for generic reference, as has already been noted.

Many languages have a word which is closer in meaning to the English number *one* than to *a* and which is used in far fewer contexts than the English indefinite article. This may be one reason why many learners frequently omit the singular indefinite article *a* where it is required in English.

For teaching purposes, it is useful to distinguish three uses of *a* and *an:* the labeling use, the first mention use, and the any use. The *labeling* use refers to its use in clauses such as *this is a book,* for example, in contexts in which objects are being labeled or classified. The *first-mention* use refers to its use in contexts such as narratives, where a character or a thing is being introduced for the first time (as in *a man-eating tiger* in Extract 4). The *any* use refers to its use in clauses such as *please bring a dish,* where its meaning may be glossed as *any (one) member of the class (I do not care which).*

2.3.5   Definite Referrers as noun group heads

Demonstrative Referrers (*this, these, that, those*) also occur as heads of noun groups, for example:

(29) This is beautiful . . .
(30) You can finish that later.

Possessive Referrers, except *its,* also occur as heads of noun groups, although most of them must change their form slightly.

my − mine
your − yours
our − ours
their − theirs
his (same)
her − hers

Demonstratives and possessives as heads can take postmodifiers like ordinary head nouns. However, they can be premodified only by the inclusive *all* or by inclusives and Quantifiers formed with *of* (these will be examined in Sections 3.1 and 3.3). For example:

(31) <u>All those who've finished</u> please put up your hands
(32) <u>Each of hers</u> was painted in a different shade of orange.

2.3.6   *Learning and teaching the reference system*

The Referrer function within the noun group clearly presents a number of potential problems for learners. The relationships between the Referrers and the reference categories of generic, indefinite, and definite are not one-to-one, and selecting an appropriate Referrer often demands considerable sensitivity to context. It is not surprising that this is an area in which even the most advanced learners are prone to error.

Attempts to teach reference through generalizations or rules about the use of each form, illustrated with example sentences out of context, are unlikely to be successful. The various types of reference and their forms need to be understood and practiced in extended contexts.

Questions for discussion

- In what order would you introduce to learners the different uses of the indefinite article *a* (i.e., generic, labeling, first mention, any; see Section 2.3.4) and the different uses of the definite article *the* (i.e., generic, backward-pointing, forward-pointing, outward-pointing; see Section 2.3.3)? Why?
- Suggest contexts in which the various uses of *a* and *the* could be introduced and practiced.
- Look back at task 2f. How could you adapt such a task for use with intermediate students or advanced learners? How useful would it be?

Summary

1. Some nouns have only one form and cannot be counted. These are known as mass nouns. Other nouns have both singular and plural forms and can be counted. These are known as count nouns.
2. Many nouns are used as both mass nouns and count nouns. When used as mass nouns their meanings are normally more general and abstract than when they are used as count nouns.
3. The basic structure of noun groups is premodifiers + head + post-modifiers.
4. The experiential function of the head is to represent the Thing.
5. Referrers are premodifiers which indicate whether the reference of the Thing is generic (to the whole class), definite (to an identified subset), or indefinite (to an unidentified subset).
6. There are four main kinds of Referrers: articles, demonstratives, possessives, and inclusives.
7. The selection of appropriate Referrers depends on the kind of reference and whether the head noun is mass, singular, or plural.
8. Demonstratives and possessives also occur as noun group heads.

Key terms introduced

This text	*Alternatives used in the field*
article	
backward-pointing	anaphoric
collective noun	
count noun	countable noun
definite reference	
demonstrative	
forward-pointing	cataphoric
generic reference	
head (noun)	
indefinite reference	
mass noun	uncountable noun
outward-pointing	exophoric
possessive	
postmodifier	Qualifier
premodifier	Modifier
Referrer	Deictic; Determiner (this term usually also subsumes Quantifiers)
Thing	

Discussion of tasks

Task 2a

The following cannot be nouns: *hear, kicked, lived, often, on.* Criteria you may have used are:

1. Word shape – certain word endings are typical of nouns. We can therefore be fairly certain that words such as *reference, activity,* and *loneliness* are nouns. We can also be fairly sure that words such as *kicked* are not nouns.

2. Adjacent words – there are certain other word classes (e.g., articles and adjectives) that commonly precede nouns. A word can therefore be tested by putting it within a frame made up of such words. For example, we can say:

Article	*Adjective*	
a	useful	reference
a	good	life
a	hard	kick
a	lively	activity
a	kind	act
a	long	talk
the	hot	sunshine
the	terrible	loneliness

	but not	
*the	quiet	hear
*the	hard	kicked

This tells us that the first eight of these words are nouns whereas the others are not.

3. Grammatical function – one grammatical function in the clause that may be realized by nouns is that of **Subject** (see Chapter 1). Thus, we can say:

Subject

The reference	can be found in this book.
Life	is not easy here.
A kick	may be painful.
Loneliness	is terrible.

	but not
*Kicked	is painful.

This is another criterion for identifying certain words as nouns.

Task 2b

cheese, wine, metal: the substance versus different kinds or types of the substance

cake, egg, chocolate: the substance as a mass versus the substance as individual units with clearly defined shapes

life, noise, war, time, kindness: the thing or activity in general versus particular instances of it

business: the activity in general versus an organization carrying on the activity

work: the activity versus a product of artistic or intellectual activity

In general, count uses are more specific and concrete and mass uses are more general and abstract.

Task 2c

1. The following are not noun groups:

   because of the large number of applicants
   are being subject to attack
   about yesterday's meeting

2. Probably the most useful test for noun groups is the grammatical function test (see Task 2a). Thus, for example, *the continual heavy rain,* like the noun *rain* alone, can function as the Subject of a clause, for example:

   The continual heavy rain is annoying.

   However, *because of the large number of applicants* cannot function as the Subject of a clause.

   *Because of the large number of applicants is dangerous.

3. The heads of the noun groups are *rain, poor, food, display, ghost, lowering, guide,* and *one.*

Task 2d

Extract 1
kiwis – generic
Australia's equally cute national symbol – definite
the nostrils on the end of their long bill – definite

Extract 2
The population of Monsoon Asia – definite
ecological niches – indefinite

these ecological niches – definite
densities – indefinite
a demographic transition – indefinite

Extract 4
the Yangzi River – definite
the town – definite
the green hills which ring the town – definite
colorful flowers – indefinite
This story – definite
the first evil – definite
a man-eating tiger – indefinite
the small children – definite

Extract 5
The constant rubbing and bumping of these materials on the river bed –
    definite
the walls – definite
the action – definite
the result – definite
the earth – definite

Extract 6
this one – definite
your piece of paper – definite
the special plastic stuff – definite
a lovely picture – indefinite

Extract 7
measurement – generic
phenomena – generic
the power to manipulate them – definite
scientists – generic
their thinking – definite
doubt – indefinite

Task 2e

The ZERO + plural noun form can be used for generic reference in nearly all contexts, although occasionally it may not be clear whether generic or indefinite reference is intended. *The* + singular noun and *a* + singular noun are both much more restricted in their use for generic reference. *The* + singular noun is common in scientific and technical writing when generalizations are made about a class of phenomena (usually defined by clear criteria). It cannot be used where the reference would be ambiguous with definite reference or where the class is viewed in terms of its individual members; for example, *the gibbon lines up in trees* is not acceptable because the action of lining up in trees entails seeing gibbons as a number of separate individuals. *A* + singular noun is also commonly used in scientific and technical writing, especially for definitions. Again, it cannot be used where there would be ambiguity with indefinite reference.

Task 2f

Extract 1
Australia's equally cute national symbol – to the country *Australia.* (That is, the possessive Refererrer itself contains the information needed for identification.)
The nostrils on the end of their nose to *on the end of their nose* (and possibly to shared knowledge that birds have nostrils)

Extract 2
The population of Monsoon Asia – to *of Monsoon Asia*
These ecological niches – to *ecological niches* (in the previous sentence)

Extract 4
the Yangzi River – to *Yangzi*
the town – to *a small town in Jiangnan* (first sentence)
the green hills which ring the town – to *which ring the town*
This story – to the whole of the surrounding text *and* the situation of the reader engaged in reading a story
the first evil – to *three evils* (the previous paragraph) and *first*
the small children – to *every house* (previous line) and *the town* (first paragraph). (This reference will be discussed later in this section.)

Extract 5
The constant rubbing and bumping of these materials on the river bed – to *of these materials on the river bed*
the walls – to *its valley* (line 1; discussed later in this section)
the action – to the whole of the previous sentence (discussed later in this section)
the result – to the first half of the same sentence (i.e., the result of the fact that the action goes on slowly over very long periods of time)
the earth – to the shared knowledge that there exists only one earth (discussed later in this section)

Extract 6

<u>*this one*</u> – to the person indicated by the teacher in the child's picture. (We
as readers of the transcript cannot identify which person; discussed later
in this section.)

<u>*your*</u> *piece of paper* – to the child the teacher is talking to

<u>*the*</u> *special plastic stuff* – to *special* and to the shared knowledge of teacher
and child that there exists plastic stuff on which the teacher sometimes
writes

Extract 7

<u>*the*</u> *power to manipulate them* – to *to manipulate them*

<u>*their*</u> *thinking* – to *scientists* earlier in the same sentence

3 *Representing things II: More on noun groups*

This chapter will first look at inclusive Referrers and then consider three other premodifying functional constituents of the noun group – Quantifiers, Describers, and Classifiers. It will then examine the major kinds of postmodifiers. Finally, the phenomenon of nominalization will be explored.

3.1 Inclusives

Inclusives indicate that the reference is to a complete group of things either positively (e.g., *all cats*) or negatively (e.g., *no cat*). With the positive inclusives, there is also a distinction between reference to the group as a whole (e.g., *all cats*) and reference to the group as composed of individuals (e.g., *every cat*).

The positive inclusives are *either, both, each, every,* and *all. Either* and *both* are used when only two things are referred to. *Either* refers to the pair as individuals, while *both* refers to the pair as a whole. For example:

(1) It can whisk away the rising air or whip the outer edges of the sheet, and in either case accelerates the circular movement.
(2) Locate both fixing screws and tighten them gradually . . .

Each, every, and *all* are used when more than two things are referred to. *Each* and *every* refer to the group as composed of individuals and *all* refers to the group as a whole. For example:

(3) Each bear had a bed to sleep in too.
(4) I have a dream that every valley shall be exalted, every hill and mountain shall be made low.
(5) We hold it self evident that all men are created equal.

The negative set includes *neither* and *no. Neither* is used when two things are referred to. *No* is used when more than two things are referred to. For example:

(6) Neither field really attracted me.

(7) . . . the first amendment grants them no special rights . . .

Inclusives can co-occur in various ways with other Referrers. *All* and *both* can directly precede definite Referrers (*the,* demonstratives, and possessives). For example:

(8) Check that all the wires are secured.

(9) Both these books say the same.

(10) . . . how race, gender, and class shape all our experiences.

The other inclusives cannot directly precede other Referrers in this way.[1] However, most inclusives have variants with *of,* such as *all of, both of,* and *each of,* which can be used before definite Referrers and are normally used when the head is a pronoun (e.g., *each of the wires* and *both of them*). The exceptions are *every* (one cannot say **every of the wires* or *every of them) and *no,* which has the form *none* before *of.*

A potential problem for learners is knowing which inclusives to use with mass, singular, and plural nouns. *Both, all,* and *no* are used with plural nouns. *Either, each, every,* and *no* are used with singular nouns. *All* and *no* are also used with mass nouns. However, learners sometimes produce sentences such as

(11) *Every citizens should be responsible for improving the environment.

3.2   Quantifiers

Like Referrers, Quantifiers limit the scope of reference of the Thing. However, they provide information not about *which* entities or entity but about *how many* entities, or *how much* entity. In other words, they indicate a quantity somewhere between *all* and *none.* A distinction can be made between inexact Quantifiers and exact Quantifiers.

3.2.1   *Inexact Quantifiers*

Inexact Quantifiers include *many, much, a lot of, several, some, any, a few, a little, few, little, fewer, fewest, less, least, more,* and *most.*

A potential problem for learners lies in the ways these Quantifiers can co-occur with Referrers. For example, *their many supporters* is acceptable, whereas *their much help is not.

---

1 One inclusive – *every* – can be *preceded* by possessive Referrers, for example, *Our every effort met with failure.* This is not very common, and introducing this usage to learners would certainly not be a high priority.

Task 3a

Which of the inexact Quantifiers listed at the beginning of Section 3.2.1 can be preceded by (1) the definite article *the,* (2) possessive Referrers?

Another potential problem for learners is knowing which of the inexact Quantifiers to use with mass, singular, and plural nouns, as seen in the following kinds of error:

(12) *There have been much arguments about this issue.

(13) *We have too few food for so much people.

Many, several, a few, few, fewer and *fewest* are only used with count nouns; *much, a little,* and *little* are only used with mass nouns. *Some, any, a lot of, less,* and *least* may be used with both count and mass nouns, although some people will not accept *less* and *least* with count nouns in formal written English.

Learners may confuse *a few* and *a little* with *few* and *little. A few* and *a little* simply indicate a small quantity, while *few* and *little* often have a negative connotation, for example, that the quantity is insufficient, less than expected or hoped for, and so on. For example:

(14) *Few people liked the taste," says Walter Brinkmann of Coca Cola Europe.

(15) A few libraries are moving beyond this . . .

Inexact Quantifiers also have *of* variants used before definite Referrers. For example:

(16) . . . all the editors of many of the world's most prestigious journals.

(17) . . . were the basis of much of my sociological imagination.

(18) . . . so she decided to eat some of the porridge.

Note that in these cases, the quantity indicated is out of a total: in example 16, *many* out of the total of *the world's most prestigious journals;* in example 17, *much* out of the total of *my sociological imagination* and in example 18, *some* out of the total of the *porridge.* Thus, the meanings of the following two sentences are quite different:

(19)   The few students who turned up were disappointed.   [*inv.*]

(19) a. Few of the students who turned up were disappointed.

3.2.1.1 *SOME* AND *ANY*

Some and *any* are classified here as Quantifiers. However, both have a range of uses that could justify their inclusion in the class of articles. For the sake of convenience, the major uses of *some* and *any* are all dealt with in this section.

Unstressed *some* (pronounced /səm/) functions like an indefinite Referrer used, like the ZERO article (Section 2.3.4), before mass nouns and plural count nouns. For example:

(20) One morning the three bears cooked some porridge for breakfast.
(21) There are some beautiful flowers in the garden.

However, *some* does have a quantifying flavor, as it indicates a restriction in the amount or number referred to, although the difference between *some* and the ZERO article can be quite subtle, as in

(22) Would you prefer coffee?   [*inv.*]
(23) Would you prefer some coffee?   [*inv.*]

Stressed *some* (pronounced /sʌm/) as in, for example,

(24) . . . now some museums really are worth seeing . . .
(25) It is in some respects like a poem.

In these examples, *some* contrasts with inclusives such as *all,* and, as such, clearly refers to a restricted quantity.

Stressed *some* can also be used with singular nouns as a kind of emphatic variant of the indefinite article in what was referred to in Section 2.3.4 as first-mention usage, for example:

(26) Some silly fool tried to dispose of glass bottles in it.   [*inv.*]

Introducing this usage to learners would probably not be a high priority.

Any has a similar range of uses. Unstressed *any* is used like an indefinite Referrer before plural and mass nouns in negative and interrogative (i.e., question) clauses, for example:

(27) I haven't got any escudos left but I've got a few pesetas.
(28) . . . do you have any information there on prices?

Stressed *any* is used as a kind of emphatic variant of the indefinite article in what was referred to in Chapter 2 as the any use, that is, to indicate that the choice is completely unrestricted, for example:

(29) Take any card from the pack.   (compare: *Take a card from the pack*)

This extends to a usage in which the meaning of *any* is close to that of an inclusive, for example:

(30) Comment briefly on each stage of the journey, deducing the values of any accelerations or retardations.
(31) Any product permitted for sale in one country can be sold in all others . . .

In these examples, *any,* like an inclusive such as *all,* refers to a whole group of things; unlike *all,* however, it suggests the possibility that the things may not actually exist or occur.

3.2.2 Exact Quantifiers

Exact quantity is indicated by numerals such as *one, two, three, four,* and so on. These are normally quite straightforward for learners. However, one source of confusion can be with the use of plural numerals such as *dozens, hundreds,* and *millions* with *of,* which are used for inexact numeric quantity (e.g., *Hundreds of people were there*). Learners sometimes produce intermediate forms, such as **three hundred of people* and **three hundreds people.*

3.3 Partitives

Partitives are structures which consist of two nouns linked by *of,* for example, *a piece of cake, an item of news, a lump of coal, a drop of water.* In these examples, the first noun (*piece, item, lump,* and *drop*) is a unit of some kind which in effect allows a mass noun to be counted. Such structures can be analyzed as noun groups with the first noun as head and the second noun as part of a postmodifying prepositional phrase, for example:

PREMODIFIER   HEAD POSTMODIFIER
    a   piece   of cake

It has already been noted that inclusives and Quantifiers can have similar *of* forms. There is, in fact, a somewhat fuzzy distinction between partitive structures and inclusives and Quantifiers formed with *of.* In a clause such as *a lot of students have arrived* it is the noun *students* which determines the number agreement of the Finite (*have* – plural). It is not normally possible to say **a lot of students has arrived.* Therefore *students* is the head of the noun group and *a lot of* is a complex Quantifier. Similarly, it is also normal to say *a number of students have arrived* not *a number of students has arrived,* that is, to treat *a number of* as a complex Quantifier.

However, expressions such as *a crowd of* and *a group of* are sometimes treated as if they were Quantifiers (i.e., the following noun determines agreement) and sometimes as if the heads were *crowd* and *group* with postmodifiers (as in *a crowd of students have arrived* and *a crowd of students has arrived, a group of students have arrived* and *a group of students has arrived*). In fact, particularly in speech, it is very common for the noun following such nouns + *of* to determine the agreement whatever may precede it, as in, for example, *a delegation of students have arrived.* However, in formal written English, many people would consider this incorrect.

For beginning learners, it may be best to introduce expressions such as *a lot of* and *a number of* as complex Quantifiers but in other cases to err on the prescriptive side and encourage agreement with the noun preceding *of.*

With the inclusives formed with *of,* there is a similar tendency to use plural Finites as well as plural possessives when the noun after *of* is plural, as in, for example, *each of the students have their own book* and *none of the students have arrived.* In the case of *each of,* this usage is heard in speech, particularly where use of the singular form would necessitate using locutions such as *his or her* for *their.* However, in written English the use of the plural Finite is usually considered incorrect. In the case of *none of* both singular and plural are normally accepted, even in writing; for example:

(32) A tap may leak for a number of reasons but none of them are difficult to deal with.

(33) None of Europe's eight manufacturers of telephone exchanges is viable on its own.

3.4   Describers

Describing words tell us something about a quality of the Thing represented by the head noun or about the speaker or writer's attitude toward the Thing, for example, *that blue vase* (quality) and *that horrible vase* (attitude). Words which perform this describing function will be called **Describers.**

3.4.1   *Types of Describers*

The class of words which most often function as Describers is that of *adjective.* Examples from the extracts in the Appendix include: *a small, tubby, flightless bird* (Extract 1); *a sleepy nature* (Extract 1); *a small town* (Extract 4); *beautiful surroundings* (Extract 4); and *peaceful and happy lives* (Extract 4).

Describers can themselves be modified by a member of the word class *adverb,* for example:

(34) These represent a very large family.

(35) Where I live there's a fairly steep rise.

The describing function can also be performed by words called *participles.* These are words which are derived from verbs and have the forms V*ing* or V*ed/en,* for example, *an interesting teacher* and *an interested student; a boring teacher* and *a bored student.*

Such participles can cause problems for learners. The difference between the V*ing* and V*ed* forms can *sometimes* relate to a time distinction – or more accurately, the distinction between unfinished and finished. For example, compare

a falling statue   (" statue which is falling")

with

a fallen statue   ("a statue which has (already) fallen")

However, very often the distinction involves not time but the role of the Thing (represented by the head) in the process represented by the participle. For example, in *a boring teacher* the relationship between the participle *boring* and the Thing *teacher* can be paraphrased as something like *a teacher who bores people* (presumably the students). In other words, when the V*ing* form is used, the Thing is in some sense the doer or causer of the action.

On the other hand, in *a bored student,* the relationship between *bored* and *student* can be paraphrased as something like *a student who is bored by something/someone* or *a student whom something or someone bores.* In other words, when the -*ed* participle is used, the Thing is the entity affected by the action. Learners whose language has nothing comparable to such participles will sometimes confuse them.

3.4.2   Order of Describers

A noun group may contain several Describers, as in the example *small, tubby, flightless bird.* When there is more than one Describer, the order of the words is not arbitrary.

Task 3b

1. How would you reorder the Describers in the following noun groups to make them sound more natural?
2. What generalization can you make about the usual order of such Describers?
   a. a square large table
   b. a green beautiful carpet
   c. a yellow new car
   d. green strange large eyes
   e. a little charming brown old pot

3.4.3   Describers as noun group heads

Describers can themselves be heads of noun groups preceded by the definite article *the.* In such cases, the reference is normally generic. Examples are: *the poor, the rich, the good,* and *the bad.*

Sometimes learners treat these as ordinary count nouns. For example:

(36) *The poors should be given more help.

3.5   Classifiers

Classifiers are words which subclassify the Thing. Thus, *assistant lecturer* is a subclassification of *lecturer,* and *assistant* is functioning as a Classifier.

3.5.1   Types of Classifiers

Classifiers may be realized by adjectives, nouns, or participles, as in the three following noun groups:

<u>urban</u> growth   (adjective as Classifier)
<u>city</u> growth   (noun as Classifier)
<u>living</u> organisms   (participle as Classifier)

When participles are used as Classifiers, the distinction between the V*ing* participle and the V*ed/en* participle can be the same as when participles are used as Describers; that is, the distinction may be interpreted as being finished versus unfinished (as in *developed economy* versus *developing economy*) or as a distinction in the relationship of the Thing to the process (as in *manufactured drug* – "a drug which people manufacture" versus *manufacturing plant* – "a plant, or factory, which manufactures things").

In some cases, it may not be immediately obvious whether a particular adjective or participle is functioning as a Classifier or as a Describer. A useful test is to try to modify the word with an adverb such as *very, quite, slightly,* etc. Where it is possible to do this, the word is functioning as a Describer; where it is not, the word is functioning as a Classifier. The reason for this is obvious. Classifiers identify a subclass which the Thing either is or is not a member of. Thus, one is *an assistant lecturer* or *a senior lecturer* or just *a lecturer.* It would make no sense in most contexts to talk of *a fairly assistant* or *slightly assistant lecturer.* Similarly, *an animal* is either *living* or it is not. It cannot be a *quite living organism.*

Task 3c

In the following noun groups (taken from Extracts 1 and 2) are the underlined words functioning as Describers or Classifiers?

1. a small, tubby, <u>flightless</u> bird
2. <u>real</u> feathers
3. a thumping <u>big</u> kick
4. their <u>long</u> beak
5. <u>monsoon</u> rains
6. <u>millionaire</u> cities

7. <u>ecological</u> niches
8. <u>rapid</u> rise

This Classifier + Thing structure will be of particular importance to learners who are studying technical or scientific subjects, in which Classifiers are much used in classification systems or taxonomies. For example, in a physics text, *weak force* refers to one of the fundamental forces which act between the particles that make up the universe. The adjective *weak* is functioning not simply to describe the force (as the adjective *weak* is used to describe the person in *he is a very weak person*), but to classify the force under discussion vis-à-vis the other kinds of force. Even learners who are not studying a technical field may encounter, in a scientific text, an adjective they know in its function as a Describer but which is functioning in the new context as a Classifier.

3.5.2 Meaning relationships between Classifier and Thing

A great deal of information may be implicit in a Classifier + Thing structure, and the meaning relationship between the Classifier and the Thing is not always predictable. For example, *an ant heap* is "a heap which is *created by* ants," whereas *a rubbish heap* is "a heap which *consists of* rubbish."

Similarly, not every Classifier ending in -*ing* or -*ed* can be interpreted as a participle, as in Section 3.4.1. For example, *disabled access* clearly means an access for the disabled, not an access which has been disabled. *Shopping mall* does not, of course, mean a mall which goes shopping.

A certain amount of knowledge, often subject-specific knowledge, on the part of the hearer or reader may be necessary to interpret a given Classifier + Thing structure, as in the example *weak force* cited in Section 3.5. This can become quite complex where there is more than one Classifier in a noun group. It may not always be immediately apparent whether a particular Classifier is classifying another Classifier or is classifying the Thing. For example, *an electric circuit breaker* is a breaker of electric circuits, but *an electric egg beater* is not a beater of electric eggs.[2] An even more complex example, which is hard to interpret without subject-specific knowledge, is *an automated nozzle brick grinder* (cited in Trimble 1985: 134). According to Trimble, this means an automated grinder of a kind of brick (a nozzle brick), not a grinder of bricks with an automated nozzle.

2 For this example I am indebted to an anonymous Cambridge University Press reviewer of the manuscript of this book.

3.5.3 *Noun or adjective as Classifier*

Learners sometimes have difficulty knowing whether to select a noun or an adjective as a Classifier. For example, *urban growth* and *city growth* are both acceptable, with little difference in meaning (although the former is much more common). However, *economic growth,* with an adjective as Classifier, is acceptable, but *economy growth,* with a noun as Classifier, is not. On the other hand, *economy drive* is acceptable. In this case, the noun *economy* means something like "saving money," not "the system of production and distribution of wealth," as in *growth in the economy.*

Unfortunately, it is not possible to come up with a generalization that will allow students in all cases to choose appropriately between a noun and an adjective as Classifier. The appropriate combinations are probably best learned as vocabulary items within the contexts of the relevant subject areas.

Note that count nouns as Classifiers are usually singular. For example, *she collects model trains,* but *she has a large model train collection.* Learners sometimes inappropriately use the plural forms of nouns as Classifiers. Again, there are exceptions to any rule one might want to set up about this; for example, it is *complaints department* not *complaint department.*

Task 3d

For the following noun groups, try substituting the nouns in parentheses for the adjectives functioning as Classifiers.

the financial sector (finance)
the artistic world (art)
linguistic analysis (linguistics)
a mathematical equation (mathematics)
a grammatical mistake (grammar)
a scientific journal (science)

Where the noun cannot be substituted for the adjective, are there other contexts in which the same noun **could** function as a Classifier? Where either the adjective or the noun could be used, does using the noun change the meaning?

3.5.4 *Classifiers and compound nouns*

There is a very fuzzy borderline between Classifier + Thing structures and what are usually called **compound nouns.** These are instances in which two (or sometimes more) nouns are commonly found together as a unit, for example, *swimming pool* and *tea bags.* They can be regarded as forming a compound head of a noun group. Some long-established compound nouns are written with hyphens, for example, *gas-guzzler, head-hunting,* and *tea-chest.* Some words that were originally compound nouns are now normally regarded as single words, for example, *bedroom* and *hayrack.*

Questions for discussion

- Suggest ways of contextualizing and practicing V*ing* and V*ed* participles functioning as Describers that would bring out the meaning differences between them and might help learners who sometimes confuse them.
- Suggest some activities to raise learners' awareness of the typical order of Describers in a noun group.
- If you are working with students who are studying other subjects through English, collect some examples of Classifier + Thing structures from their textbooks. Which of them could be confusing for the students? What kinds of activities might help them interpret such structures correctly?

3.6 Postmodifiers

Constituents which postmodify the head in a noun group qualify the Thing in some way. For example, in the first noun group in the previous sentence, *constituents which postmodify the head in a noun group,* the postmodifier *which postmodify the head in a noun group* functions to narrow down the meaning of *constituents* from all kinds of constituents to a subset of constituents.[3] Since a postmodifier may function to uniquely identify a specific subset, it is not surprising that, as was seen in Section 2.3.3, postmodifiers should often be combined with forward-pointing definite reference, for example:

(37) the nostrils on the end of their long bill   (Extract 1)
(38) Those countries which are affected by the MONSOON RAINS   (Extract 2)

3.6.1 Types of postmodifiers

There are three major kinds of postmodifying constituents in the noun group:

1. Finite clauses; for example:

3 The technical term for this experiential function is *Qualifier* (see Halliday 1994). However, because all postmodifiers function as Qualifiers, the use of this additional term has been avoided.

The child <u>who is sitting in the corner</u> has been very naughty.

2. Nonfinite clauses; for example:

The child <u>sitting in the corner</u> has been very naughty.

3. Prepositional phrases; for example:

The child <u>in the corner</u> has been very naughty.

Technically, such postmodifying constituents are all embedded constituents. In other words, they are units which normally operate at group rank or above but are being used as constituents within a group (Section 1.3.4).

Note that in clauses such as *there is a child in the corner,* the prepositional phrase *in the corner* is *not* part of the noun group. It is an *Adjunct* (see Section 1.6.2). One way of determining whether a prepositional phrase is an Adjunct or a postmodifier is to see whether it is possible to move it. In this case, *in the corner* can be moved (i.e., *in the corner there is a child* is a possible clause), which confirms that the prepositional phrase is not part of the noun group.

Postmodifying clauses often cause problems for learners and are worth examining in some detail.

3.6.2   Postmodifying finite clauses

Postmodifying finite clauses are normally referred to as **restrictive** or **defining relative clauses.** In this section, they will be referred to simply as **relative clauses.** However, it should be noted that there are other kinds of relative clauses (nonrestrictive or nondefining relative clauses), which are not embedded in the noun group; these are looked at in Chapter 12 (Section 12.3.1).

Relatives clause are linked to the head by a **relative pronoun,** for example, *who* in number 1 in Section 3.6.1. *Who* is a relative pronoun because in the relative clause it substitutes for the noun group *the child.*

To master embedding of this kind, the learner must be able to (1) place the relative clauses correctly, (2) select an appropriate relative pronoun, and (3) make any necessary rearrangements of the clause constituents.

3.6.2.1   PLACING THE RELATIVE CLAUSE

The relative clause must, of course, be within the noun group, usually directly after the head. Learners sometimes place such a clause outside the noun group which it is intended to qualify, for example:

(39) *The things dropped on the floor which I bought at the supermarket.

3.6.2.2 SELECTING APPROPRIATE RELATIVE PRONOUNS

Relative pronouns always come at the beginning of the relative clause, except when preceded by prepositions.

Selection of an appropriate relative pronoun depends upon (1) its grammatical function (e.g., Subject, Object, Prepositional Object) in the relative clause, (2) whether or not the head represents a human or nonhuman entity, and (3) the formality of the language.

The following examples illustrate the main categories of relative pronouns, according to their grammatical functions and to whether the head is human or nonhuman:

                             SUBJECT
(40) . . . every author   who   writes electronically . . . (human head)

                           SUBJECT
(41) . . . the warm threshold which leads to the palace of justice. (nonhuman head)

                          OBJECT
(42) . . . the young woman whom the police took into custody . . . (human head)

                        OBJECT
(43) . . . the direction which the government has now taken . . . (nonhuman head)

                 PREPOSITIONAL
                 OBJECT
(44) . . . the person to whom I addressed myself first . . . (human head)

                 PREPOSITIONAL
                 OBJECT
(45) . . . the velocity with which it reaches the ground. (nonhuman head)

Note that in less formal English, particularly spoken English, it is usual to leave the preposition in its original position following the verb. For example, in a more informal style examples 44 and 45 might be phrased as

(44) a. the person I talked to first . . .
(45) a. the speed it reaches the ground at.

In examples 40 through 45, the relative pronouns used are *who* and *whom* for humans, Subject and Object respectively, and *which* for nonhumans, all functions. These are by no means the only possible relative pronouns.

Task 3e

The relative clauses have been deleted from the following sentences and their nonrelative variants (i.e., clauses which are not embedded) given in brackets immediately following the relevant head.

1. Turn the clauses within the brackets back into relative clauses, choosing appropriate relative pronouns from the following list: *who, whom, which, that, ZERO* (i.e., no explicit marker of embedding). The first one has already been done.
2. In each case, try substituting relative pronouns other than the one you initially selected. What generalizations can you make about the restrictions on the use of the five relative pronouns (*who, whom, which, that, ZERO*)?
   a. . . . the green hills [the green hills ring the town] are covered with colorful flowers.
      Answer: the green hills which ring the town are covered with colorful flowers.
      or: the green hills that ring the town . . .
   b. The few wood-cutters [the few wood-cutters did go into the mountains] never returned.
   c. The result is the network of valleys [the network of valleys diversify the face of the earth] and the stupendous quantity of waste [the rivers carry the stupendous quantity of waste down to the sea].
   d. He carried bags of sand and large stones and did all the heavy work [the others could not manage all the heavy work]
   e. Informants [we contacted informants personally] proved on the whole to be more reliable.
   f. . . . yeah him, he's the one [we went to Cairo with him].
   g. The man [she had lived with the man for the previous nine years] suddenly left.
   h. The tools [a river excavates its valleys with the tools] are the boulders and sand [it sweeps along the boulders and sand with it].

A further complication is the *possessive* type of relative clause, that is, a relative clause in which the relative pronoun is functioning as a possessive Referrer within a noun group. Where the referent is human, the relative pronoun *whose* is used, for example:

(46) . . . someone in whose shadow we are not fit to stand . . .

When the referent is nonhuman, *of which* may be used, as in the following example:

(47) . . . the house the ceiling of which recently collapsed.   [*inv.*]

Whose is also often used with nonhuman referents, particularly when it is felt that using *of which* would be clumsy. For example:

(48) . . . the banyan tree under <u>whose</u> branches we used to shelter . . .

However, some people do not like this use of *whose* for nonhuman referents in formal written English.

3.6.2.3   REARRANGING THE CLAUSE CONSTITUENTS

As has been noted, relative pronouns come at the beginning of a relative clause, although they may be preceded by prepositions. Where the relative pronoun functions as the Subject of the relative clause, this does not disturb the usual order of clause constituents. However, where the relative pronoun functions as an Object or Prepositional Object there is, in a sense, a gap in the clause where the Object or Prepositional Object would normally be. Learners sometimes attempt to fill this gap. For example:

	PREPOSITIONAL OBJECT		PREPOSITIONAL OBJECT
(49) *That was the apartment before.	<u>that</u>	he took us to	<u>it</u>

In fact, such forms do sometimes occur in informal spoken English. However, they are considered incorrect, especially in written English.

3.6.3   *Postmodifying nonfinite clauses*

The postmodifying nonfinite clause can be regarded as a reduced form of the finite relative clause, with the relative pronoun and the Finite deleted. For example: *the child ~~who is~~ sitting in the corner* and *the girl ~~who was~~ arrested by the police.*

3.6.4   LEARNING AND TEACHING POSTMODIFYING CLAUSES

In some languages relative clauses are handled quite differently. For example, in Chinese, relative clauses *pre*modify the head, usually with an all-purpose marker of embedding (*de* in Mandarin Chinese). For example:

	yesterday	come	see	us	DE	that	CLASSIFIER	person
(50)	zuotian	lai	kan	women	de	na	ge	ren

("the person who came to see us yesterday")

Even where relative clauses postmodify the head and relative pronouns are used, there may not be the same distinctions as in English. Dutch, German, and Arabic, for example, all make no distinction in the relative pronouns between human and nonhuman. Learners with such language backgrounds sometimes tend to use *which* for both.

Some languages allow or require an additional Object pronoun in a relative clause when a relative pronoun is functioning as Object, as in the following Arabic example:

he wrote the book which   I read it
(51) Kataba lkitāba llaðī qaraʔtuhu   (Kay 1987: 683)

This may be one reason for errors such as number 49.

Finally, learners sometimes confuse the finite and the nonfinite relative clauses, producing intermediate forms such as:

(52) *The child who sitting in the corner has been very naughty.   (with relative pronoun but without Finite)

and

(53) *The child is sitting in the corner has been very naughty.   (with Finite but without relative pronoun)

Learners also sometimes produce forms like:

(54) *The girl who arrested by the police was my classmate.

In such cases, it is not always possible to know whether the error arises from confusion between finite and nonfinite postmodifying clauses, or between active and passive voice forms.

Relative clauses are therefore an area which many learners may have problems with. As with other structures, it is comparatively easy to construct mechanical transformation exercises through which learners either practice joining two sentences so that one becomes a relative clause within the other or exercises in which learners practice changing finite postmodifying clauses into nonfinite postmodifying clauses. However, such exercises do not help learners to use the structures appropriately in context and always carry with them the danger of producing confusion between related structures, as noted above.

Questions for discussion

- Suggest ways of introducing and practicing relative clauses that make use of their identifying function (Section 3.6.1) and might help learners to be able to use them appropriately in context.
- Design some remedial activities to help students who frequently produce the kind of error represented by example 49.

3.7   Processes and qualities as Things

The following are two sentences taken from Extract 7 (lines 1–2 and 7–10):

(55)   The problems of interpretation cluster around two issues: the nature of reality and the nature of measurement.

(56)   Such accounts cast doubt on whether an understanding of reality is to
         be conceived of as the primary goal of science or the actual nature of its
         achievement.

To make the meaning of these sentences more accessible to a learner of
English as a second language, we might rewrite them as follows:

(55) a. When we try to make sense of what we observe we are faced with two
         kinds of problems. One of these problems is: how do we know how
         things really are? The second problem is: what are we really doing
         when we measure things?
(56) a. When people say such things, it makes us doubt whether the main aim
         of science is to understand how things really are and whether this really
         is what science has achieved.

There are a number of differences between the original and the rewritten
versions. In the first place, the rewritten versions are both considerably
longer. This is mainly due to the fact that content which is contained in
noun groups in the original is expanded into clauses in the rewritten
versions.

interpretation:	(we try to) make sense of what we observe
the nature of reality:	(how do we know) how things really are?
the nature of measurement:	(how do we know) what we are really doing when we measure things?
Such accounts:	When people say such things
an understanding of reality:	to understand how things really are
the actual nature of its achievement:	this really is what science has achieved

In order to understand in more depth the grammatical differences between the two versions, it is necessary to go back to the discussion at the
beginning of Chapter 2 of the word class *noun*. It was noted then that nouns
typically represent that part of our experience that we perceive as things or
entities. Consider the following examples:

(57) . . . you measure capacitors in microfarads . . .
(58) . . . you can [. . .] shoot the ball into the ring.
(59) . . . it becomes easier for them to manipulate people.
(60) I like the sound of it.
(61) I strongly believe in what we are doing.   [*inv.*]
(62) Arthur now has a new car . . .

In these examples all the doing (*measure, shoot, manipulate*), feeling and thinking (*like, believe*), and having (*has*) are represented by verbs, while all the entities which are involved in the doing, feeling, thinking, and having are represented by nouns. A term used to refer in general to *goings-on* like *doing, happening, seeing, feeling, thinking,* as well as *being* and *having,* is **process.** A term used to refer in general to entities involved in such processes is **participant.**

Much of everyday language is like the above clauses, in that the processes are represented by verbs and the participants are represented by nouns. However, it is possible to rearrange this relationship and represent processes by nouns, as in the following examples:

(57) a. the <u>measurement</u> of capacitors in microfarads . . .
(58) a. the <u>shooting</u> of the ball into the ring . . .
(59) a. their easier <u>manipulation</u> of people . . .
(60) a. my <u>liking</u> of the sound of it . . .
(61) a. my strong <u>belief</u> in what we are doing . . .
(62) a. Arthur's <u>possession</u> of a new car . . .

In numbers 57a through 62a not only are the processes represented by nouns but a good deal of the rest of the material in the clauses has been *packed into* the noun groups. What has been done here – packing the content of clauses into noun groups – is known as **nominalization.** It is the opposite of what was done in simplifying the two sentences from Extract 7; that could be called *denominalization.*

In the examples 57a through 61a, the head noun representing the process is related to the verb which represented the process in the original sentence:

measure	measurement
shoot	shooting
manipulate	manipulation
like	liking
believe	belief

This is the simplest kind of nominalization. However, any case in which a process is represented by a noun can be regarded as nominalization. For example, in the rewritten version of number 62, the noun *possession* is not related to the verb *has.* However, since 62a represents as a noun the process of having, it can be regarded as a nominalization. Also note that the representation of a process by a noun may necessitate other changes, for example, from the adverb *strongly* in number 61 to the adjective *strong* in 61a.

Nominalization can refer to more than just the representation of processes as nouns. For example, the clause *they are very tall* can be repackaged into a noun group such as *their great height.* In this case, the noun *height* represents not a process but a **quality,** which in the original was represented by an adjective (*tall*). This is also a kind of nominalization.

Task 3f

Try denominalizing the nominalizations in the following sentences.

1. This is the reason for his many successes and his few failures.
2. Industrial development did not begin until the early 1960s.
3. The constant bumping and rubbing of these materials on the river bed wear it down.
4. Accompanying the rapid rise in population is the process of URBANISATION or city growth.
5. The payoff for the rigors and longueurs of scientific research is the consequent gain in understanding of the way the world is constructed.

Texts in which there is a great deal of nominalization (e.g., in examples 55 and 56) can seem very dense and may be hard to process. Nominalization can also lead to the meaning relationships between parts of the information being inexplicit or potentially ambiguous. We have already seen how the meaning relationships between Classifiers and Things can vary. This can be a problem when the reader does not already have the knowledge needed to *unpack* a particular noun group. So, if denominalized language is easier to process than highly nominalized language, why do users (particularly writers) of English use nominalization at all?

Nominalization serves several useful functions in the language. First, as has been noted, nominalized language offers the potential advantage of conciseness. Packing information into a noun group leaves the rest of the clause available for adding new information (e.g., *my strong belief in what we are doing has never faltered; Arthur's possession of a new car took us all by surprise*).

Second, it is much easier to begin a clause or a sentence with a noun group than with a verb group. There are many reasons why a writer might want to begin a clause or sentence with a nominalized process (some of these will be explored in Chapter 11). However, one purpose can be to provide a link between parts of a text. There is an example of this in Extract 5.

(63) The action is slow . . . (line 5)

Here the noun group *The action* sums up all the processes in the previous sentence and provides a starting point for the message in the next sentence.

A third reason has to do with the nature of scientific language, which reflects science's concern with categorizing, labeling, and describing phenomena. In order to do this effectively, it is often necessary to treat processes as if they were things. Nominalization is the device in the grammar that allows scientists to do this. This can be seen in Extract 2. Nominalizations such as *population density, urbanisation,* and *demographic transition* provide a shorthand label for the complex phenomena in question. Such labels may have very precise meanings, which may have been established earlier in a text, or which the writer assumes will be understood by anyone choosing to read a text in a particular subject area. Thus, for example, within the field of optics a term like *polarization* will be taken as referring to the process by which a filter allows to pass through it only light which is vibrating in one particular direction. It would be tiresome to have to spell out in clauses the whole process every time the author wished to refer to it. For further discussion of this see Halliday and Martin (1993).

In some cases, of course, nominalization can be a useful device for writers who have not themselves fully thought through the meaning of what they are writing!

Questions for discussion

- Imagine that you are teaching high school students who are fairly competent in everyday spoken English but have a great deal of trouble with subject area textbooks which contain a great deal of nominalization. What kinds of activities might help them with reading their subject area textbooks?
- How might you help your subject area colleagues improve the comprehensibility of textbooks and handouts which use a highly nominalized style?

Summary

1. Inclusives (*either, both, each, every, all, neither,* and *no*) refer to a complete group of things either positively or negatively and either as a whole or as individuals. *All* and *both* can directly precede definite Referrers. All the inclusives (except *every* and *no*) also have variants formed with *of* (e.g., *each of*) that may precede definite Referrers.

2. Quantifiers indicate quantity between *all* and *none*. Inexact quantity is indicated by *many, much, a lot of, several, some, any, a few, a little, few, little, fewer, fewest, less, least, more, most.* Some of these are used with count nouns, some with mass nouns, and some with both. They can also co-occur in various ways with Referrers and have variants formed with *of.* Exact quantity is indicated by numerals.

3. A partitive structure consists of a unit noun (e.g., *piece, lump*) followed by *of* and a second noun. Typical partitives allow mass nouns to be counted (e.g., *two pieces of wood*). However, there is not a firm distinction between partitives and the *of* forms of inclusives and Quantifiers.

4. Describers indicate a quality of, or an attitude to, the Thing. They are realized by adjectives and participles (V*ing* and V*ed* forms).

5. Classifiers subclassify the Thing. They are realized by adjectives, participles, and nouns.
6. The commonest kinds of postmodifiers are finite clauses, nonfinite clauses, and prepositional phrases. They function to qualify the Thing.
7. To master postmodifying finite clauses (restrictive or defining relative clauses) a learner must be able to position the relative clauses correctly, select appropriate relative pronouns, and appropriately rearrange the clause constituents.
8. In much everyday language, participants are realized by noun groups, processes are realized by verb groups, and qualities are realized by adjective groups. However, these relationships can be rearranged so that processes and qualities are realized by noun groups. This is known as nominalization.

Key terms introduced

This text	*Alternatives used in the field*
Classifier	
compound noun	
Describer	Epithet
inclusive	distributive (*each* and *every* only)
nominalization	
participant	
process	situation
quality	attribute
Quantifier	Numerative
relative pronoun	relativizer, embedder
embedded clause	
relative clause	
restrictive relative clause	

Discussion of tasks

Task 3a

The inexact Quantifiers which cannot be preceded by *the* are, of course, those which themselves include the indefinite article (*a lot of, a few, a little*), *some, any* and, for some reason, *much*. The following are examples of the other inexact Quantifiers preceded by *the*.

The many dissenters at the meeting were quite ignored.
The several dissenters at the meeting were quite ignored.
The few dissenters at the meeting were quite ignored.

The little food that is left should be shared out equally.
Last year we had the most students we have ever accepted.
Last year we had the fewest students we have ever accepted.
The children received the least food.

Note that *the* before Quantifiers is most commonly used where the reference is forward-pointing to the postmodifier within the same noun group.

Note also that *the fewer, the less,* and *the more* are normally only used in expressions with a second comparative such as *the fewer students the better; the less fuss the quicker it will be done; the more students the better.*

Possessives can precede the same range of Quantifiers as can *the:*

His many friends were all there.
Your several letters have all been received.
His few friends were all there.
Our little remaining food should be shared out.
It was last year that we had our most students.
It was last year that we had our fewest students.
It was last year that we received our least money.

Note that some people may not accept a possessive before *least,* as in the final example.

Task 3b

The usual order of Describers is *attitude, age, size, shape, color.* This is not an absolute rule – there is a certain amount of variation and flexibility, particularly in the ordering of *age* and *size.* However, it can be a useful rule of thumb for learners. But note that all Describers precede Classifiers (see Section 3.3).

Task 3c

flightless – Classifier
real – Classifier
big – Describer
long – Describer
monsoon – Classifier
millionaire – Classifier
ecological – Classifier
rapid – Describer

Task 3d

This is an area of considerable variability. The consensus among speakers I have consulted is as follows:

The *art world* and *a grammar mistake* are perfectly acceptable, although some see a difference in meaning between *the art world* and *the artistic world*.

The *finance sector* and *a science journal* are odd but possible.

Linguistics analysis and *mathematics equation* are either very odd or unacceptable.

Task 3e

1. The originals of the sentences are:
   a. . . . the green hills which ring the town are covered with colorful flowers. (*which* = Subject)
   b. The few woodcutters who did go into the mountains never returned. (*who* = Subject)
   c. The result is the network of valleys that diversify the face of the earth and the stupendous quantity of waste that the rivers carry down to the sea. (the first *that* = Subject; the second *that* = Object)
   d. He carried bags of sand and large stones and did all the heavy work the others could not manage. (*ZERO* = Object)
   e. Informants we contacted personally proved on the whole to be more reliable. (*ZERO* = Object)
   f. . . . yeah him, he's the one we went to Cairo with. (*ZERO* = Prepositional Object)
   g. The man with whom she had lived for the previous nine years suddenly left. (*whom* = Prepositional Object)
   h. The tools with which a river excavates its valleys are the boulders and sand that it sweeps along with it. (*which* = Prepositional Object; *that* = Object)
2. There is a certain amount of variability in the use of relative pronouns among users of English. You may not necessarily agree entirely with the following summing up of their usage.
   a. For human and Subject *who* is commonly used. *That* may also be used, particularly in speech. Some users of the language would not accept this use of *that* in formal written English.
   b. For nonhuman and Subject both *which* and *that* are used.
   c. For human and Object *whom, who, that,* and *ZERO* are used. *Whom* is normally restricted to formal written registers. Some users of the language would not accept *who* or *that* in most written registers.

d. For nonhuman and Object, *which, that,* and *ZERO* are used.
e. For human and Prepositional Object only *whom* is used when the preposition comes at the beginning of the relative clause. This is normally restricted to formal written English. When the preposition comes at the end of the relative clause, *whom, who, that,* and *ZERO* are all possible, again with *whom* being more formal and some users not accepting *who* in most written registers.
f. For nonhuman and Prepositional Object only *which* is used when the preposition comes at the beginning of the relative clause. When the preposition comes at the end, *which, that,* and *ZERO* are all used.

Task 3f

Some *possible* answers are as follows:

1. This is why he succeeded so often and failed so seldom.
2. Industry did not begin to develop until the early 1960s.
3. These materials constantly bump and rub on the river bed and wear it down.
4. As the population increases, the cities grow larger.
5. To research scientific questions takes a long time and is very hard work. However, it is worthwhile because you are able to understand how the world is constructed..

4 Doing and happening I: The transitivity of action processes

This chapter will begin to explore the potential of the English clause for representing our experience of the world. In other words, it will consider the clause from the point of view of its *experiential* meaning. However, before "moving up" from group rank to clause rank, it will be useful to look at the structure of verb groups in a little more detail.

4.1 Verb groups

Just as a noun group can be regarded as an expanded noun, a verb group can be regarded as an expanded verb. For example:

(1) The janitor <u>found</u> the cartons in the shed.
(2) The janitor <u>must have found</u> the cartons in the shed.   [*inv.*]

4.1.1 The structure of the verb group

In sentence 2, the word *found* is the head of the verb group *must have found.* The verb group head represents the experiential meaning of the process, that is, the *doing, happening, seeing, thinking, liking, being, having,* and so on. The constituents which precede the head can, like constituents before the head in a noun group, be regarded as premodifiers. However, the term which is more commonly used for verb group premodifiers is **auxiliary verbs** or just **auxiliaries.** This distinguishes them from **lexical verbs,** that is, verbs which can be the head of a verb group and represent the process. The maximum number of auxiliaries that can precede the head is four, making a maximum possible verb group size of five constituents, including the head (but excluding negative particles; see Section 9.3.4). For example:

	AUXILIARIES			HEAD
5	4	3	2	1

(3) By now we could've been being served coffee on a terrace overlooking the Bay of Naples.

5	4	3	2	1
will	have	is	is	eat
would	has	am	am	eats
may	had	are	are	ate
might		was	was	
can		were	were	
could				
shall				
should	have	been	been	eat
must	having	be	be	eaten
ought to		to be	to be	eating
		being		
do				
does				
did				
+V	+Ven/ed	+Ving	+Ven/ed	

Figure 4.1   Verb group structure. (Adapted from Scott et al. 1968.)

Verb groups of this size are not very common, although they are not as rare as one might think, especially in spoken English.

The structure of the verb group is set out in Figure 4.1; in the figure the auxiliaries are listed in the order in which they always occur. That is, although columns may be skipped, auxiliaries in column 4 may only be preceded by auxiliaries in column 5, auxiliaries in column 3 may be preceded by auxiliaries in columns 5 or 4, but not by auxiliaries in column 2, and so on. Thus, a verb group such as *has been being eaten* (4 3 2 1) is possible (although perhaps not very common), but a verb group such as **was having been eaten* (3 4 2 1) is not possible. Only one item from each column can be selected in a verb group; thus, a group such as **will may go* (5 5 1) is impossible.

The technical term for auxiliaries in column 4 is **perfect auxiliaries;** for those in column 3, **continuous** or **progressive auxiliaries;** and for those in column 2, **passive auxiliaries.**

The auxiliaries in each column determine the form of the following auxiliary or head. This is indicated at the bottom of each column. Thus:

1. Auxiliaries in column 5 must always be followed by V, that is, the base form of the word with no *-ed, -en, -s,* or *-ing* ending added. Examples: *would kick* (5 1), *should be eaten* (5 2 1), and *may be eating* (5 3 1).
2. Auxiliaries in column 4 must always be followed by the V*ed/en* forms. Examples: *have eaten* (4 1), *has kicked* (4 1), and *had been eaten* (4 2 1).
3. Auxiliaries in column 3 must always be followed by V*ing* forms. Examples: *are eating* (3 1) and *is being kicked* (3 2 1).
4. Auxiliaries in column 2 must always be followed by V*ed/en* forms. Examples: *is kicked* and *are eaten* (both 2 1).

Note that forms of the auxiliary *be* occur in both column 3 and column 2. They are distinguished by the form that follows them, for example, *were eating* (3 1) and *were eaten* (2 1).

The forms of the verb *do* in column 5 function as Finites in negative and interrogative clauses when the verb group contains no other auxiliary that could fulfill this function (Section 8.3). Unlike other auxiliaries in this column, they must be directly followed by a column 1 item (i.e., by the head). In other words, groups such as *did have gone* are impossible.

The auxiliaries (except those in column 5) have both finite and nonfinite forms. In columns 4 to 1 the finite forms are grouped together above the nonfinite forms.

Task 4a

1. Label the constituents of the verb groups in the following clauses according to Figure 4.1. The first one has already been done.
2. Which verb groups are finite and which nonfinite?

a. . . . which $\overset{2}{are}$ $\overset{1}{affected}$ by the MONSOON RAINS . . .
b. . . . densities can reach as high as 100 per km.
c. Monsoon Asia is going through a DEMOGRAPHIC TRANSI-
TION . . .
d. For many years the people of Yixing had lived peaceful and happy lives.
e. Having committed themselves in this way, they could hardly turn back.
f. The gorge is widened . . .
g. We wouldn't have made it without them.
h. The students have been given plenty of time.
i. Having been bitten once, they may not be willing to try again.
j. Could David still have been living in New Jersey at that time?
k. We would have liked him to have been properly rewarded.

4.1.2   Modal auxiliaries

The ten top auxiliaries in column 5 of Figure 4.1 are known as **modal auxiliaries,** or simply **modals.** Their meanings are explored in Chapter 10. However, they have a number of formal characteristics that set them apart from the other auxiliaries and can present problems for learners. These will be briefly dealt with here.

The modal auxiliaries are like other auxiliaries in that they are directly followed by *not* or *n't* to form negatives (e.g., *would not, mustn't*) and form interrogatives by being placed in front of the Subject (e.g., *would you? must you?*). (The terms *negative* and *interrogative* are discussed further in Section 8.2.) Unlike other auxiliaries, modal auxiliaries are always finite, for example, *as we must be out before eleven, we can't afford to waste any time* but not **musting be out before eleven, we can't afford to waste any time*. On the other hand, although always functioning as Finites, they are never marked for number agreement with the Subject, for example, *she must arrive before ten* but not **she musts arrive before ten*. In addition, some of the modal auxiliaries have no past tense form, for example, *today she must arrive before ten* but not **yesterday she musted arrive before ten*. Other modal verbs can be considered to have past tense forms in certain contexts, for example, *could* may function as the past tense form of *can* in the context of reported speech, as in *he said that I could go*. However, in most contexts such past tense forms (i.e., *could, might, should,* and *would*) can be considered separate modals.

4.1.3 Semimodals

In addition to the ten modal auxiliaries listed in column 5 of Figure 4.1, there are four verbs which have some of the same characteristics and which are sometimes referred to as **semimodals**. These are *need, dare, have to,* and *used to*.

4.1.3.1 NEED AND DARE

Need and *dare* sometimes behave like modal auxiliaries and sometimes like ordinary lexical verbs (see Section 4.1.1).

Number agreement with the Subject (like lexical verbs)   In positive (i.e., not negative) clauses they can be marked for number agreement with the Subject. Also, unlike modal auxiliaries, the following verb is in the *to* + V form, not the V form, for example, *he needs to do it, he dares to do it,* but not *?he need do it, ?he dare do it*.

Negative and interrogative with do (like lexical verbs)   They frequently form negatives and interrogatives with the auxiliary *do,* for example, *he does not need to do it, he does not dare to do it, does he need to do it?; does he dare to do it?*

Negative and interrogative without do; no agreement (like modals)
They can also form negative and interrogative clauses without the auxiliary *do*. In such cases, the following verb takes the V not the *to* + V form, for example, *he need not do it, he dare not do it, need he do it?, dare he do it?*

In addition, unlike a modal auxiliary but like a lexical verb, *need* and *dare* can be preceded by a modal auxiliary, for example, *he might need to do it, he wouldn't dare do it.*

In current language use, there appears to be a trend toward consistently treating these two words as ordinary lexical verbs, in terms of their formal characteristics. However, as *need* can express meanings within the area of *modality,* it will be looked at again in Chapter 10. *Dare* will not be further considered.

4.1.3.2 HAVE TO

In terms of form, *have to* is even less like a modal auxiliary. It regularly agrees with the Subject, it forms negatives and interrogatives with *do,* and it can be preceded by modal auxiliaries. However, in both American and British English, the negative and interrogative without *do* are still sometimes used, although usually with the word *got* added, as in *has he got to do it?* (compare with *does he have to do it?*) and *he hasn't got to do it* (compare with *he doesn't have to do it*).

Although formally *have to* often behaves like a lexical verb, it does express meanings within the area of modality and is also considered further in Chapter 10.

4.1.3.3 USED TO

Used to also normally forms negatives and interrogatives with *do* like a lexical verb, for example, *he didn't use to do it* and *did you use to do it?* Forms like *he used not to* (or *usedn't to*) and *used you to?* (i.e., where *used to* behaves more like a modal) are now considered old-fashioned by most British and American speakers. As the meaning of *used to* has to do with the time of a process, it will be considered again in Chapter 9.

Task 4b

The following are some typical mistakes involving the forms of modal auxiliaries. In each case, state which of the formal characteristics of modals is being ignored.

1. *He might damaged it himself for the insurance.
2. *She mays be from the mainland.
3. *I musted finish the work yesterday.
4. *He should not really goes there so often.
5. *The students may not can do it.
6. *Such people do not really ought to come here.

4.1.4   Learning and teaching verb group structure

Figure 4.1, of course, only specifies what are and what are not possible combinations of auxiliaries within verb groups. It tells us nothing about the functions and meanings of the different verb group structures. These will be explored later in this chapter and in subsequent chapters.

It is extremely unlikely that any teacher would want to present beginners with the complete structure of the English verb group as set out in such a table. The various combinations of auxiliaries and head are normally introduced separately and practiced in appropriate contexts, with knowledge and mastery of the system being built up piece by piece. However, it is not uncommon to find even quite advanced learners producing impossible verb groups such as *they should been punished*. For such learners, a systematic overview of the structural possibilities of the English verb group may be useful.

Questions for discussion

- What kinds of errors in verb group *form* do your students make? How could a table such as Figure 4.1 (simplified if necessary) be used to help intermediate or advanced learners develop self-editing skills in the area of verb group form?
- Some teachers wish to avoid technical terminology and so use the 5 4 3 2 1 format as a way of describing verb groups to learners; for example, they may refer to *a 4 2 1 verb* instead of *a perfect passive verb* or *a 3 2 1 verb* instead of *a progressive passive verb*. What advantages or disadvantages do you see in referring to verb groups in this way?

4.2   Action processes

The experiential resources of clauses in English can now be explored. The following clause from Extract 5 consists of a verb group, two noun groups, and a prepositional phrase.

(4) With a quick movement of its tail, the sea-serpent would overturn fishing boats . . .

In Chapter 1, the functions of Subject, Object, Finite, Predicator, and Adjunct in this clause were identified. However, in terms of experiential meaning, the verb group (*would overturn*) tells us about an action; the two noun groups (*the sea-serpent* and *fishing boats*) represent the thing which does the action and the thing which is on the receiving end of the action, and the prepositional phrase (*with a quick movement of its tail*) tells us how the action was carried out.

Using the terms introduced in the last section of the previous chapter, we can say that the action in this clause is a kind of *process,* and the doer and the receiver of the action are kinds of *participants.* In addition, the *how* can be described as a kind of *circumstance.* This chapter and the next chapter look at configurations of participants and circumstances typical of such **action processes.** In subsequent chapters, configurations typical of other process types will be considered. The general term for the configurations of participants associated with different processes is **transitivity.**

4.2.1 Actor and Goal

The following text was written by a learner.

Text 4a

On Saturday my father made an umu [a kind of Samoan oven] for my sister's birthday. He used wood to make the umu. My mother told me to collect some leaves for the umu while she did the cabbage and the potatoes. My father then peeled the taro and took it to the umu. When I came home, my sister put the taro in the umu. We then removed the stones from the umu and put the food in it. At the end, we put the sack on it.

This is a simple narrative consisting of a series of processes in more or less chronological order. (As an account of the stages in making an umu, the text is not in fact very accurate.) All but one of the processes are action processes. (The exception is *told,* which is a *verbal* process and is considered in Section 6.3.)

Most of the action process clauses have two associated participants, for example:

(5) We then removed the stones from the umu.

The function of the first participant (*we*) is similar to that of *the sea serpent* in example 4, which was glossed as *the thing which does the action.* The technical term for this participant function is **Actor.** In example 5, as in all **active voice** action process clauses, the Actor is also the Subject, or to put it more precisely, the noun group which realizes Actor function also realizes Subject function.

The function of the second participant (*the stones*) is similar to that of *fishing boats* in example 4, which was previously glossed as *the thing which is on the receiving end of the action.* The term for this participant function is **Goal.** In this clause, the Goal is also the Direct Object.

In most cases, if we ask a question like *what did (does, do,* etc.*) X do?*, X will be the Actor. If we ask a question like *what happened (happens,* etc.*) to Y?* Y will be the Goal, for example:

ACTOR
(5) a. What did <u>we</u> do?   <u>We</u>   removed the stones from the umu.

GOAL
(5) b. What happened to <u>the stones</u>? We removed   <u>them</u>   from the umu.

Task 4c

Identify Actors, Goals, and circumstances in the other two-participant action process clauses in text 4a.

In the first clause in the text, you may have correctly identified *an umu* as Goal. However, note that *Goal* means something slightly different here. *My father* did not really do something to *the umu.* Rather *my father* created *the umu.* However, the grammar treats such participants in the same way as other Goals, so there is no advantage in using a different label to describe it.

There is one action process clause in text 4a which only has one participant.

ACTOR
(6)   When   <u>I</u>   came home . . .

This is a little deceptive, as at first glance *home* looks as if it might also be a participant. In fact, *home* is a slightly odd word. It behaves sometimes like a noun and sometimes like an adverb. In this clause it is an adverb and represents a circumstance (of place), not a participant. In other words, it answers the question *Where (did you come)?* rather than *What (did you come)?* This becomes even clearer if other place expressions are substituted for the word *home.* For example, one can say *when I came to school* but not **when I came school.* Learners sometimes try to regularize *home* and produce clauses such as **I went to home.*

Clauses with the two participants – Actor and Goal – are normally known as **transitive** clauses, while clauses with the single participant Actor are normally known as **intransitive** clauses.

The distinction between transitive and intransitive clauses is actually not quite so straightforward as it may at first seem. For example, there can be no doubt that example 6 is an intransitive (Actor-only) clause. It would not be possible to introduce a second participant into this clause (e.g., **I came something home*). Similarly, there can be no doubt that example 5 is a transitive (Actor and Goal) clause. The participant *the stones* cannot be omitted. However, with clauses such as *she eats at least four times a day,* there is what we might call an *understood* Goal – *food.* It is therefore useful to make a distinction between the types of clauses: (1) those in which there can only be an Actor (intransitive), (2) those in which there must be both an

Actor and a Goal (transitive), and (3) those in which a Goal may be implicit (implicitly transitive).

Task 4d

In the following examples, identify (1) intransitive action process clauses, (2) implicitly transitive action process clauses, and (3) transitive action process clauses with expressed Goals. Note that there may be more than one clause in some of the examples.

a. . . . he was flying through the air with one leg up in the air . . .
b. . . . color these little birds beautifully . . .
c. . . . who were you working with?
d. Every Saturday morning in the winter term I bike into town . . .
e. Later in the week the purchaser of our house phoned to ask whether we had lost a cat. (Note that *ask* is not an action process. It is dealt with in Chapter 6.)
f. . . . I'm going to write it on the special plastic stuff.
g. Where the ball goes I go. I tackle, handle, kick, run, everything.

As the clause *we had lost a cat* (in b, task 4d) shows, the use of the term *Actor* for a participant does not imply that the participant necessarily *deliberately* carries out the action. And as the clause *where the ball goes* (g, task 4d) shows, nor does an Actor have to be animate. There are, for example, many inanimate Actors in Extract 5, for example,

(7) . . . a river excavates its valleys . . .

The Actor can even be a nominalized process, for example:

(8) The constant bumping and rubbing of these materials on the river bed wear it down . . .

However, even with inanimate Actors and nominalized process Actors, it is normally possible to ask questions such as *What does a river do?* and *What does the constant bumping and rubbing of these materials on the river bed do?*

4.2.2 Recipient and Beneficiary

Some action processes can have three associated participants, as in:

(9) I'll give you your paper.

In this clause, *I* is the Actor and *your paper* is the Goal. The third participant (in the Indirect Object position) is the one who receives the Goal. This participant is called the **Recipient.** The option also exists of representing the participant as a Prepositional Object within an Adjunct, for example:

(9) a. I'll give your paper to <u>you</u>.

The following clause looks similar in structure to number 9:

(10)   I'll find you some paper.

However, if this clause is rephrased with the second noun group as a Prepositional Object, the preposition *for,* not *to,* must be used:

(10) a. I'll find some paper <u>for you</u>.

The participant *you* in number 10 is not someone who receives the Goal. Rather it is someone for whose benefit the action is carried out. The term **Beneficiary** is used to describe this participant.

Clauses which have a Recipient or Beneficiary as an Indirect Object are referred to as **ditransitive.**

Task 4e

Identify the Recipients and Beneficiaries in the following clauses.

1. Dad got me a few books.
2. The patron himself cooked us a meal.
3. This should give HAAL members a greater opportunity to . . .
4. Rena mixed us some really strong martinis.
5. The waiter brought us the wrong dish.
6. I've left you some food on the table.
7. I wrote him a letter last week.
8. She wrote me a beautiful poem.

4.2.3 *Configurations of participants and the learner*

Potential problems in learning to produce clauses with the appropriate configurations of processes and participants can come both from differences between English and the learner's mother tongue and from difficulties within English itself.

The way in which a certain phenomenon is represented in English by a particular configuration of process and participants may be different from the way in which the same phenomenon is represented in another language. Sometimes there may simply be a difference in the number of participants. For example, the meteorological phenomenon *it is raining* is represented in English as a process with just one "dummy" participant – *it.* In this clause, *it* merely functions as Subject but has no experiential function (i.e., *it* does not refer to an entity such as *the sky*). In Malay, the same phenomenon can be represented by one word, as in:

(11) Hujan (hari ini)
      Rain (day this)
      "It's raining (today)."

(Newman n.d.)

The Malay word *hujan,* like the English word *rain,* can be both a noun and a verb, so the above clause could be interpreted either as a participant with no process or as a process with no participant. At the other extreme, according to Halliday (1994), there is a dialect of Chinese[1] in which the phenomenon is represented as a process with two participants – "the sky is dropping water."

In other cases, an entity may be represented as a participant directly associated with the process in one language but in another language as part of an Adjunct (and therefore more like a circumstance than a participant). For example, the slogan *serve the people* is represented in English as a transitive clause, with *the people* as Goal/Object. However, the equivalent Mandarin Chinese clause is intransitive, with *the people* (*renmin*) as Prepositional Object within an Adjunct.

(12) wei renmin fuwu
      for people serve

Languages also often differ in how they treat Recipients and Beneficiaries. For example, French allows:

(13)   Il a bâti une maison pour son fils
         He built a house for his son

However, unlike English it will not allow the Beneficiary *son fils* to be represented as an Indirect Object:

(13) a. *Il a bâti son fils une maison.
          He built his son a house.

Monolingual speakers tend to regard the configuration of process, participant, and circumstance by which a certain phenomenon is represented in their mother tongue as natural or inevitable. They may therefore try to replicate the configuration when learning a second language.

Potential problems also come from within English itself. Although many commonly occurring verbs can be used in both transitive and intransitive clauses, individual verbs vary greatly in the configurations of participants that they allow or require. This can be a source of difficulty for learners, who may produce errors such as:

(14)   *The balloon <u>raised</u> slowly into the air.

1 In fact, a dialect of Cantonese investigated by Halliday in the late 1940s (Halliday personal communication).

Raise is, of course, one of the verbs which can only be used in transitive clauses, as compared to *rise,* which can only be used in intransitive clauses. Such pairs are further considered in Section 5.1.

It is also not immediately obvious which verbs can take Recipients and Beneficiaries as Indirect Objects and which only allow them as Prepositional Objects. For example,

(15)   He built his son a house.

is acceptable, but

(15) a. *He constructed his son a house.

is not.

A rule of thumb that might be helpful to some learners is that the verbs which allow the Recipient or Beneficiary as Indirect Object are usually one-syllable words, of Germanic origin (e.g., *give, make, pass, get, write*), while those that do not are usually longer words, of French or Latin origin (e.g., *donate, manufacture, circulate, obtain, compose*).

There are, of course, exceptions. For example, *advance* is a two-syllable word of Romance origin, but the following clause is quite acceptable:

(16)   The bank advanced us some money.   [*inv.*]

Learners should have access to a good dictionary which indicates the different patterns a verb can occur in, together with plenty of examples.

Task 4f

1. Which of the following verbs can occur in:
   a. Intransitive (Actor-only) clauses
   b. Transitive (Actor and Goal) clauses
   c. Ditransitive (Actor, Goal, and Recipient or Beneficiary) clauses

buy	catch	sleep	hand
cut	exercise	disappear	design
drop	evaporate	fly	write
descend			

2. Where a verb can occur in two or more types of configuration, which type would you consider it most useful for learners to learn first?
3. Try translating into another language some of the clauses you used to explore the possible configurations of participants with the verbs listed. How similar or different are the configurations in the two languages?

4.2.4 Action processes and voice

In all of the examples of transitive action process clauses considered so far, the noun group realizing Actor function also realizes Subject function (or, to put it another way, the Actor is mapped onto the Subject) and the noun group realizing Goal function also realizes Direct Object function, as in:

	ACTOR/ SUBJECT		GOAL/ DIRECT OBJECT
(17)	My father then peeled	the taro . . .

As mentioned earlier, clauses in which the Actor maps onto the Subject in this way are known as **active voice** clauses. It is a characteristic of transitive action process clauses, such as number 17, that they also have **passive voice** versions, in which the Goal is mapped onto the Subject and the Actor either appears in an Adjunct as the Object of the preposition *by* or is omitted, for example:

	GOAL/ SUBJECT		ACTOR/ ADJUNCT
(17) a.	The taro was then peeled	[by my father]

The change in voice is also marked by the use of a *passive voice verb group* (i.e., a "2 1" verb group – *was peeled*) instead of an *active voice verb group* (*peeled*).

Ditransitive clauses often have two possible passive voice versions, one with the Goal as Subject and the other with the Recipient or Beneficiary as Subject, for example:

	RECIPIENT	
(18)	You	will be given your paper . . .

	GOAL	
(18) a.	Your paper will be given to you . . .

	BENEFICIARY	
(19)	You	will be found some paper . . .

	GOAL	
(19) a.	Some paper will be found for your . . .

Reasons for selecting passive rather than active voice in various contexts are explored in Section 11.9.1.

4.2.5 Action processes and tense

When referring to action processes going on *now,* that is, at the moment of speaking or writing, the normal tense choice is present continuous, for example:

(20)   My father is making an umu   at this very moment.

As will be seen in later chapters, this is not necessarily the case for other process types.

4.2.6   Range

The following examples each have two participants, one of which is an Actor and the other of which looks at first sight like a Goal:

(21)   The advance party reached the summit on the third day.

(22)   . . . a cat and a dog (who) completed a fantastic trek across Canada . . .

However, it would be very odd to ask questions about the second participant in these examples, such as *What happened to the summit?* or *What happened to the fantastic trek across Canada?* That is, because nothing is really done to *the summit* or to *a fantastic trek across Canada,* they cannot be characterized as the participants on the receiving end of an action. Rather they provide information about the extent, range, or scope of the process. In this, they are semantically rather like circumstances. However, they are treated by the grammar as participants. The technical name for such participants is **Range.**

Ranges are similar to Goals in that they are mapped onto the Direct Object in active clauses (as in examples 21 and 22) and can be mapped onto the Subject in passive clauses, for example:

              RANGE/SUBJECT
(21) a.   The summit   was reached on the third day.

              RANGE/SUBJECT
(22) a. The fantastic trek was completed in a year or more.

A special kind of Range is exemplified in the following clause.

(23)   For many years, the people of Yixing had lived peaceful and happy lives.

In this case, the head of the noun group realizing Range (*lives*) is related to verb group head realizing the process (*lived*). The Range in a sense restates the process. Other examples of this are:

(24)   Why don't you sing us one of your songs?
(25)   He slept the sleep of the innocent.

Sometimes, the nouns are not directly related to the verbs in form but are related in meaning, for example:

(26) It does a lot better job than the transistors . . .
(27) At thirty-seven he could still perform a backflip somersault.

An extension of such restating of the process in the Range is represented by the following examples:

(28) . . . in <u>giving</u> whatever or whoever it is upset with a thumping big <u>kick</u>.

(29) Britain and Ireland will still <u>make</u> quick <u>checks</u> of documents.

(30) . . . but I usually <u>take</u> a huge <u>bite</u> . . .

(31) I need to <u>get</u> an early <u>start</u> . . .

In such clauses, the representation of the process has shifted entirely to the Range, and the verb has almost no experiential meaning. Such verbs are sometimes called **delexical verbs,** because their lexical meaning has been in some sense removed. According to the *Cobuild English Grammar* (Collins 1990), the most commonly used delexical verbs are *give, have, make,* and *take.* Part of the motivation for using such structures may be that by representing the process as a noun, the potential for using the noun group to modify the process is much greater than it is with verb groups. Try, for example, rewriting the clause *he gave his usual brisk military salute* with the process represented by a full lexical verb instead of delexical *gave* and with no Range (*?he saluted as usual, briskly and militarily*).

Delexical structures are very common, particularly in informal language. They can be a problem for learners because there is no rule governing which delexical verbs go with which nouns. They are idiomatic, and must be learned simply as fixed expressions. The difficulty is compounded by the fact that new delexical structures tend to come into usage, rather often, for example:

(32) Let's <u>do</u> <u>lunch</u> sometime.

However, learners who avoid delexical structures altogether run the risk of sometimes sounding stilted, for example:

(33) I would like to bathe.   (instead of *take a bath*)

Questions for discussion

- If you are currently teaching, investigate any problems your students have with using appropriate participants with action process verbs. To what extent can such problems be attributed to different transitivity patterns in their mother tongues and to what extent can they be attributed to confusion between related English verbs (e.g., *rise* and *raise, give* and *donate*).

    If you are not currently teaching, investigate a number of dictionaries intended for learners of English by looking up the verbs listed in task 4f and any other verbs you can think of that are used in more than one transitivity pattern. How well do the different dictionaries exemplify the various transitivity patterns in which the verbs can occur?

- Suggest a context and some activities to introduce the basic structure of transitive action process clauses to beginning learners.

Summary

1. Verb groups have a head, which represents the process (a lexical verb), and up to four auxiliaries. This is symbolized as 5 4 3 2 1. The auxiliaries include modal auxiliaries and forms of *do* (at 5), perfect auxiliaries (at 4), progressive auxiliaries (at 3), and passive auxiliaries (at 2). The head is at 1.
2. Modal auxiliaries differ from other auxiliaries in that they are always finite yet are not marked for number nor, except in a very few cases, for tense.
3. *Need, dare, have to,* and *used to* have *some* of the characteristics of modals, and are sometimes called semimodals.
4. Action process clauses normally have at least one participant called the Actor (the participant "doing" the action). They may also have a second participant called the Goal (the participant which is on the receiving end of the action). Actor-only clauses are called intransitive clauses and Actor + Goal clauses are called transitive clauses.
5. Other possible participants in action process clauses include Recipients (receivers of a Goal), Beneficiaries (participants for whose benefit the action is carried out), and Ranges (which typically indicate the extent, range or scope of the action).
6. A delexical verb is a verb used with a Range where the Range represents most or all of the meaning of the process; the most common delexical words are *give, have, make,* and *take.*

Key terms introduced

This text	*Alternatives used in the field*
action process	material process
active voice	
Actor	Agent
auxiliary/auxiliary verb	verbal auxiliary
Beneficiary	Client
delexical verb	
ditransitive	
Goal	Patient, Affected
intransitive	
lexical verb	
modal auxiliaries/modals	modal verbs
passive auxiliaries	
passive voice	

perfect auxiliaries
progressive/continuous auxiliaries
Range
Recipient
semimodals
transitive
transitivity

Discussion of tasks

Task 4a

     5   1
b. can reach, finite

     3   1
c. is going, finite

     4   1
d. had lived, finite

     4   1   5   1
e. having committed, nonfinite; could turn, finite

     2   1
f. is widened, finite

     5   4   1
g. would(n't) have made, finite

     4   2   1
h. have been given, finite

     4   2   1   5   1
i. having been bitten, nonfinite; may (not) be, finite

     5   4   3   1
j. could have been living, finite

     5   4   1   4   2   1
k. would have liked, finite; to have been rewarded, nonfinite

Task 4b

1. *Might* being a column 5 auxiliary, must be followed by V, that is, *damage* (A learner may know that *might* has no past form and therefore try to mark tense on the head).
2. Modals are not marked for Subject Finite agreement.
3. *Must*, like several modals, has no past tense form.
4. Modal *should* must be followed by V. (A learner may know there is no form *shoulds* and therefore try to mark agreement on the head instead.)

5. Both *may* and *can* are from column 5. Only one auxiliary can be selected from each column. (A learner may confuse auxiliary *can* and lexical verb + adjective *be able.*)
6. Like other auxiliaries, modals form negative polarity by being followed by *not/n't,* with no use of *do* (possible influence of semimodals like *have to*).

Task 4c

	CIRCUMSTANCE	ACTOR		GOAL	CIRCUMSTANCE

1.   CIRCUMSTANCE   ACTOR   GOAL   CIRCUMSTANCE
   On Saturday   my father made an umu for my sister's birthday.

2.   ACTOR   GOAL
   He   used wood . . .

3.   GOAL
   . . . to make the umu.

4.   ACTOR   GOAL
   . . . me   to collect some leaves . . .

5.   ACTOR   GOAL   GOAL
   . . . she   did the cabbages and the potatoes.

6.   ACTOR   GOAL
   My father then peeled the taro . . .

7.   GOAL CIRCUMSTANCE
   . . . and took   it   to the umu.

8.   ACTOR   GOAL   CIRCUMSTANCE
   . . . my sister put the taro   in the umu.

9.   GOAL   CIRCUMSTANCE
   . . . and put the food   in it.

10.   ACTOR   GOAL   CIRCUMSTANCE
  . . . we   put the sack   on it.

Note that numbers 3 and 4 are nonfinite *to* + V (infinitive) clauses. In each case they "share" a participant with the finite clause on which they are dependent. In the case of number 3, the Actor is the Subject of the finite clause (i.e., *he*). Number 7 and the clause which precedes it are linked clauses (see Chapter 12); they share the same Subject/Actor (omitted in the second clause). The same applies to number 9. The Actor/Subject of this clause is understood to be the same as that of the preceding clause (We then removed the stones from the umu . . .).

Task 4d

a. Intransitive clause – *he* is the only participant (Actor); *through the air* is a circumstance (of place).

b. Transitive – *these little birds* is the Goal; the Actor (you) is understood.
c. intransitive – *you* is the Actor; *who . . . with* is a circumstance (of accompaniment).
d. *I bike into town* = intransitive – *I* is the Actor; *into town* is a circumstance (of place).
e. *the purchaser of our house phoned* = implicitly transitive – *the purchaser of our house* is the Actor; the second implicit participant is "us." (Strictly speaking, this is Range rather than Goal; Section 4.2.6.)
   we had lost a cat = transitive – *we* is the Actor; *a cat* is the Goal.
f. transitive – *I* is the Actor and *it* is the Goal.
g. *where the ball goes* = intransitive – *where* is a circumstance (of place).
   I go = intransitive.
   I tackle = implicitly transitive – the Goal (other players) is understood.
   (I) handle = implicitly transitive – the Goal (the ball) is understood.
   (I) kick = implicitly transitive – the Goal (the ball) is understood.
   (I) run = intransitive.

Task 4e

1. *me* = Beneficiary
2. *us* = Beneficiary
3. *HAAL members* = Recipient
4. *us* = Beneficiary
5. *us* = Recipient
6. *you* = Beneficiary
7. *him* = Recipient
8. *me* = Beneficiary

Task 4f

buy – transitive and ditransitive.
cut – transitive and ditransitive. *Cut* is occasionally intransitive when followed by an Adjunct (e.g., *he cut into the cheese*) and in clauses such as *this wood cuts easily* meaning *is easy to cut.*
drop – transitive, intransitive and ditransitive.
descend – intransitive. *Descend* is transitive only with a *Range* participant (e.g., *he descended the stairs;* see Section 4.2.4.)
catch – transitive and ditransitive.
exercise – intransitive and ditransitive.
evaporate – intransitive and transitive.
sleep – intransitive. Transitive only in expressions such as *this room sleeps six.*

disappear – intransitive. *Disappear* is occasionally ironically transitive (e.g., the *regime disappeared thousands of its political opponents*).

fly – intransitive and transitive.

hand – transitive and ditransitive.

design – transitive and ditransitive. *Design* is occasionally intransitive with an Adjunct (e.g., *he designs very well*).

write – transitive and ditransitive. *Write* is occasionally intransitive, especially with an Adjunct (e.g., *he writes beautifully*).

The characteristics of some of the verbs in this list will be further considered in Section 5.1.

5 *Doing and happening II: Ergativity, phrasal verbs, and phase*

This chapter will first look at some action process clauses which involve "happening" rather than "doing." The chapter will then consider two phenomena which strictly speaking apply to all process types, but which can be conveniently illustrated using action process clauses. These are cases of verbs followed by prepositions and cases of two verbs representing a single process.

5.1 Causer and Affected

Consider the following two texts.

Text 5a

How Olive Oil Is Made

The olives are first washed in water and then crushed under millstones. The resulting paste is spread on to mats. The mats are stacked up to fifty at a time and pressed under 300 to 400 tons of pressure. The resulting liquid contains oil and water. It is put into tanks and left to settle. The oil rises to the surface.

Text 5b

The Rain Cycle

Water evaporates from seas, rivers, and lakes and rises into the air as vapor. As the vapor cools, it condenses into droplets around tiny particles of dust, smoke, and salt. It then falls as rain.

These two texts are similar in that they both describe a sequence of events through which something comes about – olive oil in the one case, rain in the other. However, the two texts differ fundamentally in the way they present the events.

Text 5a represents what can be called a *manufacturing process,* in which something is produced through the actions of human beings or machines. Most of the clauses in this text therefore have a participant on which an action is performed and an implied participant which performs or does the action. This is consistent with the Actor-Goal type of analysis of action process clauses that has been adopted so far, for example:

```
                  PROCESS
     GOAL     ┌─────────────┐                           ACTOR
(1)  The olives are first washed   (implying by someone/something)

       GOAL         PROCESS                              ACTOR
(2)  The resulting paste is spread on to mats   (implying by someone/something)
```

Text 5b, however, represents what might be called a natural process. It consists less of "actions" than of "happenings," which are presented as coming about more or less spontaneously. The clauses in this text might at first be regarded as the same as the intransitive (i.e., Actor-only) action process clauses considered in Section 4.2.1. However, if the participants in this text, such as *water* in the first clause of the first sentence and *the vapor* in the first clause of the second sentence, are examined more closely, they do not seem to function as doers, or Actors. We would, in fact, be more likely to ask questions about them like *What happens to water?* and *What happens to the vapor?* than questions like *What does water do?* and *What does the vapor do?* In other words, they seem as much like Goals as Actors.

In addition, it would be possible to introduce a second participant into most of the clauses in text 5b, not in the Object position but in the Subject position, making the original Subjects the Objects. For example:

(3)   The sun evaporates water . . .   [*inv.*]
(4)   As the cold air cools the water vapor . . .   [*inv.*]

These two clauses could also have passive versions:

(3) a. Water is evaporated (by the sun) . . .
(4) a. As the vapor is cooled (by the cold air) . . .

To continue with the Actor-Goal type of analysis, we would have to label as Actors *water* and *the vapor* in the original clauses (*Water evaporates . . .* and *As the vapor cools . . .*), but as Goals in numbers 3a and 4a. This clearly exaggerates the difference between *water evaporates* and *water is evaporated* and between *the vapor cools* and *the vapor is cooled. Water* and *the vapor* in fact have the same participant role in both versions. They are neither Actors nor Goals but the participants that are affected by or undergo the processes. The label **Affected** can be used to refer to such participants. In the transitive clauses, the participants *the sun* and *the cold air* are also not so much Actors as **Causers** of the processes. In other words, numbers 3 and 4 are in some ways similar to clauses such as *the sun causes the water to evaporate* and *the cold air causes the water vapor to cool.* (These are *causative structures;* see Section 5.3.1.) The analysis of the three versions of the first clause thus becomes:

(5)   AFFECTED PROCESS
Water   evaporates . . .

(5) a. CAUSER PROCESS AFFECTED
The sun evaporates   water   . . .

(5) b. AFFECTED   PROCESS   CAUSER
Water   is evaporated (by the sun) . . .

These three versions can be regarded as three options in the voice system which English allows with some verbs, typically verbs representing processes of movement and change. Active voice and passive voice as represented by numbers 5a and 5b, respectively, have already been examined. Number 5 represents what is known as *middle voice.* In some languages, middle voice is distinguished from the other voices by the use of a different form of the verb or by case marking on the noun. In English, the verb form is the same as for active voice.

The Causer-Affected type of analysis is an analysis of **ergativity.** It brings out the fact that the grammar of English allows representation of processes not only in terms of *actions* which have a doer (the Actor) and which may or may not be extended to a second participant (the Goal), but also in terms of *happenings* which affect one participant (the Affected) and which may or may not be caused by another participant (the Causer).

Following an ergative analysis, all one-participant clauses in which the single participant is an entity to which something happens (i.e., with the one participant Affected) rather than an entity which does something can be interpreted as middle voice, for example:

(6)   AFFECTED
The branch he was sitting on suddenly broke with a sharp crack.

(7)   AFFECTED
The economy developed very fast during the 1980s.

(8)   AFFECTED
An accident happened outside the school this morning.

(9)   AFFECTED
Her grandfather died last night. [*inv.*]

However, not all verbs in such clauses can also be used in clauses with a Causer added in, as the following examples show.

(6) a. CAUSER   AFFECTED
His weight broke the branch he was sitting on

(6) b. AFFECTED   CAUSER
The branch he was sitting on was broken (by his weight)

(7) a. CAUSER   AFFECTED
The government developed the economy very fast in the 1980s.

(7) b. AFFECTED   CAUSER
The economy was developed very fast (by the government) in the 1980s.

CAUSER   AFFECTED
(8) a. * A bus happened an accident outside our school this morning.

AFFECTED   CAUSER
(8) b. *An accident was happened (by a bus) outside our school . . .

CAUSER   AFFECTED
(9) a. *A heart attack died her grandfather last night.

AFFECTED   CAUSER
(9) b. *Her grandfather was died (by a heart attack) last night.

Similarly, there are two verbs in text 5b that will not allow Causers to be introduced:

(10) *. . . the heat rises the water into the air as vapor.
(11) *The particles then fall these as rain.

It is therefore useful to make a distinction between ergativity in the broad sense, which refers to the Affected-only and Affected + Causer representation of goings-on, and **ergative verbs,** which refer only to those verbs which allow the three-voice option of active, middle, or passive – or in terms more accessible for learners, verbs which allow the Object of a transitive clause to become the Subject of an intransitive clause, without any change in the voice of the verb. Thus, *evaporate, cool, condense, break,* and *develop* are all ergative verbs, but *rise, happen,* and *die* are not.

Task 5a

Which of the following verbs are ergative verbs? In each case, give one example of the verb used in a one-participant (Affected-only) clause and one example of the verb used in a two-participant (Causer and Affected) clause.

drop	move	run
descend	jump	drown
raise	leap	ignite
widen	save	sink
lift		

It is worth noting that even with nonergative verbs, options for representing a process as having or not having a Causer may be available. However, the option may depend upon the choice between two different verbs. Sometimes they are pairs of verbs which are related historically, for example:

Without	*With*
causer	*causer*
rise	raise
lie	lay

see   show
sit   seat

There are also pairs of unrelated words which *could* be interpreted in this way, for example, *die* and *kill, flee* and *chase, fall* and *push.*

5.1.1   Teaching and learning ergative patterns

Most learners will no doubt begin to use middle voice clauses along with ordinary intransitive clauses without being aware that there is anything different about them. However, some learners tend to avoid middle voice and to overuse passive voice with ergative verbs in contexts in which the implication of a Causer may be inappropriate, as in the following examples:

(12) ?The economy was developed very fast during the late 1980s.
(13) ?Prices were dropped sharply in the first quarter of the year.

The mother tongue of the writers of these sentences is Cantonese, which would not normally have anything analogous to passive voice in such contexts. Thus sentences like these may well represent a kind of overcorrection by learners who have been taught that verbs must be either active or passive and have been often corrected for using active instead of passive voice.

Some learners also try to use passive voice with verbs which will allow only one participant, for example:

(14) *An accident was happened outside our school this morning.
(15) *Her grandfather was died last night.

It may well be that the learners are simply trying to use these verbs, which as we have seen can have an ergative interpretation in the broad sense, as if they were ergative verbs.

Finally, learners sometimes produce clauses such as the following:

(16) *Many of the old buildings in the center of the city have recently demolished.

A teacher might assume that the learner has a general problem with passive versus active voice. However, it is possible that the learner assumes that the verb *demolish* can be used in a middle voice clause in the same way that an ergative verb such as *change* can be used, for example:

(17) Many of the buildings in the center of the city have recently changed.   [*inv.*]

Questions for discussion

- If you are currently teaching, look at the kinds of errors in the area of active versus passive voice that your students make. Can any of them be plausibly related to problems with ergative patterns? If so, suggest some activities that might help your students.

  If you are not currently teaching, consider how you might deal with the kinds of problems evident in examples 12 through 16.
- Think of how Texts 5a and 5b (or similar texts) could be used to help advanced learners understand the notion of ergativity.

5.2   Verbs followed by prepositions

In most of the clauses analyzed in the previous chapter, prepositional phrases were treated as Adjuncts representing circumstances, called *Circumstantial Adjuncts* for short.[1] For example:

(18) Something sparkled <u>at the bottom of the trunk</u>.   [*inv.*]

This underlined constituent has the following characteristics typical of Circumstantial Adjuncts

1. The preposition + noun group could answer a question about circumstances:

   <u>Where</u> did something sparkle? At the bottom of the trunk.

2. Both preposition and noun group can be omitted and the clause will still be grammatical and the basic meaning of the verb will not change:

   Something sparkled.

3. The preposition and noun group can be moved to the beginning of the clause:

   At the bottom of the trunk something sparkled.

4. The noun group following the preposition *cannot* become the Subject of a passive version of the clause:

   *The bottom of the trunk was sparkled at (by something).

These characteristics confirm that (1) *at* and *the bottom of the trunk* go together to form a prepositional phrase, (2) the prepositional phrase represents a circumstance which is peripheral to the process, and (3) the noun group *the bottom of the trunk* is not a participant in the process.

---

1 One exception is the *by* + Actor structure in passive voice clauses. By analyzing the Prepositional Object as an Actor, we are treating it as a participant in the process, not as part of a circumstance.

The following example, however, is quite different.

(19) We have already set up the database.

This clause has the following characteristics:

1. The preposition and noun group could not answer a question about circumstances:

   *Where/how/why have you already set? Up the database.

2. The preposition and following noun group cannot be omitted without either producing an ungrammatical clause or changing the basic meaning of the verb.

   *We have already set.

3. The preposition and following noun group cannot be moved as one constituent to the beginning of the clause

   *Up the database we have already set.

4. The preposition *can* be moved to a position following the noun group and in fact *must* be moved to this position when the noun group is a pronoun:

   We have already set the database up.
   We have already set it up.

5. The noun group following the preposition could become the Subject of a passive version of the clause:

   The database has been already set up.

6. The verb group head (i.e., the lexical verb) plus preposition can be replaced by a single word verb with a similar meaning:

   We have already established the database.

These characteristics clearly show that the preposition *up* is attached to the verb *set* and together they represent the process. In fact, strictly speaking, *up* is not a preposition in such a structure, as it is not "pre-posed" before anything. Technically it is a **particle.** Such verb + particle structures are usually called **phrasal verbs.** The noun group *the database* is not part of a Circumstantial Adjunct but is a participant (the Goal) in the process. From the point of view of the learner, such phrasal verbs are best regarded as single vocabulary items to be learned in the same way as any single word verbs.

Unfortunately (for the learner and for the grammarian who dislikes indeterminacy), the distinction between phrasal verb + Goal (or Range) structures and verb + Circumstantial Adjunct structures is not always so clear-cut. There is, in fact, something of a continuum between the two. In many cases of verb + preposition or verb + particle, following noun groups have some of the characteristics of participants and some of the characteristics of constituents within Circumstantial Adjuncts.

Task 5b

By putting ticks or crosses in the appropriate places, use Figure 5.1 to decide whether the sequences in the following examples are more like *sparkled at the bottom of the trunk* (i.e., verb + Circumstantial Adjunct) or more like *set up the database* (i.e., phrasal verb + Goal or Range).

1. Then it sucks up the nectar . . .
2. Then I get to the top and there's a long steep slope going down.
3. Perhaps I should have allowed him this privacy, but I ran after him
   . . .
4. He behaved in a very strange way.
5. Someone has been sleeping in my bed.
6. We've never come across this problem before.
7. The advance party arrived at the summit on the third day.
8. The plants um sort of breathe out water . . .

5.2.1   Learning and teaching verbs + prepositions

Many learners have problems with verb + preposition structures. In some cases, a preposition may be omitted:

(20) *Giovanni is searching a new job.
(21) *All students are encouraged to participate sports.
(22) *They arrived Berlin yesterday.

In other cases, an unnecessary preposition may be inserted:

(23) *The procession entered into the hall.
(24) *Nowadays, the Republic produces out many highly advanced products.

Another problem can be knowing which clauses with Prepositional Objects can be made passive and which cannot. For example, even native speakers may disagree about the acceptability of a passive version of *many visitors have fallen down these steps* (*?these steps have been fallen down by many visitors*).

Because of the variety of clause patterns associated with different verbs, it is of limited use for learners to learn verbs simply as isolated vocabulary items. The patterns in which the verbs commonly occur (including any prepositions which characteristically accompany them) need to be learned at the same time.

	Answers question about circumstances	Can be omitted	Can be moved to the front	NG can be subject	Preposition can follow NG	Verb + preposition can be replaced by one word	
at the bottom of the trunk	✔	✔	✔	✗	✗	✗	Circumstantial Adjunct
up the nectar							
to the top							
after him							
in a strange way							
in my bed							
across the problem							
at the summit							
out water							
up the database	✗	✗	✗	✔	✔	✔	Phrasal verb + participant

Figure 5.1   Verbs and prepositions.

5.3   Phase

The analyses so far have involved single verbs representing single processes. However, in each of the following examples there are two closely linked verbs:

(25) Fishermen soon <u>stopped fishing</u> in the river.
(26) . . . when Mrs. Hamlyn first <u>began restoring</u> this fast-crumbling historical monument . . .
(27) The whirlwinds of revolt <u>will continue to shake</u> the foundation of our nation . . .

In each case, the two verbs (strictly speaking, two verb groups) form a structure in which the second verb is dependent on the first verb. The second verb is always nonfinite; the first verb is often finite, but may be nonfinite. In terms of experiential meaning, there is really only one action involved. The first verb adds some information about the action represented by the second verb, but does not in itself represent a complete process. This kind of structure is known as **phase.** In examples 25 through 27, the first verb provides information about the starting, stopping, and continuing of the action. This can be glossed as *time.* However, phase is not restricted to information about the time of a process. The notion can be extended to cover other sequences of verbs in which the first verb adds information about the process represented by the second verb but does not itself constitute a separate process. In addition to those phase verbs whose meanings can be glossed as time, it is possible to recognize the following subclasses:

- Verbs which add information about how real the speaker feels the action is. The meaning of this type can be glossed as *reality.* The verbs of this type commonly used with action processes are *appear* and *seem.* For example:

  (28) They <u>seem to walk</u> about in threes . . .

- Verbs which add information about the effort involved and extent of success in carrying out the action. The general meaning of this type can be glossed as *effort.* Verbs of this type include *try, attempt, endeavor, get, manage,* and *succeed,* as well as verbs with negative meanings, such as *avoid* ("manage not to") and *fail* ("not succeed in"). For example:

  (29) . . . have you actually <u>tried to assemble</u> and dis – or whatever the opposite is of assemble – a radio?
  (30) . . . institutions of learning <u>have managed to provide</u> adequate and substantial training . . .
  (31) That they <u>would succeed in overcoming</u> the difficulties of a multitude of languages . . .
  (32) . . . would find it difficult <u>to avoid encountering</u> one . . .

- Verbs which add information such as how an action is carried out, how it comes about, how frequent it is, and whether it is accompanied by someone or something. The general meaning of this type can be glossed as *manner.* Verbs of this type include *hurry, hesitate, venture, tend, happen,* and *help.* For example:

(33) He hesitated to enter without hearing the customary "come."   ("entered reluctantly")

(34) It picks up any insects that happen to be feeding on the nectar.   ("feeding by chance")

(35) It tends to tilt to the left.   ("often tilts")

(36) . . . need for German speaking EC experts to help save the former East German economy.   ("save along with others")

As already mentioned, the second (dependent) verb in a phase structure is always nonfinite. It may take one of the following forms:

1. *to* + V (infinitive), for example, *to enter* (number 33)
2. *V* (sometimes called **bare infinitive**), for example, *save* (number 36 above)
3. *Ving,* for example, *encountering* (number 32); sometimes following a preposition, for example, *in overcoming* (number 31)

This can be a problem for many learners, both because it is sometimes difficult to predict which form is likely to follow which verb and because in some cases their mother tongue may suggest a different form. For example, many languages use a form analogous to the English *to* + V both in contexts in which English uses the infinitive and in contexts in which English would use a V*ing* form. Some languages may also use a construction analogous to the English *that* clause where English would use an infinitive or V*ing* form.

Not surprisingly then, learners sometimes produce errors such as the following (from Celce-Murcia and Larson-Freeman 1983):

(37) *It has stopped to rain.

(38) *The company avoided to pay them overtime

(39) *I avoided that I should talk to him

Some languages may also express some of the meanings of phase verbs in quite different ways. In Mandarin Chinese, the meanings expressed by the time type would normally be expressed through particles such as *le,* which indicates a change from one state of affairs to another, for example:

(40) Bu xia yu le
Not fall rain LE
"It has stopped raining."

A general rule of thumb sometimes suggested to help students choose the right forms for the second verb group is that the *to* + V form is used when the action is unreal, unfulfilled, or potential, and the V*ing* form is used

voice, the Causer is mapped onto the Subject and the Affected onto the Object.

3. The grammatical representation of a process as a happening which has an Affected participant and may or may not have a Causer (instead of as an action which has an Actor and may or may not have a Goal) is described as ergativity.

4. Verbs which can be used both in Affected-only clauses and in Affected + Causer clauses are called ergative verbs.

5. Some verb + preposition + noun group sequences can be analyzed as verbs followed by a Circumstantial Adjunct. Others can be analyzed as phrasal verbs followed by a Goal or Range; that is, the prepositions are actually particles attached to the verbs.

6. In phase structures there are two verbs (or verb groups) representing a single process. The second verb is always dependent on the first.

7. Phase verbs (the first verb in such structures) are categorized according to the information they add about the processes. The categories can be glossed as time, reality, effort, and manner.

8. The dependent verb in a phase structure may take the form of *to* + V (infinitive), V*ing,* or (less commonly) V.

9. Causatives are extended phase structures with two participants. The first participant in some way causes or facilitates the process.

Key terms introduced

This text	*Alternatives used in the field*
Affected	Medium
bare infinitive (V)	
causatives	
Causer	Agent
ergative verbs	
ergativity	
particle	
phase	catenative verbs; the term *phase* is sometimes extended to cover aspect (see Section 8.3)
phrasal verbs	

Discussion of tasks

Task 5a

The clearly ergative verbs are *drop, widen, lift, move, drown, ignite,* and *sank.* In addition, some speakers may accept pairs such as the following: *he jumps his dogs through the hoops at every performance / his dogs jump through the hoops at every performance; I cannot save this file/this file won't save.* The latter occurs in computer-speak.

Task 5b

Of these examples, *sucks up the nectar, come across the problem, get to the top,* and *breathe out water* are most like phrasal verbs + Goal or Range. Note the following, however:

Up the nectar could be omitted and the sentence would remain grammatical (but odd). It is also hard to find a single word similar in meaning to *sucks up* (*drinks* will not do).

Across cannot be moved to a position following *the problem.* (Note that *across the problem* could be omitted, but this would change the basic meaning of the verb.)

Out water could be omitted without changing the basic meaning of the verb.

To cannot be moved to a position following *the top.* Also, most speakers would not accept *the top is then got to.*

The examples most like Circumstantial Adjuncts are *(ran) after him, (behaved) in a strange way,* and *(has been sleeping) in my bed.* Note, however:

Ran after could be replaced by the verb *chased.* Also, some speakers might accept *he was run after.*

Omitting *in a strange way* somewhat changes the meaning of the verb, to "behaved well." *Behave,* in fact, belongs to a category of verbs which nearly always occur with an Adjunct. Omission alone cannot therefore be a conclusive test.

My bed could become the Subject of a passive clause (*my bed has been slept in by someone*). It is therefore in this respect more like a participant than part of a circumstance.

Example 8, *arrived at the summit,* could be interpreted either way. Like a Circumstantial Adjunct *at the summit* answers a circumstantial question such as, *Where did they arrive?* It can also be omitted. However, *arrived at* could be replaced by the single word *reached,* and most native speakers would probably accept the passive version *the summit was arrived at on the third day.*

Task 5c

The reality and manner type are all normally followed only by *to* + V.

Most of the effort type are also followed by to + V, with the exception of *avoid* and *succeed in,* which are followed by V*ing.*

The time type of phase verb includes those which can be followed only by V*ing,* for example, *finish* and *keep on,* and those which can be followed by either to + V or V*ing,* for example, *start.* As they can all be followed by V*ing* and any difference between using V*ing* and *to* + V is very subtle, it would seem sensible to introduce beginning learners only to the V*ing* forms. A further advantage of this is that V*ing* is the only form used after these verbs in causatives (see Section 5.3.1).

6 Seeing, liking, thinking, wanting, and saying: The transitivity of mental and verbal processes

Text 6a

Marlene:	Is it all right?
Angie:	Yes, don't worry about it.
Marlene:	Does Joyce know where you are?
Angie:	Yes of course she does.
Marlene:	Well does she?
Angie:	Don't worry about it.
Marlene:	How long are you planning to stay with me then?
Angie:	You know when you came to see us last year?
Marlene:	Yes, that was nice wasn't it?
Angie:	That was the best day of my whole life.
Marlene:	So how long are you planning to stay?
Angie:	Don't you want me?
Marlene:	Yes yes, I just wondered.
Angie:	I won't stay if you don't want me to.

(Churchill 1990: 110)

In this dialogue the two speakers question and answer each other about such things as what they know and what they want. Unlike text 4a (the umu text), this is not a world of actions but a world of what are called **mental processes.** This category includes processes like *thinking* and *believing, seeing* and *hearing, liking* and *hating,* and *wanting* and *hoping.*

On first consideration such mental processes may seem to be not very different grammatically from action processes. Like a transitive action process clause, a mental process clause such as number 1 has two participants that we might regard as Actor and Goal.

(1)   Nearly everybody believed her.

In addition, this clause, like an action process clause, has a passive version in which the "Goal" becomes the Subject:

(1) a. She was believed by nearly everybody.

However, there are a number of differences between such clauses and action process clauses which justify treating them as a separate process type.

First, it would be very odd to ask a question about the "Goal" in number 1 like *What happened to her?* or a question about the Subject like *What did nearly everybody do?* This is because the clause is not really about someone doing something to someone. There are in fact no general words we can use for questioning mental processes in the way that we can use *do* and *happen* to question action processes.

Second, "Goals" in mental process clauses are often not simply people or things but complete *states of affairs,* with their own processes, participants, and circumstances. Such states of affairs may be expressed in ways different from the ways Goals are typically expressed in action clauses, for example:

(2)   Does Joyce know where you are?
(3)   There is no reason to believe that another truffle will develop in the same spot.

Third, it is possible to find pairs of related mental process clauses (both active voice) with very similar experiential meanings but in which the two participants are in reverse order, for example:

(4)   The way George put it pleased her very much.
(4) a. She liked very much the way George put it.

It would certainly be very unsatisfactory to label *the way George put it* Actor in number 4 but Goal in number 4a and to label *her* Goal in number 4 but *she* Actor in number 4a.

There are other differences between the two process types, as will become clear later. However, the preceding examples are enough to show that there are good reasons for treating them separately. This chapter will consider the structure of various types of mental process clauses, in particular those which can prove difficult for learners. Processes of *saying* (i.e., **verbal processes**), which share many features with mental processes, will also be looked at.

6.1 Mental processes

Typical participants in mental process clauses will be looked at first , and then the main subtypes of mental processes will be considered.

6.1.1 Senser and Phenomenon

Mental process clauses normally have at least one participant representing the one who thinks, sees, likes, wants, and so on. Unlike Actors in action process clauses, this participant must always be animate and is usually human.

(5) I can see much better without them on.

Apparent exceptions to this are cases of personification, that is, cases in which a nonanimate participant is treated as if it were human, for example:

(6) My car knows I am about to sell it. [*inv.*]

This participant is known as the **Senser.**

Most mental process clauses also have a second participant – the thing, idea, or fact which is thought, seen, liked, wanted, and so on. For example:

(7) Don't you want me?
(8) Most Hollanders know English . . .
(9) Here and there you see a tank . . .

This participant is referred to as the **Phenomenon.**

6.1.2 Types of mental processes

It is possible to recognize four subtypes of mental processes. The first type, **perception,** includes processes such as *seeing, hearing, noticing, feeling, tasting,* and *smelling.* The second type, **affection,** includes processes such as *liking, loving, admiring, missing, fearing,* and *hating.* The third type, **cognition,** includes processes such as *thinking, believing, knowing, doubting, remembering,* and *forgetting.* The fourth type, **volition,** includes processes such as *wanting, needing, intending, desiring, hoping,* and *wishing.*

Task 6a

Decide which of the four subtypes (perception, affection, cognition, or volition) each of the underlined mental processes in the following examples belongs to.

1. Don't you want me?
2. Yes, yes I just wondered.
3. . . . I kind of appreciate her . . .
4. . . . when I smell pigs.
5. I remember Iosefa's voice.
6. You must know your address.
7. If you'd like their number . . .
8. I didn't understand that bit about miles apart.

The Phenomenon in mental process clauses can be expressed by a wide range of structures, which can be quite confusing for learners. It is worth looking in some detail at the different kinds of Phenomenon, the ways they are realized, and their relationships with the different subtypes of mental processes.

The Phenomenon in number 10 is very different in nature from the Phenomenon in number 11:

(10) Lots of people hate turnips.
(11) She thought that the best thing to do would be to just ignore him.

In number 10, the Phenomenon is a noun group representing a *thing,* which is the *stimulus* for an affection-type mental process. In number 11, the Phenomenon is a finite clause representing a *thought,* which is in a sense *created* by the cognitive-type mental process. In other words, it is a kind of "saying to oneself."

There are other differences between the two. The Phenomenon in number 10 could become the Subject of a passive version of the clause (i.e., *Turnips are hated by lots of people*). It could also be replaced by the pronoun *them.*

The Phenomenon in number 11, however, could not normally become the Subject of a passive version of the clause (most people would not accept *That the best thing to do would be to just ignore him was thought by her*), and normally it would be replaced not by *it* but by *so.* In fact, strictly speaking *that the best thing to do would be to just ignore him* is not a participant in the clause at all. It is a separate clause operating at clause rank (i.e., a *ranking* clause). In other words, it is not a *nominal clause* (a clause that has been shifted down to group rank and is operating like a noun group; see Section 1.6.1.1) but a *dependent* clause (covered in Section 12.1). However, for the sake of simplicity, it is treated here as a realization of the participant function Phenomenon.

There is something of a continuum between these two types of Phenomenon. In other words, Phenomena can semantically be more like thoughts or more like things. The glosses *situations, events,* and *facts* are used below to characterize some of the points along the continuum. There is also a structural continuum paralleling the semantic continuum: Phenomena can structurally be more like ranking clauses or more like noun groups.

There are clear relationships between the subtypes of mental processes and the types of Phenomenon. These relationships are explored in the next few sections.

6.1.3   The Phenomenon in perception processes

In perception processes the Phenomenon is most typically a thing, realized by a noun group, or an event, realized by a nonfinite V*ing* or V clause, for example:

(12) I don't get a chance to notice things very much.   (thing).
(13) I saw a proctor help him out of the hall.   (event)
(14) I noticed him helping Doreen with the answer.   (event)

Note that when the Phenomenon is an event, if the V form of the verb is used, as in number 13, then the process is presented as finished. When the V*ing* form is used, as in number 14, the process is presented as unfinished (relative to the moment of perception).

Less typically, the Phenomenon can be a fact, expressed by a finite *that* clause (although note that the *that* can be omitted in such clauses).

(15)   A clerk had noticed that the passport had expired.   (fact)
(16)   He could sense all was not well with them.   (fact)

The main difference between events and facts is that the former are directly perceived while the latter are not.The following pair of examples may help to make this clearer.

(17)   I saw someone leave the gate open.   (event)   [*inv.*]
(17) a. I saw that someone had left the gate open.   (fact)

Note that the use of a *that* clause after a verb which normally represents a perception process will often lead to its interpretation as a cognitive process. For example, in the following clause, *see* could be replaced by *understand* with little difference in meaning:

(18)   I can see that changing to superannuable terms gives you more security
but . . .

6.1.4   *The Phenomenon in affection processes*

In affection processes, the Phenomenon is typically a thing, situation, or fact, for example:

(19) I love Grandma.   (thing)
(20) I like them coming round here every day.   (situation)   [*inv.*]
(21) She loathed him even being in the same room.   (situation)
(22) I like the fact that you can see the screen no matter where you sit.   (fact)
(23) She now bitterly regrets that they did not take the warnings
seriously.   (fact)

Situations in affection processes are typically expressed by V*ing*[1] clauses, and there is no distinction between finished and unfinished situa-

---

1 Traditionally, some prescriptive grammarians have advocated use of the possessive before such V*ing* forms on the grounds that the V*ing* form is a nominalization (gerund) in such clauses, e.g., *I like their coming round here every day; she loathed his even being in the same room.* Some users of English still favor this form in formal written contexts, although the possessive is rarely used with a "full" noun (i.e., not

tions in the way that there is a distinction between finished and unfinished events in perception processes.

Less typically, *to* + V clauses are also sometimes used after affection process verbs. For example, numbers 20 and 21 could be rephrased as:

(20) a. I like them to come round here every day.
(21) a. She loathed him even to be in the same room.

This in fact represents an area in which situations shade into desires (see Section 6.1.6).

Note also that facts are often expressed by relative clauses embedded in noun groups with a word like *fact* as head, as in number 22. There is in fact some variation among affection verbs. With some verbs, such as *like* in number 22, facts are always or nearly always embedded in this way, although there is also a slightly more colloquial variant of such clauses with the pronoun *it*, for example:

(22) a. I like it that you can see the screen no matter where you sit.

6.1.5   *The Phenomenon in cognition processes*

In cognition processes the Phenomenon is typically a thing, a fact, or a thought, for example:

(24) . . . and are now ready to believe the implausible.   (thing)
(25) You have to recognize the fact that the kinds of conditions we've been getting can't, it can't go on like that forever.   (fact)
(26) But we tend to forget that Andrei is a very noble man indeed.   (fact)
(27) I believe you know what I am talking about.   (thought)
(28) Most people think that when you get old, you either freeze to death or you burn up.   (thought)
(29) I wondered why there were so many tuis [New Zealand birds] in one place.   (thought)

Note that when the thought is related to a statement, a finite *that* clause (again with the possibility of omitting the *that*) is used. When the thought is related to a question, a finite clause beginning with *if* or *whether* (for yes-no question; see Section 9.2) or one of the *wh-* words (for *wh-* questions; see Sec. 9.3.1) is used. (As stated previously, *wh-* stands for one of the question words *how, what, when, where, which, who, whom, whose,* and *why.*)

In number 25 the clause is embedded in a noun group with *fact* as head. It is therefore presented explicitly as a fact, that is, as something which in a sense exists prior to the mental process. In number 26, *the fact that* could also be inserted with no significant difference in meaning. In addition, the

pronoun), as in *?She liked the children's coming round here every day* and *?She loathed John's even being in the same room.*

Phenomena in both these examples could be paraphrased using a noun group, for example:

(25) a. . . . to recognize the temporary nature of our present conditions.
(26) a. But we tend to forget Andrei's nobility of character.

In numbers 27, 28, and 29, on the other hand, the Phenomena are dependent clauses. They could not normally be embedded in a noun group with a head like *fact,* and it would be much harder to paraphrase them using a noun group. They are presented not as facts but as thoughts which, as noted earlier, are in a sense created by the mental process.

There are also some less typical ways in which thoughts can be expressed with cognition processes. With a few verbs, thoughts can take the form of *to* + V clauses, for example:

(30)   I believe him to be an honest man.
(31)   . . . she would automatically consider herself to be "bad" . . .

There are also a small number of cognition verbs which take different patterns, for example:

(31) a. . . . she would automatically consider herself "bad" . . .   (i.e., as number 31, but with the verb omitted)
(32)   . . . even though we might regard them as very important . . .[2]

Finally, with some cognition verbs, thoughts can also be directly quoted, which brings out clearly their saying to oneself nature, for example:

(33)   "What a mess!" he thought.

6.1.6   The Phenomenon in volition processes

In volition processes, the Phenomenon can be a thing or a desire, for example:

(34) Don't you want me?   (thing)
(35) I'd like you to go and . . .   (desire)
(36) They intend us to be completely discredited.   (desire)
(37) I just wish those people would go somewhere else.   (desire)
(38) I desire only that you should be happy.   (desire)

Note that *'d like (would like)* is here regarded as representing a process of volition, while *like* as in numbers 20 and 22 is regarded as representing a process of affection. In other words, the modal auxiliary *would* in this context does not indicate that the mental process is conditional or hypothetical. Rather it indicates that a volition rather than an affection process is involved.

2 In such clauses, a relational process (see Chapter 7) is in a sense built in to the mental process.

Some volition process verbs can take both nonfinite *to* + V clauses and finite *that* (usually *that* + modal) clauses, for example:

(39)   I wish you to leave my kingdom immediately.
(39) a. I wish that you would leave my kingdom immediately.

In such cases, the version with the *to* + V clause normally implies a kind of order or command, whereas the version with the *that* clause simply states the desire.

Some verbs of volition can take only one of the forms or at least take the other form only rarely, for example:

(40)   I hope that you will remember this.
(40) a. *I hope you to remember this.
(41)   I want you to remember this.
(41) a. ?I want that you should remember this.

Finally, sometimes the desire can be expressed as a nonfinite clause with a V*ed/en* participle, for example:

(42)   I don't want <u>unpleasant words said to other people</u>, thank you.

This can be regarded as a case of the *to* + V pattern with a passive verb group (i.e., the *passive infinitive*) but with the *to be* omitted, that is, *I don't want unpleasant words ~~to be~~ said to other people, thank you.*

Table 6.1 summarizes the most typical kinds of Phenomena.

6.1.7 *Two processes with one Subject*

In the following examples a mental process verb is followed by a nonfinite verb (of any process type) and there is only one Subject for both processes.

(43) She now bitterly <u>regrets having</u> ignored the warnings.
(44) He <u>enjoys being</u> the center of attention.
(45) Tuis <u>like to eat</u> the sweet nectar they find in many flowers.
(46) I <u>don't want to exaggerate</u> the danger . . .
(47) If you <u>wish to fit</u> a flush socket into a lath-and-plaster wall . . .
(48) I should <u>like to hear of</u> the injuries done to you by My Court.
(49) If you <u>do forget to loop</u> the cable over the platform . . .

The underlined structures in these examples look very similar to the phase structures discussed in the preceding chapter (Section 5.3), and it is possible to treat them as such. However, strictly speaking, rather than one phased process, these examples involve two processes, a mental process followed by a process of any of the types. They are, therefore, more accurately regarded as two clauses, the second dependent on the first.

For teaching and learning purposes, the priority is to give the learner a way to determine what form the second verb should take. As with the structures looked at in the previous section, we can generalize about the

Table 6.1   *Phenomena in mental process clauses*

Structure	Example	Gloss
Perception		
noun group	I saw them.	thing
V clause	I saw them leave.	event (finished)
V*ing* clause	I saw them leaving.	event (unfinished)
that clause	I saw that they had left.	fact
Affection		
noun group	I hate them.	thing
V*ing* clause	I hate them leaving.	situation
relative clause	I hate the fact that they are leaving.	fact
Cognition		
noun group	I believe them.	thing
that clause	I believe that they are leaving.	thought
wh-/if clause	I wonder why they are leaving.	thought
relative clause	I recognize the fact that they are leaving	fact
Volition		
noun group	I want them.	thing
to + V clause	I want them to leave.	desire
that clause + modal	I wish that they would leave.	desire

typical forms the second verb may take according to the different types of mental processes involved.

With affection processes, the second verb is typically in the V*ing* form, as in numbers 43 and 44. However, as 45 illustrates, the second verb can sometimes also be in the *to* + V form. There is sometimes very little difference between the use of the V*ing* form and the *to* + V form. However, as with the affection process clauses discussed above, the use of the latter form can be interpreted as representing the shading of affection into volition. For example, a clause such as:

(50) I like swimming (especially when the weather is warm).   [*inv.*]

could be paraphrased as *I enjoy (the activity of) swimming,* while a clause such as:

(51) I like to swim (whenever I can).   [*inv.*]

is closer in meaning to *I desire to swim.*

Other affection process verbs which can take both forms include *hate, prefer,* and *love.*

Such differences are very subtle, and the V*ing* form can normally be substituted for the *to* + V form with no more than a slight loss of idiomaticity. In most teaching contexts, it therefore makes sense to initially generalize the use of the V*ing* form to all cases of verbs following an affection process verb.

One exception to this is the verb *regret.* With the V*ing* form, *regret* indicates that the Senser feels sorry about something he or she has already done (or not done), as in number 43. With the *to* + V form, however, *regret* indicates that the Senser does something regretfully. In this case, it is much more like a phased process of the manner type, for example:

(52) I regret to inform you that you will not be offered a renewal of contract
  . . . ("inform you regretfully")

Volition process verbs are normally followed by the *to* + V form, as in numbers 46, 47, and 48.

Very few cognition process verbs can be followed by a second verb in this way. Two verbs which can be are *forget* and *remember,* which can be followed by either V*ing* or *to* + V. When followed by *to* + V they are more like phase verbs, suggesting successful completion of a process or failure to carry out a process, for example:

(53) He had forgotten to have his passport stamped.

Followed by V*ing* they are more like full mental process verbs, expressing the recall or lack of recall of a past process, for example:

(54)   I clearly remember agreeing with what they said . . .
(55)   Jeremy had completely forgotten ever having visited the city.

6.1.8   The Phenomenon-Senser order of constituents

The following pair has already been noted:

	SENSER		PHENOMENON
(56)	She	liked very much	the way George put it.

	PHENOMENON		SENSER	
(56) a.	The way George put it	pleased	her	very much.

There are many verbs of the affection type and a few of the cognition type which take the *please* pattern (i.e., Phenomenon followed by Senser). Pairs such as numbers 56 and 56a, in which the meanings of the processes are very similar, are easy to find, for example:

(57)   I don't understand that bit about a mile apart.
(57) a. That bit about a mile apart puzzles me.
(58)   I have to admit that I still fear flying.   [*inv.*]
(58) a. I have to admit that flying still frightens me.

With perception processes please-type verbs are rarer and usually some-what metaphorical, but it is possible to find pairs such as:

(59)   We smelled the stench as soon as we opened the door.
(59) a. The stench hit us as soon as we opened the door.

Task 6b

1. Which of the following mental process verbs are of the *please* (i.e., Phenomenon followed by Senser) type and which of the *like* (i.e., Senser followed by Phenomenon) type?
2. Using these verbs, construct as many pairs of clauses as you can with roughly similar meanings using a *please*-type and a *like*-type verb.

love	annoy	impress
escape	realize	delight
worry	excite	strike
dislike	convince	forget
believe	admire	

Mental process verbs of the *please* type are also very commonly used in passive voice, for example:

(60) She was very pleased by the way George put it.
(61) . . . the small children were too frightened[3] even to cry.
(62) You may be puzzled by another question also.

This, of course, results in the Senser being mapped onto the Subject, as it is with active *like*-type verbs.

A further complication with the *please* type is that where the Phenomenon is represented by a finite *that* clause it normally occurs after the verb and the Subject position is filled by a "dummy" *it,* for example:

(63)   It annoys me that they do all these things without consultation.
(64)   It puzzles me that it took them so long to figure it out.

Clauses such as 63a and 64a, in which the *that* clause is at the beginning of the clause, are possible but much less common.

(63) a. That they do all these things without consultation annoys me.
(64) a. That it took them so long to figure it out puzzles me.

---

3 An alternative interpretation of words like *pleased* and *frightened* as Attributes will be explored in Chapter 7.

6.1.9 Tense in mental process clauses

When the time reference is *now,* that is, the moment of speaking or writing, the tense choice for mental process verbs is typically simple present. This contrasts with action processes, for which the tense choice is typically present continuous, for example:

(65) I just wish those people would go somewhere else . . .   (not: **I am just wishing . . .*)
(66) Does Joyce know where you are?   (not: **Is Joyce knowing . . .*)

The other continuous tenses are also typically not used with mental process verbs, for example:

(67) I have known her since she was a little girl.   (not: **I have been knowing her . . .*)
(68) She had always believed that honesty was the best policy.   (not: **She had always been believing . . .*)

With many perception process verbs it is also very common to use the modal auxiliary *can* when the time reference is now, for example:

(69) I can see wonderful things.

Tense use will be further explored in Chapter 8.

6.1.10 Learning and teaching mental processes

At the initial stages, mental process clauses with noun groups (things) as Phenomena can be introduced. Apart from choice of tense, such clauses differ little from action process clauses.

At later stages, to minimize confusion among the various structures which can represent more complex Phenomena in mental process clauses, it is logical to deal separately with the four types – perception, affection, cognition, and volition – first associating them with the *most typical* expressions of the Phenomenon in each category.

In most cases, one would expect learners to have least difficulty with the *that* clause following cognition process verbs, as the form of the dependent clause is identical to that of an independent clause (i.e., a clause that can stand alone), apart from the word *that* (which can be omitted). However, with *wh-/if-* dependent clauses (i.e., where the thought is related to a question), the word order is normally Subject followed by Finite, that is, the word order characteristic of statements instead of the word order characteristic of questions. (Word order in statements and questions will be further explored in Chapter 9.) Learners sometimes produce errors such as:

```
                          FINITE    SUBJECT
(70)    *I don't know where  are     the books.
```

It has also been noted that learners are potentially faced with at least three ways of expressing a mental process, for example:

(71)   All of us hate such hypocrisy.
(71) a. Such hypocrisy disgusts all of us.
(71) b. All of us are disgusted by such hypocrisy.

Another possible form is, of course, the passive version of number 71:

(71) c. Such hypocrisy is hated by all of us.

It is perhaps not surprising that learners sometimes produce forms such as:

(71) d. *I disgusted such hypocrisy

Even when the learner's mother tongue possesses structures analogous both to the English like type and to the English please type, they may not necessarily be used in the same contexts. In French, the Phenomenon followed by Senser clause, for example,

(72)   Il me plaît.
        it (to) me pleases
        "It pleases me."

is used in many contexts in which English would prefer the Senser followed by Phenomenon clause *I like it.* Similarly, the order of participants in the next example, a French clause in which Phenomenon is followed by Senser, is opposite to its English equivalent:

(73)   Tu me manques.
        You (to) me miss
        "I miss you."

In English, mental process clauses in which the Senser is mapped onto the Subject (numbers 71 and 71b) are in fact more common than those in which the Phenomenon is mapped onto the Subject (numbers 71a and 71c), and most learners would probably first need to develop control over the active voice *like* type (number 71). It will be suggested in the next chapter that the passive voice *please* type (e.g., number 71b) could be first introduced as a special form of relational process clause. The active voice please type will on the whole be of a lower priority for most learners.

Questions for discussion

• In what order would you teach the different types of Phenomena used with mental process verbs? Why?

- Outline an activity for teaching each of the subtypes of mental process with its most typical realization of Phenomenon.
- Suggest an activity for raising the awareness of relatively advanced learners about the difference between the *please* and *like* types of mental process clauses.

6.2   Mental-action processes

Some processes are on the borderline between mental processes and action processes and have some of the characteristics of both, for example:

(74) First she tasted the porridge from Papa Bear's great big bowl.

(75) I watch that ball . . .

(76) . . . then I know they are listening carefully.

(77) That course encouraged me to think about the relevance of race

These can be referred to as **mental-action processes.**

Mental-action processes must normally have a participant which, like the Senser in mental processes, must be animate and is usually human. However, unlike Sensers, but like many Actors in action processes, this participant normally acts deliberately. Like action processes, questions can be asked of mental-action processes, for example, *What did she do first?* and *What did that course encourage you to do?* Finally, the normal tense choice for mental-action processes when the time reference is *now* is present continuous, as it is with action processes but not mental processes.

Some verbs can be used for both mental processes and mental-action processes. In other cases, different verbs must be used. The following examples illustrate this:

Mental processes	*Mental-action processes*
I think there is a problem here	I am thinking about the problem
I can taste garlic in this	I am tasting the soup
I can see the screen	I am watching the screen/I am looking at the screen
I can hear the radio	I am listening to the radio

6.3   Verbal processes

Verbal processes are processes of *saying* and are expressed by verbs such as *say, tell, ask, reply,* and *suggest.* Verbal process clauses normally have one participant, the **Sayer,** plus in most cases a representation of what is said, called the **Saying.** In addition, many verbal process clauses have a participant which represents the person toward whom the words are directed. This participant is called the **Addressee.** For example:

	SAYER		SAYING	SAYER	SAYING
(78)	I	didn't say	"move,"	I	said "sit still."

(79) <u>Philosophers of science</u> have latterly been explaining
                     SAYING
  <u>that science is about correlating phenomena</u>.

        SAYER   ADDRESSEE SAYING
(80) Once, <u>my uncle</u> told   <u>me</u>   <u>a story</u> . . .

        SAYER   ADDRESSEE   SAYING
(81) Could <u>you</u> ask <u>Mrs. R.</u> <u>to bring a table back</u>?

In all the above examples the Sayer is human. However, this need not always be the case, for example:

(82) . . . <u>neon indicators</u> which tell you at a glance whether the socket is switched on.

Note that in number 80, the participant Addressee is mapped onto the Indirect Object. However, with some verbs, the Addressee (if any) must be expressed in an Adjunct as a Prepositional Object, for example:

(83) There is something I must say <u>to my people</u> . . .

In some cases, the Saying may be realized as a noun group representing a *label* for the subject matter of the verbal process, or for a particular kind or unit of speech, for example, *story* in number 78, and *the various options, nonsense,* and *lies* in the following clauses:

(84) We discussed <u>the various options</u>.
(85) You always talk <u>nonsense</u>.
(86) Harold really does tell <u>the most awful lies</u>.

Other examples of labels are *(explain) the mistake, (ask) questions, (make) a statement, (speak) Italian, (tell) a joke,* and *(tell) the truth.* However, like the Phenomenon in mental processes, the Saying in verbal processes is more often than not itself a state of affairs, with process, participants, and sometimes circumstances expressed by finite or nonfinite clauses, as in most of the above examples. Such Sayings may be **quotes** (traditionally called *direct speech*) or **reports** (traditionally called *indirect speech*). Quotes present the Saying as being (more or less) the original words. In writing they are surrounded by quotation marks, as in number 78. Reports are a restating of the meaning of the original words. Quotes and reports can be of *statements* or *questions,* as in the following examples:

(87) "<u>Well, I've never seen one,</u>" he said.   (*quoted statement*)
(88) He told me <u>that the tongue has a little brush at the tip</u>.   (*reported statement*)
(89) "<u>Doesn't it worry you?</u>" asked Tauilopepe.   (*quoted question*)

(90) . . . phoned to ask <u>whether we had lost a cat.</u>   (*reported question*)

Reported statements take the form of *that* clauses (as in 88), while reported questions take the form of *wh-/if* clauses (as in 90). Reported statements and questions may be compared to thoughts in mental process clauses.

Quotes and reports can also be of directives. Briefly, a *directive* refers to such things as commands, suggestions, and requests which aim to get people to do things, for example:

(91) "Be careful!" he warned.   (*quoted directive*)
(92) Each would be requested <u>to select</u> . . .   (*reported directive*)
(93) The notice warned us <u>not to take this path.</u>   (*reported directive*)
(94) . . . he had the damn nerve to suggest <u>that I should repeat the exam</u>
     . . .   (*reported directive*)

Reported directives (like desires in mental process clauses) take the form either of *to* + V clauses (as in numbers 92 and 93) or *that* clauses, usually with a modal auxiliary (as in number 94). (Directives are explained more fully in Chapter 9.)

Finally, quotes and reports can also be of *offers,* as in the following examples:

(95) "Let me help you with that," he offered.   (*quoted offer*)
(96) Most of the first year students volunteered <u>to help.</u>   (*reported offer*)
(97) The sales rep promised <u>she would bring all the software with her.</u>   (*reported offer*)

Like reported directives, reported offers can take the form of either *to* + V clauses (as in number 96) or as *that* clauses, usually with a modal auxiliary (as in number 97).

Finally, the subject matter of the verbal process is often realized not as a participant (a Saying) but as part of a Circumstantial Adjunct, most commonly after the preposition *about,* for example:

(98) Well, we haven't talked <u>about that little brown blob there.</u>

Task 6c

Use Figure 6.1 to explore some of the constituents with which each of the following verbs is typically associated.

say	reply
tell	request
talk	persuade
ask	warn

	Say	Tell	Talk	Ask	Reply	Request	Persuade	Warn
Saying								
Quote (" ")								
Reported statement (*that* clause)								
Reported question (*if/wh* clause)								
Reported offer or directive (*to* + V clause)								
Reported offer or directive (*that* clause + modal)								
Addressee								
Object								
Prepositional Object (*to*)								

Figure 6.1 Saying and Addressee.

6.3.1   Learning and teaching verbal processes

The variety of configurations of constituents typically associated with different verbal process verbs can be a problem. Learners sometimes produce errors such as:

(99)   *The man told to us we must leave the country.
(100) He said me that he lived nearby.
(101) *They always discuss about the weather.
(102) *She asked that would I go too.

It is probably best to introduce the most common verbs and their typical patterns first:

say + reported statement, for example, *She said (that) it was too late.*
tell + Addressee + reported statement, for example, *She told us (that) it was too late.*
ask + Addressee + reported question, for example, *She asked us if we had a problem.*
tell + Addressee + reported directive, for example, *She told us to leave.*
tell + Addressee + label, for example, *She told us a story.*
talk + *to* Addressee + *about* + subject matter, for example, *She talked to us about the problem.*

Other verbal process verbs can in most cases be related to these basic patterns.

A traditional way of teaching indirect speech (i.e., reports) is to treat it as a transformation of direct speech (i.e., quotes), for example:

(103)   "I will do it for you tomorrow," he said.
(103) a. He said that he would do it for us the next day.

Rules are sometimes given along these lines:

Change the tense of the verb one step back into the past.
Change *I* and *you* to *he, she* and *they* as appropriate.
Change words like *now* and *at present* to *then* and *at that time.*
Change *tomorrow* to *the next day.*
Change *here* to *there.*

There are a number of potential problems with such an approach. The major difficulty is that it does not help learners appreciate the different functions of quoting and reporting. As has already been noted, quotes represent more or less the exact words spoken. Reports, on the other hand, represent the meaning of what was said and do not necessarily include any of the words actually spoken, for example:

(104)   "They've gone," said the doorman.

(104) a. The doorman told us that the two men had already left the building.

Quotes are typically used in narratives for the vivid representation of dialogue. Reports tend to be used for the reporting of information in a much wider range of contexts.

In addition, although *Change the tense of the verb one step back into the past* may seem at first to be a useful rule of thumb, more advanced learners will need to be aware that the essential factor is the status of the reported information at the time of the report. For example, present tense is more likely to be used where the information is believed to be still true at the time of reporting and is likely to be of relevance to the speaker and listener, as in:

(105) I heard her say she comes from Lima. (*I am referring to a person still in the room – and I have no reason to doubt the information.*) [*inv.*]

(106) He told me that the tongue has a little brush at the tip. (*This is a fact about the bird being described which is still true and will be of interest to the reader.*)

Sometimes, a slight difference in attitude can be conveyed by the choice of tense, for example:

(107) David said he'll be here by two. (*It is not yet 2 o'clock and I fully expect David to arrive by then.*)

(107) a. David said he would be here by two. (*I am merely reporting what he said – he may or may not actually arrive by then* or *It is now 2 o'clock and I am annoyed because David isn't here yet.*)

Such subtle distinctions will not, of course, be of high priority for most learners. However, learners need to be aware from the beginning that selecting one form rather than another is a question of meaning in context and cannot be done successfully by the mechanical application of rules. This also applies to the choice of Circumstantial Adjuncts such as *tomorrow* or *next day, at present* or *at that time,* and so on. The selection of an appropriate Adjunct can only be made by reference to the time of the original words and the time of the report. No rule can prescribe the appropriate choice out of context.

Questions for discussion

- Suggest some ways of introducing and practicing reported speech that do not involve the mechanical transformation of quoted clauses into reported clauses.
- Suggest an activity for raising the awareness of advanced learners about the possibilities of using different tenses in reported statements and questions.

Summary

1. There are four subtypes of mental processes: perception (e.g., seeing, hearing, smelling, and feeling); affection (e.g., liking, hating, admiring, and fearing); cognition (e.g., thinking, believing, knowing, and forgetting), and volition (e.g., wanting, wishing, intending, and hoping).
2. The Senser in a mental process is the participant that sees, likes, wants, thinks, and so on. It is normally animate (usually human).
3. The Phenomenon is the participant that is seen, liked, wanted, thought, and so on. Different kinds of Phenomena include things (typically noun groups), events (typically V*ing* or V clauses), situations (typically V*ing* clauses), facts (typically embedded clauses), and thoughts (typically dependent *that/if/wh-* clauses). There is a relationship between the four subtypes of mental processes and the kinds of Phenomena typically associated with them.
4. It is possible to find many pairs of semantically related mental process clauses (both active voice) one of which has the order Senser followed by Phenomenon (the *like* type) and the other of which has the order Phenomenon followed by Senser (the *please* type).
5. The typical tense in mental process clauses for reference to *now* is simple present.
6. Mental-action processes lie between mental processes and action processes. They are to do with mental activity and normally have an animate participant similar to a Senser in a mental process. However, this participant acts deliberately like an Actor in an action process. The typical tense in mental-action process clauses for reference to *now* is present continuous, as in action process clauses.
7. Verbal processes are processes of saying. Verbal process clauses normally have a Sayer – the participant that says, tells, informs, etc. – and a Saying – a representation of what is said, told, informed, etc. They may also have an Addressee – the person to whom the Saying is directed.
8. Quotes present the Saying as more or less the original words. Reports restate the meaning of the original words. Both quotes and reports can be of statements, questions, directives, and offers.

Key terms introduced

This text	*Alternatives used in the field*
Addressee	
affection	
cognition	
label	Verbiage

mental process
mental-action process behavioral process
perception
Phenomenon   Stimulus (note that in Halliday 1994,
          Phenomenon excludes ranking clauses)
quote   direct speech
report   indirect speech
Sayer
Saying
Senser   Experiencer
verbal process
volition   affection (in Halliday 1994, volition-type
          mental processes are not distinguished from
          affection-type)

Discussion of tasks

Task 6a

1. *want* – volition
2. *wondered* – cognition
3. *appreciate* – affection
4. *smell* – perception
5. *remember* – cognition
6. *know* – cognition
7. *'d like* (*would like*) – volition
8. *understand* – cognition

Task 6b

1. *Like type* *Please type*
 love   escape
 dislike   worry
 believe   annoy
 realize   excite
 admire   convince
 forget   impress
      delight
      strike

2. I love it/it delights me
   I dislike it/it annoys me
   I believe it/it convinces me
   I admire it/it impresses me
   I forget it/it escapes me
   I realize it/it strikes me (more likely in a context such as *I suddenly realized the solution / the solution suddenly struck me*)

Task 6c

See Figure 6.2 on the next page.

Saying	Say	Tell	Talk	Ask	Reply	Request	Persuade	Warn
Quote (" ")	✓	✓		✓	✓	✓		✓
Reported statement (*that* clause)	✓	✓			✓		✓	✓
Reported question (*if/wh* clause)		✓		✓		✓⁷		
Reported offer or directive (*to* + V clause)		✓		✓		✓	✓	✓
Reported offer or directive (*that* clause + modal)	✓¹	✓²		✓⁵		✓	✓	✓
Addressee								
Object		✓³		✓⁶			✓⁸	
Prepositional Object (*to*)	✓	✓⁴	✓	✓	✓	✓		

1. *Say* can report both offers and directives, for example:
   She said that she would do it.   (offer).
   She said that I had to leave.   (directive)
2. Again, *tell* can report both offers and directives, for example:
   She told us that she would do it.
   He told me that I had to leave.
3. The Addressee is normally an obligatory participant except when the Saying is a label, for example:
   He always tells wonderful stories.   (*wonderful stories* is a label)
4. Only when combined with a label, for example:
   He told the same story to both of us.
5. For example, sentences like
   He asked that we should not say anything about it.
   These are less common than *to* + V clause reported directives, such as
   He asked us not to say anything about it.
6. Only when combined with a label, for example:
   He asked a question to the whole class.
7. Very restricted. Note that sentences like
   She requested whether it would be possible to extend the deadline.
   could also be interpreted as directives (asking for permission).
8. Normally an obligatory participant in all contexts.

Figure 6.2   Saying and Addressee (suggested answers).

125

7 Being and having: The transitivity of relational and existential processes

The following text was written by a teacher.

Text 7a

> *Red Deer*
> The adult male (stag) stands one and a half meters high at the shoulder and weighs up to 200 kilograms. The adult female (hind) is considerably smaller. The young deer (calf) weighs approximately 7 kilograms at birth. It is fully grown at 4 years. The stag has antlers on the top of the head. These are bony growths up to one and a half meters from base to tip, which are used as weapons in fights with other stags during the mating season (rut). Hinds and calves live together in groups separately from the stags, except during the rut, which begins in early April and lasts 6 to 8 weeks. Survival and safety of the group depend on a highly developed sense of smell and hearing, and on the wisdom of the leader, who is always a hind.

This is a generic description of an animal. It is not mainly about actions (although it does contain some actions), nor is it about perceptions, thoughts, and feelings. Rather, it is about what things are, what they are like, and what they possess. The name for the process type dominant in this text is **relational process**.

Three subtypes of relational processes can be identified – **attributive, identifying,** and **possessive.** Each of these will be looked at in turn. In addition, this chapter will consider **existential** processes, as in clauses such as *there are fairies at the bottom of our garden.*

7.1 Attributive relational processes

The following clauses from text 7a all have one participant to which an **Attribute** of some kind is assigned. This participant is referred to as the **Carrier** of the Attribute. The Carrier is normally mapped onto the Subject, and the Attribute is normally mapped onto the Complement (see Section 1.6.2).

126

CARRIER ATTRIBUTE
(1) The adult female (hind) is considerably smaller.

CARRIER ATTRIBUTE
(2) These are bony growths up to one and a half meters from base to tip

CARRIER ATTRIBUTE
(3) . . . the leader, who is always a hind.

Carrier and Attribute are linked by a relational process verb, which can be called simply a **linking verb.** In the above three examples, the linking verbs are all forms of the verb *be*.

7.1.1   Types of Attributes

Numbers 1 to 3 illustrate two kinds of Attributes. In number 1 the Attribute is some kind of quality of the Carrier, while numbers 2 and 3 are the class of entity to which the Carrier belongs. The quality type of Attribute is typically expressed by an adjective or adjective group, while the class type of Attribute is typically expressed by a noun or noun group.

In Sections 3.4 and 3.5 it was noted that adjectives also function within the noun group as Describers and Classifiers. However, a number of adjectives function commonly as Attributes, but never or very rarely (usually with a specialized meaning) as Describers or Classifiers, for example, *ill, asleep, awake, afraid, late.* and *alive.*[1]

Like Describers, Attributes of the quality type can also be expressed by V*ing* and V*ed* forms, for example:

(4) The density and range of bird life along the harbor was still amazing.
(5) In 1788, these sheltered coves were densely wooded.

In most cases, these are best interpreted simply as adjectives (but see Sections 7.1.5 and 7.1.6). There is a third kind of Attribute, which is exemplified in the following clauses:

(6) Somebody was in the house.
(7) The next meeting will be on Wednesday.

Such Attributes represent circumstances, in the above examples providing information about place and time. Circumstance Attributes are typically expressed by prepositional phrases.

Task 7a

1. Identify the Carriers and Attributes in the following examples.
2. Which Attributes would you characterize as quality, which class, and which circumstance?

---

1 Note that what are here called adjectives functioning as Attributes are sometimes called *predicative adjectives* and what are here called adjectives functioning as Describers are sometimes called *attributive adjectives*.

   a. But the first white Australians were so conspicuously unfit for survival in the new land . . .

   b. As far as I remember the first session was about process writing.

   c. Most of the trees were eucalypts.

   d. Another basic difference is in how the sockets are mounted.

   e. Journalists are not a privileged class . . .

   f. Participation by both will be necessary.

   g. The eyes are bulbous and set on the side of the head.

   h. All his music is very romantic.

   i. It's probably a late romantic violin concerto.

   j. The whole package is a lot less than you might think.

7.1.2   Linking verbs

In all the examples so far, the verbs linking the Carrier to its Attribute have been forms of *be*. However, many other verbs can be used. A wide range of meanings can be expressed by such verbs. Some of the major categories are exemplified below.

7.1.2.1   PERCEPTION-TYPE LINKING VERBS

One kind of linking verb has to do with what can be glossed as the *perception* of the Attribute, for example:

(8) Moaula <u>looked</u> amazed.

(9) Yes, well they <u>seem</u> very, very intricate to me.

(10) Incredible as it may <u>sound</u> . . .

(11) It <u>smelled</u> so good!

Other verbs in this category are *taste* and *feel*.

   Such verbs clearly have a semantic relationship with mental process verbs of perception. In the previous chapter, it was noted that mental processes and mental-action processes could be related, sometimes sharing the same verb, sometimes using different verbs. The semantic relationships between mental, mental-action, and attributive processes can now be compared, as in the following examples:

Process	*Example*
Mental:	I can see the sea.
Mental-action:	I am looking at the sea.
Attributive:	The sea looks very blue.
Mental:	I can taste a lot of salt in the soup.
Mental-action:	I am tasting the soup.
Attributive:	The soup tastes salty.

Mental: I can hear some strange music.
Mental-action: I am listening to some strange music.
Attributive: This music sounds very strange.

Note that Attributive process verbs, like mental process verbs, normally select simple present tense for *now* time references.

7.1.2.2 CHANGE-TYPE LINKING VERBS

A second kind of linking verb used in attributive process clauses has to do with change, for example:

(12) The beautiful town of Yixing had become a frightening place to live in.
(13) . . . but it would often turn into a harsh croak or long gargle.
(14) It's getting hot in here.

Other verbs in this category are *grow, go, turn,* and *fall.*

Unlike other linking verbs, this category typically selects present continuous tense for *now* time references, presenting an Attribute as not yet complete but in the process of becoming (e.g., number 14). These verbs also often take perfect (i.e., relative past; see Section 8.1) tenses to show that the change to the Attribute is complete, as in number 12 and the following:

(15) You've got very cynical in your old age.

Learners sometimes have a problem with this and may produce errors such as:

(16) *Abortion becomes very controversial these days.

7.1.2.3 CIRCUMSTANCE-TYPE LINKING VERBS

A third type is where some circumstantial meaning is incorporated into the verb itself rather than being expressed entirely in the Attribute. A range of different circumstantial meanings that can be expressed in this way, as, for example, in numbers 17 through 20:

(17) and [the rut] lasts 4 to 6 weeks.   (time)
(18) This meeting concerns teaching loads.   (matter)
(19) The adult male (stag) stands one and a half meters high.   (quantity)
(20) . . . and weighs up to 200 kilograms.   (quantity)

Task 7b

1. Try substituting the following linking verbs for the forms of *be* in the attributive clauses in task 7a.

   Perception: look, seem, appear

the Attribute (i.e., they have been *postponed*). The pronoun *it* has then been "inserted" to function as Subject. In other words, numbers 39 and 40 can be related to the following versions:

CARRIER	ATTRIBUTE

(39) a. That America has defaulted on this promissory note is   obvious.

CARRIER	ATTRIBUTE

(40) a. To get them to read is practically impossible.

Versions like 39a and 40a do occur but the postponed versions are much commoner. The Attributes which commonly combine with postponed Carriers in this way fall into four main types:

1. Attributes expressing an evaluation of the state of affairs, for example:

   (41) It is good that you were able to see him before he left.
   (42) It's odd that nobody saw anything.

2. Attributes expressing judgments of the likelihood of the state of affairs, for example, number 39 and

   (43) It is certain that things will get worse before they get better.

3. Attributes expressing degrees of facility and *potentiality*,[3] for example, number 40 and

   (44) It would be easier for you to do it yourself. [*inv.*]
   (45) It is not possible to get an appointment before next month. [*inv.*]

4. Attributes expressing degrees of obligation and necessity, for example:

   (46) It is compulsory for all students to attend tutorials.
   (47) It is necessary to set the batten back from the front edges of the stud.

The meanings expressed by many such Attributes come within the area of **modality,** which will be further considered in Chapter 10.

7.1.5 *Mental process or attributive process?*

In the previous chapter, mental process clauses such as the following were considered.

(48)   She was pleased by the way George put it.

The combination of the words *was pleased* in this clause was interpreted as a passive voice (2 1) verb group.

---

3 The term *potentiality* rather than *possibility* is used here to avoid ambiguity. The adjective *possible* is used both for what will be called *likelihood* (e.g., *it is possible that they will come;* see Section 10.1.8) and what is here being called *potentiality* (*it is possible for them to come*).

In this chapter, we have seen how similar meanings can be expressed by attributive process clauses, for example:

(48) a. She was happy at the way George put it.

The combination of words *was happy* in this clause is interpreted as a linking verb followed by an Attribute (realized by an adjective), which is postmodified by the prepositional phrase *at the way George put it.*

However, the distinction between the two process types is not always clear-cut. For example, number 48 can be related to an active voice clause:

(48) b. The way George put it pleased her.

This is why it was interpreted as a passive voice mental process clause. However, if the preposition *by* in number 48 is replaced by *at,* then it becomes more plausible to interpret it as an attributive process clause, with *pleased* as an Attribute postmodified by *at the way George put it.*

Example 48 has other characteristics which make it possible to interpret it as an attributive clause. For example, *pleased,* like an Attribute such as *happy,* can be premodified by adverbs such as *very* and *quite.* In addition, the verb *was* could be replaced by one of the other linking verbs used in attributive process clauses, for example, *she looked very pleased at the way George put it.* Note also that clauses such as

(49)   They were determined to put a stop to the protests.

and

(50)   As a boy, he was very attached to his grandmother.

can be interpreted *only* as attributive process clauses, as it is very difficult or impossible to plausibly express them as active voice clauses, for example,

(49) a. ?Something determined them to put a stop to the protests.
(50) a. ?As a boy, something attached him to his mother.

7.1.6   Action process or attributive process?

As Task 7c and the discussion of Task 7c at the end of the chapter demonstrate, the borderline between attributive processes and action processes is also fuzzy.

Task 7c

State which of the following clauses you think are best interpreted as passive voice action processes and which as attributive process clauses, and give the criteria you used in making your decision. (Note that in some cases two interpretations may be possible, each assuming a different context.)

1. It is fully grown at 4 years.
2. The premises are located on the fourth floor.
3. The dormitories have been located too far away from the stadium.
4. The child was very well brought up.
5. They were all highly educated.
6. She is very widely read.
7. The population of Monsoon Asia is distributed in ecological niches.
8. The newsletter is distributed to all members.
9. He was drunk.
10. The wine was soon drunk.

7.1.7 *Learning and teaching attributive clauses*

Some languages have no verbs linking Carriers and Attributes in some types of attributive clauses. Number 51 is an example from Malay:

(51) Ali guru   *and*   Ali marah
     Ali teacher   Ali angry
     "Ali is a teacher."   "Ali is angry."

(Prentice 1987)

This may be one reason learners sometimes omit the linking verb in English, producing errors such as:

(52) *I said to my mum they kind to me.
(53) *Before, he just a small puppy.

Many learners have difficulty with the expansion of Attributes for comparison. In some languages, comparison of Attributes is handled quite differently. In Mandarin Chinese, for example, the basic structure is: *X bi (literally "compare with") Y Attribute,* as in:

(54) Ta   bi   wo gao.
     S/he compare with me is tall.
     "S/he is taller than me."

The practice in English of marking the comparative twice – first by *-er* attached to the adjective or premodifying *more* and second by postmodifying *than* – can be confusing, and it is perhaps not surprising that learners sometimes either mark the comparative only once or mark it three times, for example:

(55) *She intelligent than me.
(56) *She is more taller than me.

The postponed Carrier structure can also cause problems for learners, particularly if their mother tongues have nothing comparable. Learners may, for example, produce errors such as:

(57) *I am very easy to get to the college from my home.
(58) *Dr. Taylor is not convenient to see you now.

Learners may also sometimes try to use the structure when the Carrier is not a clause but a noun group, producing errors such as:

(59) *It is very difficult differential equations.

The different ways in which the general meaning of affection can be expressed by mental process clauses and by attributive process clauses may be partly responsible for the kinds of hybrid clauses learners sometimes produce, for example:

(60) *They afraid to tell them.
(61) *Now I don't scare of dogs anymore.
(62) *They are fear of unemployment.

Questions for discussion

- Design some tasks or games that would require learners to produce and interpret attributive clauses.
- Clauses such as *I am bored, I am scared, I am interested,* and so on are often first presented to learners as structurally identical to clauses such as *I am sad, I am afraid,* and *I am happy,* that is, as ordinary attributive clauses rather than as passive voice mental process clauses. What are the advantages or disadvantages of this approach?
- Could any of the activities you suggested in Chapter 3 for dealing with confusion between V*ing* and V*ed* Describers be adapted to help learners who also confuse forms like *boring* and *bored* functioning as Attributes?

7.2 Identifying relational processes

The following clauses look at first glance much the same as attributive process clauses.

(63)   The best known of New Zealand's birds is the kiwi . . .

(64)   The result is the network of valleys that diversify the face of the earth
        . . .

(65)   A mammal is an animal that suckles its young.

However, one significant difference between these clauses and attributive clauses is that they can be reversed, for example:

(63) a. The kiwi is the best known of New Zealand's birds.
(64) a. The network of valleys that diversify the face of the earth is the result.
(65) a. An animal that suckles its young is a mammal.

Attributive clauses cannot normally be reversed in this way. (When reversal is acceptable, it produces a very unusual, or *marked* clause; see Section 11.4.1.) The reason for this is that clauses like 63 through 65 do not simply assign an Attribute to a Carrier. They *identify* one participant by *equating* it with another participant. This is why they are called **identifying process** clauses. And if participant A equals participant B, then of course participant B also equals participant A. In other words, the clauses are reversible.

The participant which is identified is called the **Identified** and the participant which does the identifying is called the **Identifier.** One can think of Identifiers as answering questions such as *What is X? Which is X?* and *Who is X?* Thus, in numbers 63 through 65 the Identifiers are *the kiwi, the network of valleys that diversify the face of the earth,* and *an animal that suckles its young.* Note that unlike Attributes, Identifiers cannot be realized by adjective groups. They must be noun groups or nominal clauses. The only apparent exception to this is when the Identifier is realized by a superlative adjective, that is, an adjective pre-modified by *most* or with the suffix *-est,* as in *John is the tallest.* In such a clause, a form like *the tallest* can, in fact, be interpreted as a noun group with the head noun (e.g., *boy* or *student*) omitted because it is understood.

There is a strong tendency for the Identifier to be the second participant, as in numbers 63 through 65. This is because the Identifier contains the new or important information in the clause and such information normally comes at the end of the clause. However, sometimes the Identifier can be the first participant. When the Identifier does come first, it is usually marked, in speech at least, by carrying a major pitch movement (called the *tonic;* see Section 11.8). For example:

(66) (Who is the fat guy?)

<pre>
IDENTIFIED   IDENTIFIER
┌─────────┐ ┌───────────┐
The fat guy is the principal.
</pre>

(67) (Who is the principal?)

<pre>
IDENTIFIER   IDENTIFIED
┌─────────┐ ┌───────────┐
The fat guy is the principal.
</pre>

Task 7d

1. Assuming normal intonation, identify the Identifieds and the Identifiers in the following identifying clauses.

2. Where two interpretations seem equally likely, construct a different context for each.

   a. Well, "joyous" is the word I think of when I smell the pigs.
   b. The topic for the next session will be "process writing."
   c. This will be the day when all of God's children will be able to sing . . .
   d. That is the antenna.
   e. Now is the time to make real the promise of democracy . . .
   f. This is our hope.
   g. (A _____ liked Paris most) but for me Barcelona was the high point of the trip.

7.2.1 *Linking verbs in identifying processes*

As in attributive clauses, a wide range of linking verbs can be used in identifying clauses. These include the categories of perception, change, and circumstance that were identified with attributive linking verbs, excluding those which can only be used with adjectives and adjective groups. For example:

(68) From where I was standing, Early Riser <u>appeared</u> the winner
   . . . (perception)
(69) Such writings <u>have become</u> the most important means of discovering Greece. (change)
(70) I <u>was surrounded</u> by birds. (circumstance: place)
(71) The meeting <u>took up</u> the whole of Wednesday afternoon. (circumstance: time)
(72) . . . and most frequently nothing <u>follows</u> [the question]. (circumstance: time)

With the circumstance type, the line is often hard to draw between attributive and identifying clauses. The basic principle is if the sequence of participants can be reversed (often necessitating a change in voice), then it is an identifying clause. For example:

(70) a. Birds surrounded me.
(71) a. The whole of Wednesday afternoon was taken up by the meeting.
(72) a. . . . the question is most frequently followed by nothing.

In addition, there is a type of linking verb used in identifying clauses that can be called a *symbolizing* verb, such as *mean, represent, signify, exemplify, define,* and *equal.* For example:

(73) These signals <u>mean</u>: Go forward! Go away from me!
(74) The electronic research library <u>symbolizes</u> the cutting edge . . .

Such linking verbs are much used in writing of a technical nature.[4]

Questions for discussion

- Design some tasks or games that would require learners to accurately produce and interpret identifying clauses.
- It is important for learners wishing to study subjects such as science through the medium of English to be able to distinguish between *generalizations* expressed by attributive clauses (e.g., *a reptile is a cold-blooded animal*) and *definitions* expressed by identifying clauses [e.g., *a reptile is a cold-blooded animal which has a scaly skin and lays eggs* (Collins 1987: 1229)]. Suggest some activities for sensitizing relatively advanced learners to the difference between generalizations and definitions, making use of the different grammatical properties of the two process subtypes.

7.3   Possessive relational processes

In possessive process clauses, two participants are related through one being the **Possessor** of the other (the **Possessed**), for example:

	POSSESSOR		POSSESSED	
(75)	The stag	has	antlers	on the top of the head.

	POSSESSOR		POSSESSED
(76)	Each of them	had	their own porridge bowl.

As these two examples suggest, possession processes include relationships of part to whole (as in number 75) and of ownership (number 76). Other verbs of possession are *own* (although not in the part-whole sense) and *possess*. *Have got* is also used as a more colloquial (usually spoken rather than written) variant of *have*. For example:

(77) Porter's father had owned a feed and farm merchandise store.
(78) Most offices did not even possess a computer.
(79) We've all got 486's now.

Also included in this category are possession in the sense of *inclusion* and what can be called *negative possession*. For example:

(80) The library of the future will still contain millions of books . . .

---

4 Some of these processes in fact lie on the borderline between relational and verbal processes. For example, in a clause such as *Conductors which obey Ohm's law are called ohmic conductors;* the process of calling could be interpreted as verbal. However, in this context it clearly expresses a symbolizing relationship.

(81) Monsoon Asia includes those countries which are affected by the monsoon rains.

(82) They lack a professional membership association . . .

Like most attributive and identifying processes, possessive process clauses normally select simple present for now references, and continuous tenses in general are seldom used, for example:

(83) Deutsche Bank and Credit Lyonnais now own whole networks of banks . . . (not: *are now owning*)

Possessive processes are very common in English and have, in a sense, colonized many other process types, often involving some kind of nominalization (Section 3.5) in the Possessed, for example:

(84) It has no real beginning or end . . . ("It does not really begin or end . . .")

(85) The warm moisture-laden air of the tropical ocean possesses an enormous capacity for heat energy. (" . . . can produce an enormous amount of heat energy.")

(86) Gibbs has certain calls and whistles which tell Bob what to do. ("Gibbs calls and whistles in a certain way according to what he wants Bob to do.")

(87) I have a splitting headache. (?"My head aches splittingly.")

This extends to cases of *have* as a delexical verb (see Section 4.2.6), where the meaning of possession is not really present at all.

These extended uses of possessive processes can present problems for learners, particularly if there are no comparable metaphorical uses in their mother tongues.

7.4 Existential processes

Existential process clauses consist of just one participant, known as the **existent,** for example:

EXISTENT
(88) Once upon a time there were three bears.

In such clauses, *there* functions as the Subject. However, it is not a participant (or circumstance) in the clause.

It was noted in Chapter 1 that number agreement on the Finite in existential clauses is determined by the number of the following noun group (i.e., the Existent). In informal spoken English there is a tendency to use *there's* and *there was* with both singular and plural Existents, for example:

(89) There's some students still waiting outside.

However, this is generally considered incorrect in written English.

It is quite common for the Existent to be an event or situation, usually involving some kind of nominalization, for example:

(90) There has been <u>a huge explosion and fire</u> at a warehouse in S _____
. . .
(91) There is a <u>growing tendency to bar access to computers</u> . . .

Occasionally, a verb other than *be* is used in existential clauses, for example:

(92) There came a sudden knock at the door.
(93) There remains the question of compensation.

The use of such verbs tends to be restricted to more formal English.

It is also possible sometimes to omit the *there* when the clause begins with a Circumstantial Adjunct, for example:

(94) Inside every university will be an electronic virtual university.

7.4.1   *Learning and teaching possessive and existential processes*

Some learners may have difficulties with the difference between possessive and existential processes. In many languages existential and possessive processes are not distinguished quite as they are in English. For example, the Malay word *ada* translates both English *there is* and *have:*

(95)   saya ada banyak buku
       I ADA many book
       "I have many books."
(96)   disini ada banyak buku
       here ADA many book
       "There are many books here."

In English also, the two processes can come very close. For example, a speaker can express the existence of overhead projectors in all classrooms with either a possessive or an existential process clause:

(97)   Every classroom has an overhead projector.   [*inv.*]
(97) a. There is an overhead projector in every classroom.

The speaker can also move the Circumstantial Adjunct to the front of the existential process clause and omit the *there:*

(97) b. In every classroom is an overhead projector.

However, the following clause is not acceptable in Standard English, as a prepositional phrase cannot function as Subject (in number 97b *there* remains the Subject, even though it has been omitted):

(97) c. *In every classroom has an overhead projector.

Not surprisingly, learners sometimes produce errors like number 97c.

Questions for discussion

- Suggest ways of introducing and practicing possessive and existential clauses that clearly distinguish them by exploiting the fact that possessive clauses typically involve relatively permanent part-whole or ownership relationships whereas existential clauses often involve relatively temporary location.
- Suggest some activities to be used with more advanced learners for exploring the more subtle distinctions between possessive clauses and existential clauses such as in numbers 97 and 97a.

Task 7e

This task should help you to review some of the material covered in this and the previous two chapters.

1. Extract 1 consists of a general description of a class of animals (a New Zealand bird called the *kiwi*), and the first part of extract 3 is a short narrative describing how a Chinese emperor discovered how to prepare tea. Without looking at the two extracts, describe the types of processes and participants you would expect to find in each of them. To which aspects of the experiential meaning of the texts would you expect each process type to contribute?
2. Look at extract 1 and extract 3, lines 1 through 7. To what extent are your expectations borne out?

Summary

1. There are three types of relational processes: attributive, identifying, and possessive.
2. Attributive relational clauses have a Carrier to which an Attribute of some kind is assigned. The Carrier is mapped onto the Subject and the Attribute onto the Complement.
3. Attributes are realized by adjective groups, noun groups, or prepositional phrases.

4. Attributes and Carriers are linked by relational verbs, also known as linking verbs. The most common linking verb is *be*. Other categories of linking verbs can be glossed as perception (e.g., *look, seem*), change (e.g., *become, turn*), and circumstance (e.g., *stand, concern*).
5. Adjective group Attributes can be expanded for comparison. They can also be expanded for comparison of equality.
6. Carriers realized by *that* clauses are often placed after the Attribute, with *it* taking up the Subject function. Such Carriers are referred to as postponed Carriers.
7. Identifying relational processes identify one participant by equating it with another.The identified participant is called the Identified and the participant which does the identifying is called the Identifier. Unlike attributive relational clauses, identifying relational clauses are normally reversible.
8. Possessive relational clauses have a Possessor and a Possessed linked by a verb of possession (most typically *have*). Possessive processes include part-whole relationships as well as ownership relationships.
9. Existential process clauses consist of one participant (the Existent), the word *there* (functioning as Subject), and an existential verb (usually *be).*

Key terms introduced

This book	*Alternatives used in the field*
Attribute	Characterization, predicative adjective
attributive (relational) process	
Carrier	Characterized
comparative	
comparison	
comparison of equality	
Existent	
existential process	
Identified	
Identifier	
identifying (relational) process	
linking verb	copula
Possessed	
possessive (relational) process	
Possessor	
relational process	
superlative	

Discussion of tasks

Task 7a

Carrier	Attribute
a. the first white Australians	so conspicuously unfit for survival in the new land (quality)
b. the first session	about process writing (circumstance)
c. Most of the trees	eucalypts (class)
d. Another basic difference	in how the sockets are mounted (circumstance)
e. Journalists	a privileged class (class)
f. Participation by both	necessary (quality)
g. The eyes	bulbous and set on the side of the head (quality)
h. All his music	very romantic (quality)
i. It	a late romantic violin concerto (class)
j. The whole package	a lot less than you might think (quality)

Task 7b

Look is commonly used with adjective Attributes (e.g., . . . *the first white Australians looked so conspicuously unfit*). Its use with noun Attributes is much more restricted (e.g., **Most of the trees looked eucalypts* is not acceptable.) *Look* can normally be used before noun Attributes only when the Attribute can be interpreted as more like quality than class, (e.g., *In his new uniform, he looked a real soldier*). Note that the clause *?in his new uniform, he looked a soldier* would be very odd. *Look* can, of course, be used before a prepositional phrase Attribute beginning with *like* (e.g., *the trees looked like eucalypts*).

Seem and *appear* can be used before both adjective and noun Attributes. However, they are usually followed by *to be* before noun Attributes.

Become can be used before both noun and adjective Attributes, whereas *get* and *turn* cannot be used with noun Attributes. *Turn* can also be used only with a semantically restricted range of quality Attributes (e.g., colors) and evaluative Attributes (e.g., *vicious* and *bad*). Note that *turned into* is used before noun Attributes. *Concern* and *cost* are used only with noun Attributes, which must, of course, be compatible with their circumstantial meanings.

Task 7c

Possible criteria for recognition as a passive voice action process clause are:

- The possibility of introducing an Actor with a *by* phrase (e.g., *The newsletter is distributed by the committee to all members*).
- Tense selection compatible with interpretation as an action. For example, number 2 would be very odd interpreted as an action process (suggesting somebody regularly or always performs the action of locating), whereas the tense of number 3 is perfectly compatible with an action interpretation.

Possible criteria for recognition as attributive process clause are:

- Presence or possibility of introducing an adverb modifier, such as *very,* typically used with adjective Attributes. For example, *he was very drunk* is possible, but *the wine was soon very drunk* is not.
- Tense compatible with interpretation as a relational process.

As the two sets of criteria are not mutually exclusive, there will inevitably be some indeterminate cases. Note also that number 6 is not indeterminate but *ambiguous* out of context; that is, it could be interpreted as *people in many different places read her books* (passive clause interpretation) or *she has read a great deal* (implying that she is well-educated, an attributive interpretation).

Task 7d

The *most likely* distribution of participant roles is:

Identifier	*Identified*
a. joyous	the word I think of when I smell pigs
b. process writing	the topic for the next session
c. the day when all of God's children will be able to sing	this
d. the antenna	that
e. the time to make real the promise of democracy	now
f. our hope	this
g. Barcelona	the high point of the trip

Task 7e

Extract 1

In such a text, one might expect mainly relational process clauses, particularly of the attributive type, with Carriers representing the kiwi or parts of its body, and of the possessive type, listing its body parts and inherent characteristics. There might also be some action processes describing some of the bird's typical patterns of behavior and perhaps a few mental processes of the perception type giving information about the senses of the bird.

Analysis of the extract on the whole confirms these expectations. There are many attributive process clauses used to describe physical as well as some behavioral characteristics of the bird, with either the bird or a body part as Carrier (e.g., *It's a small tubby flightless bird; it is nocturnal; feathers . . . are more like hair; they are still fairly lazy*).

There are also possessive process clauses used for the listing of body parts and behavioral characteristics (e.g., *they have no wings, feathers . . . short sight and a sleepy nature; the kiwi has something in common . . . a shocking temper*). One possessive process clause (*. . . the All Blacks have nothing on them when it comes to strength of leg*) is part of a somewhat metaphorical sentence, and even when this clause is "de-metaphorized," it still comes out as a possessive process: *they have legs even stronger than those of members of the All Black rugby team.*

In addition, there are three identifying clauses. The first two clauses in the extract are identifying clauses which introduce the bird by identifying it as *the best known of New Zealand's birds* and as *the symbol of New Zealanders.* The other identifying clause is *the night time is when they are most active.*

A few action or mental-action process clauses in the extract describe typical behaviors of the bird, for example, *giving . . . a kick* (involving a delexical verb structure); *sleeping for . . . a day,* and *which they sniff out.*

The one mental process in this extract is embedded within an Attribute (*easy to observe*).

Extract 3

One would expect the backbone of such a narrative to be a series of action process clauses, with most of the Actors representing the individual involved and sometimes with Goals representing the materials involved in tea making and drinking. One might also expect some of the action processes to be of the ergative type, either with Causers representing the discoverer (e.g., *he boiled the water*) or without Causers (e.g., *the water boiled*). As the narrative is about discovering the pleasures of tea drinking, one might also expect a few mental processes of the perception type (e.g., *see, smell,* and *taste*). Relational processes might be expected to occur only occasionally – for background description of the individual involved, the setting, and perhaps some of the ingredients. One or two existential process clauses might be expected near the beginning of the narrative, introducing the individual involved or aspects of the setting.

Analysis of the extract on the whole confirms these expectations. Most of the finite clauses represent action processes, with Chen-nung (or *he*) as Actor. However, one action process clause has a natural phenomenon as Actor (*a slight breeze*). Another action process clause (*They fell into the boiling water*) can be interpreted as ergative, with a potential ingredient as Affected (note that this clause is ergative in the broad sense – the verb *fell* itself is not a verb which also allows a Causer as Subject; see Section 5.3). There is just one mental process clause (*Chen-nung did not notice . . . the subtle aroma*). There is also only one relational process clause (*hot water is more refreshing than iced water*), which is clearly marked as background information by the use of brackets. There is also one existential process clause (the first clause), which introduces the whole narrative (the label *legend* is the Existent).

8 Representing time: Tense and temporal Adjuncts

This chapter will explore some of the ways in which the notion of *time* may be represented in the grammar of English. The following extract is from a newspaper feature.

Text 8a

It happened when we moved house to a village about three miles from our former home, taking our cat with us. For a couple of months she settled in, apparently quite content. Then one morning she was missing. Later in the week the purchaser of our house phoned to ask whether we had lost a cat. A stray had suddenly appeared in one of his outbuildings. We went to investigate and, sure enough, it was our missing tabby.

(Whitlock 1992)

The expressions of time in this paragraph can be grouped in the following ways.

1. Time is expressed within the verb group through the system of **tense.**

   happened, moved, settled, was, phoned, had lost, had appeared, went, was

This is the most frequent type of time expression, as every finite verb group[1] selects for tense.

2. Time is expressed within the clause by a **Circumstantial Adjunct:**

   for a couple of months
   one morning
   later in the week

3. Time is encoded in the structural relationship between two clauses, marked by the word *when* (a *binding conjunction;* see Section 12.2.2):

   When we moved house to a village about three miles from our former home
   . . .

4. Time is expressed by a **Conjunctive Adjunct,** which provides a temporal link between this sentence and the previous text:

---

1 As will be seen, many nonfinite clauses select for *relative* tense.

Then . . .

A large part of this chapter will be devoted to exploring the system of tense. Circumstantial and Conjunctive Adjuncts of time will also be looked at. Structural relationships between clauses involving time will be dealt with in Chapter 12.

8.1   The tense system

A basic distinction can be made between **absolute tense** and **relative tense.** Absolute tense essentially locates a process in time relative to the here and now. Relative tense further locates the process relative to the absolute tense, for example:

(1) They <u>arrived</u>.
(2) They <u>have arrived</u>.
(3) They <u>had arrived</u>.

All three verb groups present processes as taking place at a time before now. In number 1, the absolute tense is *past;* there is no relative tense. The process is simply located at a time in the past. This explains why this tense form often co-occurs with Circumstantial Adjuncts of absolute past time, such as at *3 p.m.* or *on the 31st of August.*

In number 2, the absolute tense is *present* and the relative tense is *past.* This represents what can be glossed as *past in the present.* In other words, the past is in a sense viewed from the present, which is why this tense form is typically used where a process is located in the past but has some consequence in or relevance to the present. Thus, number 2 implies not only that their arrival took place in the past but also that *they* are here *now;* number 1 lacks this latter implication. This also explains why this tense form occurs rarely with Circumstantial Adjuncts of absolute time but often occurs with Circumstantial Adjuncts of relative time, such as *recently* and *just.*

In number 3, the absolute tense is *past* and the relative tense is also *past.* This represents *past in the past.* In other words, the process is located at a time before a time in the past. This again explains why this tense form often occurs with Circumstantial Adjuncts of relative time, such as *recently, just, the day before,* and *previously.*

There is a selection of three absolute tenses:

1. *Present:* location at the moment of speaking or writing, or an extended period including the moment of speaking or writing
2. *Past:* a time before the moment of speaking or writing
3. *Future:* a time after the time of speaking or writing.

Table 8.1   *Absolute and relative tense selections*

Relative tense	Absolute tense	Example	Usual name
Present in	present	*is walking*	present continuous/progressive
Past in	present	*has walked*	present perfect
Present in	past	*was walking*	past continuous/progressive
Past in	past	*had walked*	past perfect
Present in	future	*will be walking*	future continuous/progressive
Past in	future	*will have walked*	future perfect

Table 8.2   *Further relative tense selections*

Relative		Absolute	Example	Usual name
Present in past	in	present	*has been walking*	present perfect continuous/progressive
Present in past	in	past	*had been walking*	past perfect continuous/progressive
Present in past	in	future	*will have been walking*	future perfect continuous/progressive

These are the three tense forms normally called *simple present* (e.g., *walk/walks*), *simple past* (e.g., *walked*), and *simple future* (e.g., *will walk*).

The system then allows a selection between two relative tenses. The selections are *present* (that is, *at the same time* as the absolute tense selection) and *past* (that is, *before* the absolute tense selection). Table 8.1 gives absolute and relative tense selections for present and past.

There are in addition limited possibilities for adding a second relative tense selection, which further locates the process relative to the previous selections (Table 8.2).

8.1.1   Relative future

The notion of **relative future** – that is, a time later than the absolute (or absolute + relative) tense selections – can be expressed by forms of the verb *be* + *going to* (usually reduced to "gonna" in speech), for example:

Future in present: *is going to walk*
Future in past: *was going to walk*

In addition, the following forms are possible, although they occur only rarely and one would almost certainly not wish to teach them to learners.

Future in past in present: *has been going to walk*

Future in past in past: *had been going to walk*
Future in future: *will be going to walk*
Future in past in future: *will have been going to walk*

Most grammar books do not regard the *going to* forms as tenses, and there is no generally accepted set of terms to describe them. However, in terms of their function, there is no reason why they should not be included in an account of the tenses of English (as is done in Halliday 1994: 198–207).

There are other ways in which the notion of relative future can be expressed, with different nuances of meaning, for example, *be about to* (immediate future), *be to* (predestined or arranged future),[2] and *would* (future in past only). For example:

(4) . . . young people who are <u>about to</u> embark on a career . . .   (*future in present*)
(5) We were later to become firm friends.   (*future in past*)
(6) Despite such a very unpromising start, he would one day outshine us all.   (*future in past*)

8.1.2   Tense and modals

In origin, *could, might, should,* and *would* are the past tense forms of the modal auxiliaries *can, may, shall,* and *will. Could, might, should,* and *would* do function as past tense forms in certain contexts, such as in dependent clauses following mental or verbal processes, as in:

(7) (I <u>can</u>'t move it.)
    He told me that he <u>couldn't</u> move it.   [*inv.*]
(8) (He <u>may</u> not come.)
    I knew that he <u>might</u> not come.   [*inv.*]
(9) (I'<u>ll</u> help you.)
    He said that he <u>would</u> help us.   [*inv.*]

Could and *would* are, in fact, used as past tense forms more widely than *might* and *should,* for example:

(10) . . . we were good for each other: his maths was better than mine and I <u>could</u> help him unravel the madness of English grammar.
(11) He <u>would</u> not help us, no matter what we said.

In other contexts, however, it is more accurate to treat *could, might, should,* and *would* as separate modals rather than as past tense forms of the other modals.

All modals combine with relative past, present, and future, for example:

---

2 This is complicated by the fact that the *be to* form often also has the modal meaning of obligation, for example, *You are to report to the head office immediately.*

(12) Henry must have been out of his mind. (*modal + relative past*)
(13) They might be doing it right now. (*modal + relative present*)
(14) . . . oblivious of the fact that the whole edifice could be about to come
        crashing down. (*modal + relative future*)

Some of the meanings expressed by modals with relative tenses are explored in Sections 10.1.3 and 10.2.2.

   The semimodal *used to* (see Section 4.1.2), usually pronounced "usta," is
used with action processes to refer to repetitive or habitual actions in the
past. *Used to* usually implies that the repeated past actions no longer
continue, for example:

(15). . . because old radios <u>used to</u> go on valves . . .

Used to is similarly used with other process types, again usually with the
implication that the state of affairs is no longer the case, for example:

(16) The pub used to be a coaching inn.

8.1.3   Tense in nonfinite verb groups

Note that nonfinite verb groups cannot select for absolute tense. Thus
relative tense selections in nonfinite clauses locate the process relative to
the time established by the tense selection in a finite clause. In other words,
whereas finite verb groups can make such tense distinctions as *has walked*
(past in present), *had walked* (past in past), and *will have walked* (past in
future), nonfinite verb groups have only *having walked* (relative past), for
example:

(17)   . . . <u>having worked</u> at a number of sites en route, he was told of a stray
        dog . . .
(17) a. . . . <u>having worked</u> at a number of sites en route, we'll then be well pre-
        pared . . .

The relative tense selection in the nonfinite clause in both these sentences is
past. However, in 17 its location in absolute time is also past; in 17a its
location in absolute time is future.

   Relative tense selection in nonfinite clauses can be *past* (as in 17 and
17a), *present,* or *present in past,* for example:

(18)   They must be really disillusioned by the whole thing <u>to be talking</u> like
        that. (*present*)
(19)   I'd like you <u>to</u> at least <u>be smiling</u> when you greet them. (*present*)
(20)   <u>Having been queuing</u> all night, they were cold and hungry. (*present in
        past*)

8.2   Using tense

The above sections merely set out the bare bones of the system of tense in English. The precise meaning of any one selection from the system will depend on the process type involved and the context.

Grammar books sometimes try to cover all of the tense forms of English by going through them one by one and in each case attempting to explain their uses and meanings in different contexts. This is not the approach that will be taken in this chapter, nor is it the approach recommended for teaching tenses to second language learners. Rather, the relationships between tense and process type that have already been touched on in previous chapters will be further explored. Some typical tense selections in a number of different contexts will then be considered. It will not be possible to consider in detail all the possible nuances of meaning of all the tenses.

In the following sections the names conventionally used for the tenses of English will be used. These names are not ideal. However, they are widely known and used by learners, teachers, and textbooks.

8.2.1   Tense and process type

It has been noted in previous chapters that the typical or *unmarked* tense selection in *now* references is present continuous (present in present) for action processes (including mental-action processes) and simple present for mental and relational processes, with the exception of change-type linking verbs. For example:

(21) Who's <u>doing</u> that?   (*action*)   [*inv.*]
(22) I'm <u>looking</u> at what you are doing.   (*mental-action*)   [*inv.*]
(23) I <u>want</u> you all to sit up straight.   (*mental*)
(24) You all <u>look</u> very smart.   (*relational*)
(25) You're <u>getting</u> noisy again.   (*relational – change type*)

Some of the other combinations of tense selection and process type will now be considered.

8.2.1.1   SIMPLE PRESENT WITH ACTION PROCESSES

The combination of simple present tense with action processes expresses what are often called *habitual* and *timeless* actions – i.e. actions which are repeated regularly over a period of time including *now* – or actions which are presented as general or universal. For example:

(26) At this time of year I usually <u>walk</u> to school.
(27) The tools with which a river <u>excavates</u> its valleys are the boulders and the sand that it <u>sweeps</u> along with it.

(28) A truffle <u>absorbs</u> nourishment from the soil and the vegetation surrounding it.

One would expect most learners to encounter this very common usage early on.

Much less common (and therefore of lower priority in most teaching contexts) is the use of simple present with action processes for (1) future time references, where the event is fixed or scheduled (sometimes called the *timetabled future*), as in number 29, (2) *now* references in commentaries or demonstrations, as in numbers 30 and 31, and (3) past time actions within (usually spoken) narrative (Section 8.2.2.1).

(29) His flight <u>doesn't arrive</u> till about eight.
(30) Smith <u>passes</u> the ball to Jones, Jones <u>passes</u> it to Grimes, Grimes <u>heads</u> it beautifully into the net . . .   [*inv.*]
(31) First I <u>attach</u> the red lead to the positive terminal . . .

8.2.1.2 CONTINUOUS TENSES WITH MENTAL PROCESSES

The combination of present continuous (present in present) and other so-called *continuous* tenses (or *progressive* tenses; see Section 9.3) with mental processes often carries the sense of *beginning to,* as in:

(32) I can see that <u>you are believing</u> me at last.

Continuous (relative present) tenses also carry an implication that the mental process is temporary. This is sometimes exploited to express a certain tentativeness in polite suggestions and requests, for example:

(33) I <u>was wondering</u> whether you would be able to help us.

These two uses of continuous tenses with mental processes would probably not be of high priority for most learners.

8.2.1.3 CONTINUOUS TENSES WITH RELATIONAL PROCESSES

Where the linking verb is *be,* continuous tenses often suggest a kind of temporary behavior. In other words, the process becomes much more like an action process. For example:

(34) . . . a picture where someone <u>is being</u> kind and saying . . .   ("behaving in a kind way")
(35) You <u>are being</u> very stupid.   ("You are behaving in a very stupid way.")

It has already been noted that present continuous is the unmarked tense selection for the change type of relational process. In addition, *some* of the reality-type linking verbs can combine with either simple present or present continuous with very little difference in meaning, although the use of the continuous tense does tend to imply something temporary, for example:

(36) You're looking good today.   [*inv.*]

Again, such usages would not be of high priority for most learners.

Task 8a

Taking into account process type, time reference, and likely context, explain the tense selections in the following clauses.

1. They are all standing around waiting.
2. The statue stands in the center of the square.
3. I am seeing most of the students tomorrow.
4. I was thinking that we might go there together.
5. The river flows through the center of the city.
6. I am understanding a lot more of it now than I did in the first semester.
7. She lives in upstate New York.
8. Many of the former officials are living in poverty far from the capital.

8.2.2   *Tenses in context*

The rest of this section on tenses will look at some typical patterns of tense selection in a number of different contexts.

8.2.2.1   TENSE SELECTIONS IN NARRATIVES

Narratives are typically associated with past tenses (i.e., those with an absolute tense selection of *past*). The story line, which is the backbone of any narrative, typically consists of a chronological sequence of events each represented by verbs in the *simple past tense*. Verbs in the story line are usually action process verbs, but there may also be some mental process verbs, particularly of the perception type, representing what characters in the narrative *see, hear,* and so on.

In the simplest kind of narrative, simple past may be the only tense form used, as in text 4a (the umu text) and the following short text written by a teacher.

(37)   Last week I saw something very funny at the zoo. A man walked up to a cage and looked at a monkey inside. Suddenly, the monkey snatched the man's glasses and put them on. The monkey looked at the man and the man jumped angrily up and down. The monkey quickly gave the glasses back to the man and covered his face with his hands.

In more sophisticated narratives, the other past tenses are typically used to flesh out the narrative with processes tangential to the main narrative, the relative tense locating them before or simultaneous to a point in the story line.

Thus, the *past perfect* (past in past) typically introduces background events previous to a point in the story. In the following example, this takes the form of a flashback to events that take place before the beginning of the story proper.

(38) In light of the figure he was to become, it was a small irony that he almost hadn't made it to Vietnam. The plane he should have taken in March 1962, with ninety-three other officers and men, had disappeared over the Pacific. He had missed the flight because, in his eagerness to go to war, he had forgotten to have his passport renewed. A clerk had noticed that the passport had expired during the final document check, and he had been instructed to step out of the boarding line.

(Sheehan 1989: 37)

Sometimes the reference is to an earlier event (or absence of a previous comparable event) that provides some perspective or evaluation of something in the story, for example:

(39) I had never seen anything quite like it.

Also note that a modal + (relative) past can be used for reference to a potential earlier event which did not take place, as for example, in number 38 – *should have taken.*

The *past continuous* (present in past) with action processes and the *simple past* with relational processes typically provide some kind of descriptive background to the story line, for example:

(40) When I set out the sun was shining and I didn't have a care in the world.
(46) I was trembling and aware of being overwhelmed by a familiar feeling I could not place as I sat beside her and asked what the charge was.

Occasionally, the past continuous is used for an event in the story line itself, as in this extract from a spoken narrative about a skiing accident. Here the speaker in a sense freezes the action at a crucial moment and paints the scene for the listeners.

(42) and he found it was a ski jump (laughter) he, he'd lost one, ski at the top and he apparently he was flying through the air with one leg up in the air with a ski on it, and he landed head first in the snow . . .

(Slade and Norris 1986: 52)

Whereas the past perfect locates events prior to a point in the main story line and the past continuous locates events simultaneous to a point in the story line, *was/were going to, would,* and *was/were to* (future in past) are used to locate events *later* than a point in the story line, in other words, to *anticipate* events. For example:

(43) . . . it was clearly going to be difficult to change things in a hurry.

(44) Little did he know that his life <u>would be changed</u> by that chance meeting.
(45) In light of the figure he <u>was to</u> become . . .   (from number 38)

Task 8b

Describe and account for the tense selections of the finite verb groups in text 8a at the beginning of this chapter and its continuation below.

When we examined her we found a big lump behind one ear. We conjectured that she had been knocked down by a car; then, partially recovering but still dazed, had instinctively made for her old home. How she found her way we do not know, for she had been brought to our new house by car. She never tried the journey again.

Nonpast tenses *can* of course be used in narratives. Many narratives include quoted dialogue which is likely to contain nonpast tenses. This will be considered in Section 8.2.2.4.

Simple present tense may occasionally also be used in the *scene setting* (technically *orientation*) sections of a narrative where the scene is presented as a place which still exists, as, for example, in the first paragraph of Extract 4:

(46) Yixing <u>is</u> a small town in Jiangnan to the south of the Yangzi River.

In the same text, the narrator introduces the story in the following way:

(47) This story <u>takes</u> place in the middle of the third century A.D. . . .

The narrator is here using simple present to make a link to the here and now of the reader reading the story before switching to simple past to begin the story line.

Present tense can sometimes be used even for the story line itself. This is most common in spoken narratives to make the story more vivid. Speakers may sometimes begin with the past tense and switch to the present at the most important or exciting points of the narrative. This also occasionally occurs in written narratives, as in this extract from Gore Vidal's novel *Creation* (1993: 93):

(48) . . . instead of stretching out on the moss with the others, I wandered off into the forest.

Green laurel suddenly <u>parts</u>. I <u>see</u> the snout; the curved yellow tusks. I <u>freeze</u>, spear in hand, unable to move as the huge bristling body <u>breaks</u> through the hedge of laurel.

The boar <u>gets</u> wind of me; <u>backs</u> away. No doubt, the beast <u>is</u> as alarmed as I. But then, in an odd circling movement the boar <u>wheels</u> about and <u>charges</u>.

I am thrown high into the air. Before I reach earth again, I realize that all the wind has left my chest.

I thought I was dead . . .

Such usages of present tense forms in narratives are not typical and would not be a high priority for learners.

8.2.2.2 TENSE SELECTIONS IN DESCRIPTIONS

Descriptions of people, places, and things are typically associated with present tense forms, with the *simple present* form as the core or basic form used. Extract 1, a generic description of a kind of bird, uses present tense throughout, mainly with relational process clauses, for example:

(49) The best known of New Zealand's birds is the kiwi . . .
(55) Kiwis have no wings . . .

In such generic descriptions, simple present may also be used with action processes to further delineate what is being described – in the case of extract 1, to describe the kiwi's habits:

(51) the rest of the time they spend poking around for worms which they sniff out with the nostrils on the end of their long bill.

In specific descriptions (i.e., descriptions of specific individuals rather than classes of people, places, or things) simple present with relational and sometimes action process verbs is also typically used, as in this description of the Statue of Liberty containing attributive process verbs of the circumstance type and one action process with modal auxiliary.

(52) . . . still the most popular landmark in America after ninety years, this 152 ft. (46 m) high copper-plated statue towers green and majestic over the gateway to the United States. Its labyrinthine interior framework, designed by Gustave Eiffel of Eiffel Tower fame, can be explored by a stairway which leads to an observation gallery . . .

(*US Travel Information*)

The *present perfect* (past in present) may be used to give some depth to descriptions. With action processes, it can refer to events which took place at an unspecified time before the present but whose results are relevant to the present description, for example:

(53) Now it has been discovered by the world.   (meaning *the world now knows about it*)
(54) Now officially a part of the French patrimony, it has been classified as a "monument historique" . . .   (meaning *it is now a 'monument historique'*)
(55) The new gastronomic era has brought to our shores some delicious olive oil.   (meaning *some delicious olive oil is now available in our country*)

Similarly, the present perfect often occurs with relational processes of the change type to present Attributes or Identifiers which are part of a description but which are the result of earlier changes, for example:

(56) . . . which <u>has become</u> the symbol of New Zealanders. (meaning *it now is the symbol of New Zealanders*)

With other types of relational and existential processes, the present perfect is often used to backdate the description, that is, to extend a present situation back in time, for example:

(57) There <u>has been</u> a place of worship on this spot for at least a thousand years. (implying *and there still is*)

Descriptions can, of course, also be of people, places, and things in the past, and then simple past is the basic tense selection. In the following text extract past and present aspects of Roman Tarragona are contrasted, with a switch from simple past to simple present. Notice how the present perfect provides a link between past and present by locating a process somewhere between the past and the present, but with consequences in the present.

(58) Located on the flat land near the port, this <u>was</u> the main meeting place for locals for three centuries. The site . . . , which <u>contained</u> temples and small shops ranged around a porticoed square, <u>has been split</u> by a main road: a footbridge now <u>connects</u> the two halves where you <u>can see</u> a water cistern, house foundations, fragments of stone inscriptions and four elegant columns.

(Brown 1992: 291)

With *process* descriptions, events are sequenced in time (like a narrative). However, in descriptions of both manufacturing and natural processes *simple present* is also typically used, as in the two texts in Section 5.1, for example:

(59) The olives <u>are</u> first <u>washed</u> in water . . .
(60) Water <u>evaporates</u> from seas, rivers, and lakes . . .

The *present perfect* (past in present) is sometimes used in process descriptions for an event that either is not an important stage in the process or is providing some kind of restatement of a previous stage. In such cases, the present perfect often occurs in a subordinate clause, for example:

(61) After the bottles <u>have been</u> thoroughly <u>washed</u>, they are dried and . . .

Task 8c

Extract 8 is part of the introduction to the life and work of a Thai novelist. What tenses are used in the first two paragraphs of this extract (*excluding* verb groups with modals) and how would you account for their use?

8.2.2.3 TENSE SELECTIONS IN PREDICTIONS

Texts which are centrally concerned with prediction of future events are typically associated with the future tenses. The following is an extract from the introduction to a book about the future of information management.

(62) By the end of the century, text retrieval will have become a relatively sta-
ble computer technology, and the information community will be grappling
with the management of image databases. Research interests will be
directed towards content-based retrieval from image and sound databanks.

There will be a continuing and accelerating move away from analogue towards digital systems for the capture, storage, reproduction and distribution
of sound and of still and moving images and graphics. There will also be a
trend towards disc rather than tape storage media. Analogue recording media such as acetate records and analogue audio cassettes will increasingly
. . .

(Martyn, Vickers, and Feeney 1990: 9)

The pattern of tense selection in this extract is similar to that in the other extracts. The simple future expresses the primary location in future time, while the future perfect (past in future) – *will have become* – locates a change prior to the absolute time and the future continuous (present in future) – *will be grappling* – locates an event simultaneous with the absolute time.

However, it is in the nature of the future that we are likely to be much less certain about it than about the past and the present. Therefore, not surprisingly, in texts that are predicting future events *will* often alternates with modal auxiliaries which express degrees of *likelihood,* as in the next extract from the same text:

(63) Mass marketing computing systems will continue to be silicon-based, the
major change being in the machine architectures used, with a very rapid
take-up of parallel computing techniques. This should benefit the users of
information systems. . . . Hardware-based approaches to text retrieval may
require a move away from inverted files . . .

(Martyn, Vickers, and Feeney 1990: 7)

The use of these modal auxiliaries will be further considered in Chapter 10.

8.2.2.4 TENSE SELECTIONS IN CONVERSATION

Conversation is a rather loose term for various kinds of interactive informal spoken language and is here used to also include dialogue quoted within narratives. Clearly, a whole range of tenses can occur in conversation, and conversation can itself include chunks of, for example, narrative and description. Nevertheless, there are certain tense usages that tend to be more common in conversation than in other contexts, for example, the use of present continuous with action processes for *now* references, for example:

(64) They're still trying to figure out what it all means.
(65) You're going home? No, swimming.
(66) Your mother and brother are plotting against me.

Simple present with mental processes is also very common in conversation, as in text 6a (which opens Chapter 6), for example:

(67) Yes, don't worry about it.
(68) Does Joyce know where you are?

The use of *going to* (or *gonna*) to refer to future events (future in present) is common in conversation in predicting a future situation or event based on a present situation or on present knowledge, for example:

(69) . . . the whole system's been changed. I think . . . it's gonna be a lot simpler to get study leave in future . . .
(70) According to the program, Apache Indian's gonna be on about eight.

When the Subject is *I* or *we,* the future situation or event may be based on a decision the speaker has made. In other words, it can be a way of expressing *intention,* for example:

(71) I'm going to be a doctor, nothing less.
(72) "Don't think I'm going to touch the muck," he said.
(73) I'm gonna tell you about some rules of baseball.

This again brings us into an area where tense overlaps with modality, which will be more fully explored in the next chapter.

The use of *present continuous* to refer to future processes also tends to be associated more with conversation than other contexts. This is used for events already planned at the time of speaking. The time of the future event must be specified, usually by a Circumstantial Adjunct. Otherwise the default interpretation for the present continuous (*going on now*) would normally apply. For example:

(74) A: What are you doing, ah say, this evening?
        B: Well actually we're doing something in the evening so . . .

Task 8d

What generalizations can you make about the patterns of tense selection in the speech of the teacher in Extract 6 (*excluding* verb groups with modals)? How do these patterns relate to what the teacher is doing in this lesson?

8.3 Different interpretations of tense

The interpretation of the English tense system given in Sections 8.1 and 8.2 is not the only possible interpretation. Some linguists claim that English has only two tenses. This is based on the fact that verbs can be inflected for present tense and past tense only, for example:

Present: kick/kicks   know/knows
Past: kicked   knew

Forms such as *have gone* and *were going* are then interpreted as realizing a combination of tense and **aspect;** in the case of *have gone,* present tense plus perfect aspect; in the case of *are going,* past tense plus continuous or progressive aspect. This is, of course, the origin of the labels by which the tense forms are usually known.

As its name suggests, *aspect* is essentially a way of *viewing* processes rather than locating them in time. Many languages have systems of aspect either instead of or in addition to systems of tense. A typical aspect distinction is between processes viewed as a whole or complete (**perfective**) and those viewed as not complete or in progress (**imperfective**). For example, in Russian, *citat'* (imperfective) can be glossed as *to be reading* and *pro-citat'* (perfective) can be glossed as *to read through and finish* (Campbell 1991). Both imperfectve and perfective can denote processes located in the present, past, or future.

In English, however, it is rather difficult to separate aspect from tense. For example, both of the following forms refer to complete processes in the past viewed as a whole, despite the fact that one is usually interpreted as having perfect aspect while the other lacks it.

(75) They have arrived.
(76) They arrived.

As has already been noted, the tense selection in number 75 is a kind of past in the present, in other words a process located in the past with an orientation to the present, whereas the tense selection in number 76 simply locates the process at a time in the past.

The term *progressive* for relative present may be more useful than the term *perfect* for relative past, provided *progressive* is interpreted as meaning *in progress when viewed from the absolute tense location.* The alternative term, *continuous,* which is still commonly used by teachers and in learners' textbooks, is potentially misleading. Although the distinction between *simple* and *continuous* has different implications with different process types, in all three of the following pairs of examples, it is the continuous form which narrows down the location of the process to the here

perfect (the *passato prossimo*) and simple past (the *passato remoto*). Like the English present perfect, the *passato prossimo* is used to locate processes at an unspecified time in the past but with relevance to the present. Similarly, like the English simple past, the *passato remoto* is typically used with processes forming the story line of narratives (especially in writing). However, Italian tends to extend the use of the *passato prossimo* to any process located in the relatively recent past, including those located within completed time periods where English typically prefers the simple past. For example:

	Yesterday	(I) have	drunk	too much	wine
(85)	Ieri	ho	bevuto	troppo	vino.

"Yesterday I drank too much wine."

The Italian *passato remoto,* as its name suggests, is typically restricted to contexts in which the time location is felt to be more remote.[1]

Not surprisingly, Italian learners of English may identify these two tenses of Italian with the two English tenses, producing errors such as:

(86) *I have seen her last week.

(Duguid 1987)

Similarly, a number of languages, including Italian and French, use a form analogous to the English simple present or present continuous for processes which are going on now and extend back in time, where English typically uses the present perfect or the present perfect continuous. Errors such as the following are in fact quite commonly made by learners with a wide range of language backgrounds:

(87) *I live in this city since I was born.
(88) *They are working in this company since migrating here.

Some learners also tend to use continuous tenses inappropriately with mental and relational processes, for example:

(89) *I am seeing a dog and two cats.   (*describing a picture*)
(90) *He is possessing a large house in the suburbs.

This can perhaps be attributed to the influence of tense selection in the mother tongue or to overgeneralization from the use, in English, of continuous tenses with action processes.

The preceding examples of learners' errors are no more than a small sample, but they give an idea of the range of problems learners can have with the English tense system. Many teachers find that it is an area of grammar that needs substantial time and attention.

---

3 There is in fact considerable regional variation. In northern Italy, the *passato prossimo* is much more widely used than in southern Italy.

It is unlikely that any teacher would want to present all at once the tense system as set out in Section 8.1. And, although one still comes across syllabuses and textbooks which attempt to systematically go through the tense forms of English one at a time, attempting to explain and give examples of their various uses, it is probably not a good idea to do this. One problem with such an approach is that it leads to roughly equal time being spent on each tense form, despite the fact that some tenses are more frequent and useful for learners than others. For example, the past perfect (past in past) is much less common than the simple past, and the future perfect continuous (present in past in future) is far less common than past perfect (past in past). More important, it is hard to establish the meanings and usages of the tenses with rules, explanations, and isolated examples, and learners are unlikely to get a feel for how combinations of tenses work together to express time relations in different kinds of contexts.

Some teachers like to present tenses in contrast, for example, the simple past with the present perfect or the simple present with the present continuous. This can be useful, particularly in raising the consciousness of learners who have already become acquainted with the forms and their uses. However, a potential disadvantage of such an approach, particularly when introducing the forms for the first time, is that it may lead to some learners producing hybrid forms such as *they are now walk across the street* or *they walking to school every day* (hybrids of *they are now walking across the street* and *they walk to school every day*). In addition, when presenting two forms together in this way, it is difficult to present and practice them in rich enough contexts to enable learners to develop a feel for how they function in authentic contexts. There is a tendency to boil down the relevant features of context to a fairly small number of Circumstantial Adjuncts, for example *every day* (for the simple present with action processes), *now* (for the present continuous), *yesterday* (for the simple past), and *already* (for the present perfect). This may not be helpful for learners when they must select appropriate tense forms in contexts in which these trigger words are not provided.

An alternative approach is to start from contexts relevant to the learners and introduce first the core or basic tense form for each of these contexts. When learners are able to produce appropriate language within each context, other tenses typical of each context can be introduced.

Questions for discussion

- Suggest ways of introducing and practicing absolute (simple) present and absolute (simple) past as they are typically used in narratives and descriptions.

- Suggest how the same contexts could be elaborated to introduce and practice the past in present (present perfect), past in past (past perfect), present in present (present continuous/progressive), and present in past (past continuous/progressive).
- Suggest some contexts in which future tenses are typically used. How can these contexts be exploited for teaching?

8.5   Circumstantial Adjuncts of time

There are three basic kinds of **Circumstantial Adjuncts of time:** (1) those which express *duration* and answer questions such as *How long?* (2) those which express *location* in time and answer questions such as *When?* and (3) those which express *frequency in time* and answer questions such as *How often?*

8.5.1   Duration in time

Duration in time is typically expressed by a prepositional phrase beginning with the preposition *for* usually followed by a noun group with a Quantifier, for example:

(91) For a couple of months she settled in, . . .

(92) For many years, as he worked in the monastery gardens, he carried out . . .

Sometimes, however, there may be just a noun group with no preposition, as in:

(93) We've been waiting here nearly an hour now.

Since *for* can usually be inserted before such noun groups, from a teaching point of view it is probably best to regard these simply as cases of omission of the preposition.

8.5.2   Location in time

Location in time can be expressed by a prepositional phrase such as *on Wednesday* or an adverb group such as *once upon a time.* The selection of appropriate prepositions in prepositional phrases of time often causes problems for learners.

Prepositions commonly used to indicate a location in time are *at, on,* and *in.* The rule of thumb is that *at* is used for points of time and *in* is used for periods of time *except* days, for which *on* is used, for example:

(94) Peggy arrived at about 8.30.

(95) The gun was fired every day at noon.
(96) A number of court decisions in recent years . . .
(97) I don't really fancy being in Helsinki in winter.
(98) See you on Saturday then.

However, the use of these prepositions is somewhat idiomatic. *At* can be used for some periods, such as *at night* and *at dinner,* but not for others, such as **at day* and **at evening. At* can also be used for periods which are fixed points on the calendar, for example, *at Christmas* (compare *on Christmas Day*). *At* is also used with the noun *time,* as in *at that time* (compare *in those days*). On the other hand, *on* is used with the noun *occasion* where one might have expected *at,* for example, *on that occasion.*

A further potential problem for learners is that prepositions are normally omitted in some contexts, for example, before noun groups beginning with *last, next, this,* and *that* and before *today, yesterday,* and *tomorrow.*

(99) . . . was on display last Saturday.

However, if a learner does use a preposition in such a context (e.g., **on last Saturday*), it may not be very idiomatic, but it is hardly a grievous error.

Prepositions commonly used to refer to a time *before* or *leading up to* a location in time are *before, till, until, to,* and *by,* for example:

(100) . . . to be agreed upon and enforced before the end of 1992.
(101) By the end of the 2nd century A.D. Greece had already become a museum . . .

Prepositions commonly used to refer to a time *after* or *starting from* a location in time are *from, after,* and *since,* for example:

(102) There had been so many people in my life since our last meeting.
(103) After the game I strip off and get under the shower . . .

Adverbs and adverb groups generally indicate **relative** rather than absolute location in time. Common adverbs indicating relative location in time are *now, recently, just,* and *soon,* for example:

(104) . . . the transformation of higher education that is now in progress . . .
(105) Mr. Delors recently made a speech, haltingly, in German . . .
(106) Many Germans feel that their language will soon come into its own.

8.5.3 Frequency in time

Exact frequency is typically expressed by adverbs and adverb groups and by noun groups beginning with inclusive Referrers, for example:

(107) Meng and I found ourselves in the same class every year.
(108) . . . about 6 tons of truffles are imported annually into the United States . . .

Relative frequency is typically expressed by adverbs and adverb groups, such as *always, usually, normally, often, sometimes,* and *rarely.* For example:

(109) . . . Ziggy <u>often</u> runs out to catch fish when the tide is out . . .
(110) The characters are <u>usually</u> quickly described, and <u>seldom</u> develop or change in any way.

Questions for discussion

- In what order would you introduce the various Circumstantial Adjuncts of time to learners? Why?
- Suggest some practice activities that would make the use of different prepositions with Circumstantial Adjuncts of time seem less arbitrary than it usually does at first.

8.6 Conjunctive Adjuncts of time

Conjunctive Adjuncts of time express temporal relationships between one part of the text and another part of the text; in other words, they form a link based upon time with what has been said or written or what is about to be said or written, for example:

(111) <u>First</u> she tasted the porridge from Papa Bear's great big bowl. But it was too hot for her.
      <u>Then,</u> she tasted the porridge from Mama Bear's middle-sized bowl.
(112) Another sign that the computer age is with us can be found in many executive offices where a computer terminal is becoming increasingly common. <u>Previously</u>, managers were generally loath to touch a keyboard . . .
(113) From filtering it goes into a large vat for boiling and <u>then</u> to another one for further refining. <u>Finally</u>, it is stored as a very different material . . .

8.7 Interpersonal Adjuncts of time

There are a small number of Adjuncts concerned with time which at first glance look like Circumstantial Adjuncts. In fact, however, they are oriented more to interpersonal meaning than experiential meaning. They are therefore referred to as **Interpersonal Adjuncts of time.** In other words, they do not so much locate a process at a particular time as express an attitude toward the time location. Such Adjuncts include *already* (earlier than might be expected), *still* (longer in duration than might be expected), and *at last* (later than expected).

(114) Free at last! Free at last! Thank God almighty we are free at last!
(115) Today we already stand at the brink of the Thoughtware Revolution, . . .
(116) But a hundred years later, the Negro is still not free.

Learners sometimes miss the interpersonal meaning associated with these Adjuncts, as in the following example, where *at last* is used as if it were a Conjunctive Adjunct (meaning *this is the last point I have to make*):

(117) *At last, capital punishment does not stop people committing murder. Countries which have capital punishment still have a high murder rate.

Task 8e

Of the combinations of time Adjuncts and tenses in the following clauses, which do you consider to be inappropriate in all contexts and which acceptable in some contexts? In the case of the former, try to explain why they are unacceptable. In the case of the latter, specify contexts in which they would be acceptable.

1. The office is open since 8.30 this morning.
2. I am working in this company for two years now.
3. I've been travelling in Mexico several years ago.
4. I've been to Rio last year.
5. I just start here two days ago.
6. After this course I am a teacher.
7. I began studying in this school from the beginning of September until today.
8. In three years from now I was going to leave.
9. A plane had overshot the runway this morning.

Summary

1. The notion of time is represented in the grammar through the tense system and various kinds of Adjuncts.
2. Absolute tense (present, past, or future) locates a process in time relative to now.
3. Relative present, relative past, and relative future further locate the process relative to the absolute tense selection.
4. Nonfinite verb groups can be marked for relative tense only.
5. Unmarked tense selections in reference to *now* are present continuous (present in present) with action and mental-action processes, and simple present (absolute present) with mental and relational processes (except the change type).
6. Other combinations of tense and process type include:

   a. Simple present with action processes for habitual or timeless events, for "timetabled" future, and for commentaries and demonstrations.

   b. Continuous (relative present) tenses with mental processes with the sense of *beginning to* or temporariness.

   c. Continuous (relative present) tenses with relational processes to suggest temporary behavior.

7. The story line of a narrative typically consists of action processes with simple past (absolute past) tense. Past perfect (past in past) is typically associated with events previous to the story line (e.g., flashbacks), and past continuous (present in past) is associated with background events simultaneous with the story line.

8. Simple present (absolute present) is typically the basic tense in descriptions. Present perfect (past in present) is typically used to give time depth to descriptions.

9. Simple future (absolute future) is typically the basic tense in prediction texts, with future continuous (present in future) and future perfect (past in future) locating events simultaneous with and previous to the basic future time reference.

10. Present continuous (present in present) for reference to now with action processes, the *going to* future (relative future), and present continuous (present in present) for future reference all tend to be commonly used in conversation.

11. Circumstantial Adjuncts of time express location, duration, and frequency. Conjunctive Adjuncts of time express temporal relationships between one part of the text and another. Interpersonal Adjuncts of time express attitudes toward the time location.

Key terms introduced

This text	*Alternatives used in the field*
absolute future	will future; primary future
absolute past	past; primary past
absolute present	present; primary present
absolute tense	tense; primary tense
aspect	
Circumstantial Adjunct of time	temporal adverbials
Conjunctive Adjunct of time	
imperfective	
Interpersonal Adjunct of time	temporal adverbial
perfective	
relative future	going to future, secondary future
relative past	perfect; secondary past

relative present	continuous; progressive; secondary present
relative tense	aspect; secondary tense
tense	tense-aspect

Discussion of tasks

Task 8a

1. The verb group *are standing* represents an action process (*What are they doing?*). The present continuous is therefore the unmarked tense selection.
2. The verb *stands* represents a relational process (*Where is the statue?*). Simple present is therefore the unmarked tense selection.
3. The verb group *am seeing* represents an action process, which might be glossed as *am meeting*. The present continuous can be used to refer to planned future actions where the time is specified (see the examples in Section 8.2.2.4).
4. Here the marked tense selection (past continuous) with a mental process verb makes the suggestion sound more tentative and open to disagreement.
5. The verb *flows* can be interpreted as representing a relational process (*Where's the river?* rather than *What does the river do?*). The selection of simple present is therefore unmarked.
6. The use of present continuous with a mental process verb is marked – simple present would be more usual. It can be interpreted here as suggesting something like "now beginning to understand" or "right now in the process of understanding."
7. The process represented by *lives* can be interpreted as relational. In other words, the clause might answer questions such as, *Where is she? What's her address?* rather than *What does she do?* This would explain the selection of simple present. However, *live* does lie on the border between action and relational processes (see the explanation for 8).
8. The use of the present continuous (present in present) narrows down the location of the process to now (thereby suggesting a more temporary state of affairs) in the same way as it would with a more typical action process. Note that this sentence could answer a question such as, *What are the former officials <u>doing</u> these days*?

Task 8b

Simple past tense is used for the introductory scene setting in the first sentence, establishing that this is to be a past-time narrative, and for the events in the story line. (Note that *was missing* is simple past relational process verb followed by participle functioning as Attribute, not past continuous tense.)

Past perfect is used for out-of-sequence events – first in the recount by the purchaser of the house of events prior to his phone call and second in the reconstruction by the author of events prior to the cat's arrival at their old house, that is, a flashback. Note that one out-of-sequence event – *she found her way* – selects simple past not past perfect. This illustrates that once the past in past time location has been established, the past perfect is not always consistently used. In this case, the selection of simple past might have been influenced by the fact that the event in the following clause refers back to a time before the reconstructed events (*she had been brought*) had even begun.

Task 8c

The first paragraph is a description of the present status of Pira Sudham as a novelist. It therefore selects mainly simple present with relational processes. In one case present perfect is used with a change-type relational process verb (*has become*) for a present situation resulting from a completed change.

Paragraph two switches to a mininarrative of Pira Sudham's life history, and simple past with action processes is used in the first two finite clauses. In the final finite clause of the paragraph, the action (*departure*) is nominalized and therefore has no tense selection. It is, however, a participant in a relational clause which selects simple present. The past action is thus, in a sense, universalized and made relevant to a present situation.

Task 8d

In the lesson in Extract 6, the teacher is *managing the class* (making sure the pupils are on task, checking who is working with whom, and telling them what to do next). She is also *evaluating the pupils' work.* The tense selections reflect this.

Classroom management   *Simple present* with relational processes is used as the teacher checks who is partnered with whom, whose picture is whose, and whether the pupils have what they need (e.g., *Who's your partner? Whose is this? Have you got your piece of paper . . . ?*).

Occasionally, past tenses are used, suggesting that some pupils have finished their work (or are no longer working with their partners). Note that simple and continuous past tenses are used, not present perfect. That is, the orientation is to the past situation, not its present relevance (e.g., *Who was your partner? Who did it with you? Who were you working with?*).

Simple future and *future in present* (*going to* future) are used as the teacher informs the pupils of her intentions (e.g., *Mrs. S will write on there; I'll give you your paper; I will copy your story; This is going to go on the wall; When you've written it on your piece of paper I'm going to write it on the special plastic stuff*). Note in the last of these the use of present perfect in the dependent clause. The reference is of course still future. However, in dependent clauses the *will* is omitted.

Evaluation of pupils' work   *Simple present* with relational processes is used in describing the pupils' pictures (e.g., *This looks to me as if it is a picture . . .* ; *This is a lovely one*).

One case of *present continuous* is used to describe the seeming behavior of people in the pictures (e.g., *. . . a picture where someone is being kind and saying . . .*). Note that *being kind* can be interpreted here as a kind of action process (behaving in a kind way).

Task 8e

Some *possible* answers (you may not agree with all of them):

1, 2. Not acceptable – both processes are backdated, that is, projected back in time, and require the addition of relative past (perfect).
   3. Probably not acceptable – the present in past in present (present perfect continuous) suggests an orientation to present time that conflicts with the absolute past time reference of the Circumstantial Adjunct.
   4. Usually considered incorrect for reasons similar to number 3 – however, such clauses are not uncommon in speech. The past in present (present perfect) suggests a past event with present relevance (*this is an experience that I now possess*) that seems to override the absolute time reference of the Circumstantial Adjunct.
   5. Unacceptable – absolute past time reference of Circumstantial Adjunct requires simple past.
   6. Unacceptable – the Circumstantial Adjunct refers to future time, and the future tense is needed.
   7. Unacceptable – the Circumstantial Adjunct refers to a continuous period from the past until now, whereas the Phase of the process expressed by *began* was completed in the past.
   8. Odd out of context – but possible if the meaning is *in the past it was my intention to leave at a point in future time which is now three years from now.*
   9. Odd – but just possible in a context such as *the airport was closed this afternoon because a plane. . . .*

9 *Interaction: Speech acts and mood*

Chapters 4 through 8 have been concerned with the resources of the grammar for representing various aspects of our experience of the world and for locating them in time, in other words, with language as expressing *experiential* meaning. This chapter will explore some of the ways in which speakers and writers structure clauses in order to interact with one another; it will be concerned primarily with *interpersonal* meaning.

9.1 Speech acts

The following extract is from a spoken text in which one person is explaining to another how a radio works. The interaction in the text thus involves the *exchange of information.*

(1) A: What's a resistor for?
   B: A resistor is when you've got a current that needs to be reduced you use a resistor.
   A: How do you mean, excuse me, how do you mean, uh, reduced?
   B: Well, if you've got an electric current, it's running along through your circuit board . . .
   A: Yes . . .
   B: . . . and it's too powerful, if you put the resistor there . . .
   A: Mmm . . .
   B: . . . going by the different values of it you can reduce it by different amounts.
   A: Mmm . . .

(Courtesy Marilyn Lewis, University of Auckland)

Speaker A's initial request for information and subsequent request for clarification are both kinds of **questions.** Speaker B responds to the questions with **statements,** which provide the information requested. *Question* and *statement* are not labels for grammatical structures. Rather they are basic categories of what are usually called **speech acts.** In other words, they are labels for the kinds of things we are doing when we act upon one another through language.

174

However, asking for and giving information are not the only ways in which we act upon one another through language. We also use language to *exchange services* – to get people to do things and to offer to do things ourselves. The following extract is from the speech of a primary school teacher (the same one as in Extract 6), who is trying to elicit certain kinds of behavior from her pupils.

(2) Sit beautifully. Fold your arms everyone please. Now be patient and button up those lips, tightly. Sit on your bottom T_____, sit on your bottom. I didn't say move I said sit still, cross your legs, fold your arms and button up your lips, thank you.

The speech acts in this extract belong to the category of **directives.** The pupils respond to the teacher's directives nonverbally, by doing what she asks (eventually).

In the following extract from the speech of two people in a restaurant, speaker A is not trying to get speaker B to do something. Rather he is offering to do something (pay the check) himself.

(3) A: Let me get this.
    B: Mmm, I can . . .
    A: You paid for dinner.
    B: Okay.

Speaker A's initial speech act can be described as an *offer.* When speaker B appears to be about to contest the offer, speaker A makes a statement serving as a reminder of whose turn it is to pay. Speaker B then acknowledges the offer with an *okay.*

Questions, statements, directives, and *offers* are basic categories of speech acts. Within these categories it is possible to recognize a large number of subcategories. For example, the category of directives includes orders, prohibitions, suggestions, permissions, and requests. However, most language interaction can be analyzed (initially at least) in terms of the four basic categories. Note that this applies equally to writing as to speech (*Language acts* would in fact be a better term than *speech acts.*) In writing we also exchange information, try to get people to do things, and offer to do things. However, because writing normally lacks the face-to-face interaction of speech, one category of speech act, that of statement, tends to dominate in most kinds of writing.

One kind of speech act which falls outside the above four categories is exemplified by the following:

(4) A: . . . and by the time I'd found a copy it was already too late.
    B: What a pity you didn't ask me first!

Speaker B in the above extract is not giving or requesting information, nor is she trying to get someone to do something or offering to do some-

Table 9.1   *Mood*

Mood	Speech act typically realized	Example
Declarative	Statement	They put the books into the boxes.
Interrogative (yes-no type)	Question	Did they put the books into the boxes?
Interrogative (*wh-* type)	Question	Where did they put the books?
Imperative	Directive	Put the books into the boxes.
Exclamative	Exclamation	What a mess the books are in!

thing. She is simply expressing her attitude concerning the state of affairs stated by speaker A. Such a speech act is known as an **exclamation.**

9.2 Mood

The grammatical system of **mood** and the relationship between the different moods and the basic speech act categories, are illustrated in Table 9.1.

The speech act *offer* does not have a separate mood category typically associated with it. A clause such as *let me get this* is a kind of imperative mood clause.

It is important to note that although declarative, interrogative, imperative, and exclamative moods typically realize the speech acts statement, question, directive, and exclamation, respectively, mood and speech act are not the same thing. The mood of a clause can be identified simply from its structure (this will be examined in more detail later in the chapter). However, the interpretation of a speech act (which may or may not be realized by a single clause) normally depends upon structure, context and intonation. The typical relationships between mood and speech act can in fact be skewed, producing what are called **indirect speech acts.** For example, a clause such as

(5) Why don't we take a short break now . . .

is interrogative in mood. However, in most contexts, for example, when the speaker is a college instructor talking to a class, it is likely to be interpreted as a strong suggestion or even an order. It therefore can be categorized as a kind of directive. It is unlikely that any hearer would take such a clause as a question and reply with a statement such as *We don't take a short break now because we have too much to do.*

Task 9a

1. Identify the mood of each clause in the following examples.
2. Identify the most likely speech acts involved. To do this, you may need to reconstruct likely contexts and intonation (all punctuation marks related to speech acts have been removed). Note that one clause need not necessarily equal one speech act.
   a. What were some of the causes of the revolution. Jason, you might just know.
   b. Who's sitting up nicely. Who's ready to learn.
   c. Would you go off and finish coloring yours please.
   d. I want you to do another big person because you've done little wee people and I can't see them.
   e. I was wondering whether I could get another extension.
   f. Can I help you.
   g. If I were you I'd just forget it.
   h. You're sure you haven't made a mistake somewhere.
   i. Isn't it gorgeous today.
   j. Can't you see I'm busy.

9.3 Mood structure

The two functions Subject and Finite (see Section 1.5.1) are crucial to the structural realization of mood in English.

9.3.1 Declarative and interrogative moods

The distinction between declarative and interrogative moods depends on the ordering of Subject and Finite. The basic system, where $^\wedge$ means *followed by,* is as follows:

Declarative:	Subject$^\wedge$Finite
Wh- interrogative:	*wh-* Finite$^\wedge$Subject
Yes-no interrogative:	Finite$^\wedge$Subject

It was noted in Chapter 1 that the Finite is always the first constituent of a verb group, while the remaining constituents of the verb group function as Predicator, for example:

Declarative

	SUBJECT	FINITE	PREDICATOR	
(6)	You	should	insulate	yourself with a sleeve . . .

	SUBJECT	FINITE	PREDICATOR	
(7)	We	have	already been searcing	for the answer . . .

Interrogative

	FINITE	SUBJECT	PREDICATOR	
(8)	Can	you	be leaving	before eight?

	FINITE	SUBJECT	PREDICATOR	
(9)	Will	you	be leaving	before eight?

Note that in declarative mood, Finite and Predicator are often fused (i.e., the finite verb group consists only of a head), for example:

	SUBJECT	FINITE/ PREDICATOR	
(10)	They	put	the books in the box. [*inv.*]

	SUBJECT	FINITE/ PREDICATOR	
(11)	Examples of these ecological niches	include	. . .

For *emphatic* versions of such declarative clauses, Finite and Predicator are separated and the Finite is realized by forms of the auxiliary *do,* for example:

	SUBJECT	FINITE	PREDICATOR	
(10) a.	They	did	put	the books in the box.

	SUBJECT		FINITE	PREDICATOR	
(11) a.	Examples of these ecological niches		do	include	. . .

Similarly, in interrogative mood clauses where there is no other auxiliary, forms of *do* function as Finite, for example:

	FINITE	SUBJECT	PREDICATOR	
(10) b.	Did	they	put	the books in the boxes?

	Wh-	FINITE	SUBJECT	PREDICATOR	
(11) b.	When	did	you	come	here?

One exception to the use of *do* where there is no other auxiliary is with the verb *be.* Even when it is a lexical verb (i.e., is not an auxiliary), it does not form interrogative mood or emphatic declarative mood with *do.* Instead, the Finite and Predicator remain combined and both precede the Subject. Thus, the *yes-no* interrogative form of

	SUBJECT	FINITE/ PREDICATOR	
(16)	Last Monday	was	a holiday.

is

                FINITE/
                PREDICATOR   SUBJECT

(16) a.   Was   last Monday a holiday?

not

                FINITE   SUBJECT   PREDICATOR

(16) b.   *Did   last Monday   be   a holiday?

An exception to the Finite^Subject ordering of interrogative mood clauses is where the *wh-* word is itself the Subject. In such cases, the order is simply *wh-*^Finite, as in:

         Wh-/SUBJECT FINITE

(17)   Who   has   been eating my porridge?

9.3.2 Imperative mood

Imperative mood clauses are typically realized by a Predicator in the V (base) form of the verb, with no explicit Subject or Finite, for example:

(18)   . . . sit on your bottom . . .
(19)   . . . leave me alone.

The Subject in such imperative clauses is understood to be *you,* and many grammarians would regard such imperative mood clauses as cases of Subject omission (technically **ellipsis**). The Subject is in fact sometimes stated, as in these directives given by the same primary teacher quoted earlier.

(20)   . . . you make it beautiful.
(21)   . . . you boys go and sit over there.

The Finite auxiliary *do* may also sometimes be used in imperative mood clauses. This normally has the effect of making the directive more polite – in some contexts to the extent of being an invitation rather than an order (depending as always on the intonation used), for example:

(22)   Do come in. [*inv.*]

However, many speakers find these forms rather old-fashioned and prefer to mark the politeness by using *please* rather than *do* (e.g., *please come in).*

9.3.3 Exclamative mood

Exclamative mood clauses typically have the form *what*-Object/ Complement^Subject^Finite or *how*-Complement/Adjunct^Subject Finite, for example:

	OBJECT	SUBJECT	FINITE/ PREDICATOR	
(24)	What nonsense	you	talk!	[*inv.*]

	COMPLEMENT	SUBJECT	FINITE	PREDICATOR	
(25)	What a fool	I	've	been!	[*inv.*]

	COMPLEMENT	SUBJECT	FINITE/ PREDICATOR	
(26)	How foolish	you	are!	[*inv.*]

	ADJUNCT	SUBJECT	FINITE	PREDICATOR
(27)	How quickly	it	has	changed!

Note also that the speech act *exclamation* is also often realized by a clause with no Subject, Finite, or Predicator (technically a *minor clause*), as in the following.

(28) What a mess!
(29) How stupid!

Such clauses cannot be analyzed for mood at all.

9.3.4   *Mood and polarity*

Declarative, interrogative, and imperative mood can each be combined with positive or negative *polarity.* Most of the examples considered so far have had positive polarity. For negative polarity, the **negative particle** *not* (or *n't*) directly follows the Finite. Where there is no other auxiliary, the auxiliary *do* again functions as Finite. The following are examples of declarative, interrogative, and imperative clauses with negative polarity (Finite and negative particle are underlined).

(30) Developing countries may not benefit at all from the new order.
(31) She probably didn't mean to hurt him.
(32) Don't you believe me?
(33) What haven't we done yet?
(34) Don't just rest on your laurels.
(35) Don't you touch that!

9.4   Questions

This section and the following sections will look at typical ways in which some of the different moods function in interaction and explore further the relationships between moods and speech acts.

9.4.1 Yes-no *interrogative questions*

As their name suggests, questions realized by *yes-no* interrogative mood clauses expect the addressee to confirm or deny information, typically with the answers *yes* or *no* (or variants of these), for example:

(36) A: Is it yours Violet?
     B: No.
(37) A: Have you finished both of them?
     B: Yup.

Very often, the *yes* or *no* may be followed by a declarative clause consisting of only the Subject and the Finite from the question, together with the negative particle *not* (*n't*) where relevant, for example:

(38) A: Well, does the fact that there's no antenna make it weaker?
     B: No it doesn't.
(39) A: Is that a special price?
     B: Yes, it is.

In such clauses there is ellipsis of the Predicator (unless it is fused with the Finite, as in number 39) and any Objects and Adjuncts. In other words, they have been left out in the answer because they are understood from the question.

Note that to confirm the information in a *yes-no* question, the polarity of the answer agrees with the polarity of the question. In other words if the question has negative polarity, the answer *no* confirms the information, for example:

(40) A: Haven't you finished that chapter yet?
     B: No, I haven't. But I'm getting there.

To deny the information, the polarity must be reversed by giving an answer such as *Yes, I finished it last night. I'm writing the next one already.*

One basic interactive exchange is thus:

Question: *yes-no* interrogative
Answer: *yes* or *no*
                or
            yes or *no* + elliptical clause consisting of Subject^Finite

There are, of course, numerous possible variations of this basic exchange. Sometimes, the answer *no* will be followed by a declarative clause (again usually elliptical) providing different information, for example:

(41) A: Linda, did you touch those?
     B: No, Paul did.

Occasionally, the answer will contain a full declarative clause, repeating the information in the question.

(42) A: Is it twelve?
     B: Yah it's twelve.

Sometimes, the question itself may be elliptical. In the following extract, B is trying to remember the name of an Australian ski-slope.

(43) A: . . . was it Perisher?
     B: no it wasn't uh, I forget where it was
     A: Smiggins?
     B: no no er – Guthega

(Slade and Norris 1986: 239)

The word *Smiggins,* as used by A, can be interpreted as a *yes-no* interrogative question with the Finite and Subject (*was it . . .*) ellipsed. It is clearly interpreted as such by B, who complies with the request for confirmation of information by answering (again elliptically) *no no Guthega.* Note that in this context, the word *Smiggins* would carry rising intonation, which is normally associated with *yes-no* interrogatives.

It was noted earlier that the typical relationships between moods and speech acts can be skewed, as in the following exchange on the telephone.

(44) A: Do you have any information there on prices?
     B: Sydney to Melbourne return eighty dollars.
     A: Right, okay. Is there any student concession on that?
     B: Fifty percent reduction with a Railways of Australia Student card.
     A: Er – sorry? Could you say that again?
     B: Fifty percent reduction with an Australian Railways Student Card.
     A: Ah okay. Thank you very much. Okay, bye.

B treats A's first two *yes-no* interrogatives not as requests for confirmation of information but as requests for new information (in a sense, as if they were *wh-* interrogatives). The third *yes-no* interrogative is treated as a request for action (i.e., as a kind of directive). Note how inappropriate it would have been for B to have replied simply *yes* or *no* to each *yes-no* interrogative.

9.4.2 Wh- interrogative questions

Questions realized by *wh-* interrogative mood clauses request specific pieces of information. A typical response is simply to provide the information requested, as in the following:

(45) A: What do ohms measure?
     B: Resistance.
     A: Oh.
(46) A: When did you hear that?
     B: This morning.

A: Well they certainly don't believe in giving a lot of notice.

In number 45, the *wh-* word in the question is an Object and in number 46 the *wh-* word is an Adjunct. Both answers can be interpreted as elliptical declarative mood clauses, with only the constituents which directly correspond to the *wh-* words in the questions actually expressed. In other words, *resistance* is an Object and there is ellipsis of the Subject (*ohms*) and Finite/Predicator (*measure*); *this morning* is an Adjunct and there is ellipsis of the Subject (*I*), Finite/Predicator (*heard*), and Object (*that*).

Often, particularly after *wh-* words such as *why, how,* and *when,* the answer will be a *dependent clause* (a clause which would not normally stand alone; see Section 12.1), for example:

(47) A: Well, why don't they just not make it so powerful to start with?
<u>Because it's not so easy</u>. And also um it's, it's a lot cheaper to do it that way, because you've got this battery here.

This can be interpreted as a case of ellipsis of the independent clause (*they do not make it so powerful to start with*) to which the dependent clause (underlined) is subordinate.

Another basic interactive exchange thus is:

Question: *wh-* interrogative
Answer: elliptical clause (questioned constituent only) *or* dependent clause

Again, there are many possible variations on this basic exchange. For example, the answer may sometimes be a full declarative mood clause, as in the following:

(48) A: So what's this value here?
    B: That is a uh 1.5.

Answers can, of course, extend well beyond single clauses or sentences, as in number 47 and in number 1 at the beginning of this chapter, in which B answers A's second question in six clauses (five finite clauses and one nonfinite clause).

The addressee can even violate the expectation that the information requested by the *wh-* word will be given, as in the following.

(49) A: Well, but when do I do all these things?
    B: You don't.

Here, instead of providing the requested information, B negates the assumption of the question that "I do all these things at some time" with an elliptical clause consisting of Subject, Finite, and negative particle.

The asker of a *wh-* interrogative usually also responds to information given in reply. The response may simply be an acknowledgment, such as *yes* and *mmm* (as in number 1), or *oh, yes, I see* (as in the last clause in the extract in task 1a). It may also be a more extended reaction to the information, such as *Well they certainly don't believe in giving a lot of notice* (number 46) above.

It would therefore be more accurate to represent the typical interactive exchange as having three parts rather than just two, as follows:

Question: *wh-* interrogative
Answer: elliptical clause (questioned constituent only) *or* dependent clause
Response: acknowledgment *or* extended response

9.4.3 Tag questions

Tag questions are questions formed by adding a *tag* consisting of Finite^Subject (combined with positive or negative polarity) to an otherwise declarative mood clause (Section 1.5.1.1), for example:

(50) A: He's still there now, <u>isn't he</u>?
     B: Yeah, I suppose so.
(51) A: The MTR [mass transit railway] doesn't normally run all night, <u>does it</u>?
     B: No, it's just because it's new year's eve tonight.

The tag usually has a different polarity from the rest of the clause, as in these examples. Such questions normally expect that the information will be confirmed. If the tag is combined with falling intonation, this expectation is even stronger than if it is combined with rising intonation.

Notice that the use of *yeah* in number 50 and *no* in number 51 both confirm the information by agreeing with the polarity of the main part of the clause . To deny the information, something like *no, he isn't* would have to be used in number 50 and something like *yes, it does* in number 51.

Less commonly, the polarity of the tag can be the same as in the rest of the clause, for example:

(52) A: It was a boring movie, was it?
     B: Sure was.

This implies that speaker A did not go to the movie but has surmised that speaker B found the movie boring. If a negative tag had been used, the most likely implication would be that speaker A had also gone to the movie and was seeking confirmation of his opinion that it was a boring movie.

Note that there is an exception to the rule that the tag picks up the Finite form of the main clause. This is when the Finite is *am*. The negative tag is not *amn't I,* as one might expect, but *aren't I.*

9.4.4 Declarative mood questions

It has already been noted that declarative mood clauses can sometimes realize the speech act of question. These normally have the rising intonation typically associated with *yes-no* interrogatives, for example:

(53) A: You did it yourself?
     B: Yeah, it's not that hard.
(54) A: They haven't called or anything?
     B: No. There hasn't been a word.

Such questions normally expect the information to be confirmed. In other words, if the question has negative polarity (as in number 54), the expected answer is *no;* if the question has positive polarity, the expected answer is *yes.*

9.5 Directives

Although imperative mood clauses are typically (although not always[1]) directives, the opposite is not necessarily the case. The relationship between mood and speech act is in fact much less close with directives than with statements and questions. A wide range of structural options is available to the speaker for expressing directives with varying degrees of force. Some of these will be touched on here.

9.5.1 Imperative mood directives

In many contexts directives expressed by imperative mood function as commands or orders which the speaker expects to be obeyed. However, this is not always the case. The directness or strength of the directive may vary greatly, for example:

(55) Use a large, soft wall brush or pasting brush to apply the paste. Mix the paste in a plastic bucket . . . (instruction)
(56) Mind your head as you come in. (warning)
(57) Don't forget to take some warm clothing. (advice)

9.5.2 Interrogative and declarative mood directives

Several examples of interrogative and declarative mood directives have already been examined (see, for example, task 8a). Following are some further illustrations:

(58) You must go and apologize to her right now. [*inv.*]

1 For example, in many contexts *give me a break* would be an exclamation.

(59) Could you just move a bit further in?   (*from a photographer*)
(60) Would you boys please stop chattering!

Note that all of these examples include a *modal auxiliary*. Such auxiliaries are frequently used in directives and are important in moderating the force of the directive. They will be considered in greater detail in Chapter 10. Note also that interrogative mood directives are typically the least direct or least strong directives, and hence the gloss *requests* can often be applied to them. However, intonation and context must always be taken into account. Number 60 (from a teacher), for example, is certainly stronger than a mere request.

An appropriate response to a directive may sometimes be simply to perform the action one is directed to perform. However, in many cases, particularly with interrogative mood directives, a verbal compliance is also given, for example:

(61) A: Could you get me a cup too?
      B: Yeah, sure.

Of course, it is also possible for the addressee to refuse to comply entirely, in other words, to challenge the directive. One strategy for doing so is apology followed by excuse, as in:

(62) A: Would you mind picking them up on the way?
      B: Sorry, I don't finish class till eight and I'll have to go straight there.   [*inv.*]

Task 9b

Look at Extract 6 in the Appendix.

1. Find at least one example of each of the following.
    a. Declarative mood statement
    b. *Wh-* interrogative question followed by full declarative answer
    c. *Wh-* interrogative question followed by elliptical declarative clause answer
    d. *Yes-no* interrogative followed by a denial
    e. Imperative mood directive
    f. Declarative mood directive
    g. Interrogative mood directive with (verbal) compliance
2. What generalizations can be made about the range of moods and speech acts in the speech of the teacher and pupils in this extract? How do the moods and speech acts used by teacher and pupils reflect their respective roles in this context?

9.6 Learning and teaching mood and speech acts

Many languages have quite different ways of distinguishing statements from questions. In some languages, declaratives and *yes-no* interrogatives are structurally distinguished not at all or much less frequently than in English, with intonation and context being relied on to make it clear whether a statement or question is intended. For example, the Italian clause

(64) ha lavorato molto oggi
     have worked much today

could be translated *you have done a lot of work today* or *have you done much work today?* depending on intonation.

Many languages use question particles to form interrogatives, either as well as or instead of word order. In French, for example, the particle *est-ce-que* is placed at the beginning of a clause to form *yes-no* interrogatives (although Subject Finite inversion is also possible), and in Mandarin Chinese the particle *ma* is placed at the end of the clause. Otherwise in both languages the word order is the same as for declarative mood. For example:

         PARTICLE   it is true
(65) est-ce que c'est vrai?   (French)
     "Is it true?"

       is true   PARTICLE
(66) shi zhende   ma?   (Mandarin)
     "Is it true?"

Many languages also use the same word order for declaratives and *wh-*questions, merely substituting a *wh-* word for the constituent being queried, for example:

     you have how-many   children
(67) Nei yaau   geigo   sailoujai?
     I   have   three   children.
     Ngo yaau saamgo sailoujai   (Cantonese)

The formation of interrogatives in English may therefore seem rather complicated to some learners. Learners often have problems with the use of the auxiliary *do* and may produce errors such as:

(68) *What means this?
(68) *You how know her?

Some learners also have difficulty with tag questions, and tend to use the invariant form *isn't it*. Sometimes a contributing factor is that their mother tongue has only one invariable form for such tag questions, for example, the French *n'est pas* and German *nicht wahr* (usually shortened to *nicht*).

Answers to negative questions can also be a problem. As already noted, *yes-no* questions are confirmed by agreeing with the polarity of the question. In other words, *no* confirms a negative question and *yes* confirms a positive question. In some languages (for example, Japanese), a form analogous to English *yes* is regularly used to confirm a question (whatever its polarity), and a form analogous to English *no* is regularly used to deny a question. Learners may transfer this into English and answer *yes* to a negative question that they wish to confirm, for example:

(70) Teacher: So you didn't enjoy the film?
     Student: Yes. (meaning: "That's right, I didn't")

Most beginners will probably learn first to make statements with declarative mood clauses, although it may be useful early on to learn some basic interrogative mood questions (such as, *What does this mean?*) as unanalyzed chunks.

The forms of interrogative clauses are sometimes taught as transformations of declarative clauses. This may be useful in alerting learners to the structural differences between the two moods, although it may do little to help them use the structures appropriately in context, and, as is always the case when two structures are taught in contrast, there is a danger that some students will come up with hybrid forms. If we want learners to be able to use interrogatives and to respond to them appropriately, then they are probably best presented and practiced in more authentic interactive contexts. Note also the inappropriateness of some traditional exercises that require students to answer questions in full sentences. Learning to use ellipsis is an important part of learning to interact appropriately.

Imperative mood clauses present no particular structural problems, and they are relatively straightforward to present and practice through activities in which learners complete tasks by responding appropriately to instructions and by giving instructions themselves.

Control over the range of other options for expressing directives of varying strengths can only be developed slowly through practice in a variety of real or simulated contexts. In presenting examples of directives to learners care should be taken that the relative strength of the directives and the role relationships between speakers are clear.

Questions for discussion

- Suggest some activities for practicing *yes-no* questions and answers, *wh-* questions and answers, and tag questions and answers. Try to make the activities as interactive and authentic as possible.

- Suggest an activity to help learners who make the kind of error represented by numbers 68 and 69.
- Imagine you are working with learners who can produce simple imperative clauses, but no other kinds of directives. Which kinds of directives would it be most useful for them to learn next? How would you introduce and practice the directives so that their interpersonal force would be very clear to the learners?

Summary

1. Question, statement, directive, and offer are four basic speech act categories. A fifth, more minor, category is that of exclamation.
2. Declarative, *yes-no* interrogative, *wh-* interrogative, imperative, and exclamative are grammatical moods.
3. The relationships between moods and speech acts are as follows:

   Declarative mood clauses typically realize statements.
   Interrogative mood clauses typically realize questions.
   Imperative mood clauses typically realize directives.
   Exclamative mood clauses typically realize exclamations.

   However, these relationships can be skewed, producing indirect speech acts.
4. The structural realizations of mood are as follows:

Declarative:	Subject^Finite
Wh- interrogative:	*wh-*^Finite^Subject (unless the *wh-* is Subject)
Yes-no interrogative:	Finite^Subject
Imperative:	(Subject) Predicator
Exclamative:	*what*-Object/Complement^Subject^Finite
	how-Complement/Adjunct^Subject^Finite

5. Interpretation of moods depends on grammatical structure. Interpretation of speech acts depends upon interaction of grammatical structure with intonation and context.
6. Some typical interactive exchanges involving questions are as follows:

Question:	*yes-no* interrogative
Answer:	*yes* or *no*
	or
	yes or *no* + elliptical clause consisting of Subject^Finite
Question:	*wh-* interrogative

Answer: elliptical clause (questioned constituent only) *or*
               dependent clause

Response: acknowledgment *or* extended response

7. Tag questions are formed by adding a tag (Finite^Subject, with negative or positive polarity) to a declarative clause. The tag typically has a different polarity from the rest of the clause. Such questions normally expect a confirmatory answer.
8. Declarative mood clauses combined with rising intonation can function as questions.
9. Imperative mood directives are typically direct commands. However, they can also function as instructions, warnings, and advice.
10. Interrogative mood clauses and declarative mood clauses, often containing modal auxiliaries, can function as directives with varying degrees of force.

Key terms introduced

This text	*Alternatives used in the field*
declarative	
directives	commands
ellipsis	
exclamations	
exclamative	
imperative	
indirect speech acts	metaphors of mood
interrogative	
minor clause	verbless clause
mood	
negative particle	
questions	
speech act	speech function
statements	
tag question	

Discussion of tasks

Task 9a

The moods and *most likely* speech acts are as follows:

a. Clause 1 is interrogative mood, question; clause 2 is declarative mood, directive.
b. Both clauses are interrogative mood, directives.

c. Interrogative mood, directive.
d. Declarative mood, directive. (Note that it is the three clauses together that express the directive speech act.)
e. Declarative mood, directive. [Note that the second *dependent* clause is a reported question (see Section 6.2), but like all dependent finite clauses it must be declarative in mood. Note also that again, it is both clauses together that express the directive speech act – *requests* are a type of directive.]
f. Interrogative mood, offer.
g. Declarative mood, directive (advice).
h. Declarative mood, question, or directive ("check it!").
i. Interrogative mood, exclamation.
j. Interrogative mood, directive ("go away!").

Task 9b

1. Possible answers are as follows
   a. This looks to me as if it is a picture where someone is being kind and saying . . .
   b. T: . . . what is the person saying to his one P_____?
      P: He said go away
   c. T: Who's your partner P_____?
      P: R_____?
   d. T: P_____ have you got your piece of paper to write it on?
      P: No
   e. Make it really nice 'cos that's gonna be a lovely picture.
   f. you boys have to go over and color it in really nice
   g. T: Would you finish coloring them?
      P: yah
2. The moods and speech acts in this extract are a direct reflection of the roles of teacher and pupils. The teacher manages the lesson by (i) telling the pupils what to do (hence the directives – including direct directives (commands) expressed by imperative mood, which her authority over the young pupils makes it appropriate for her to use) and (ii) keeping a check on what the pupils are actually doing or have done (hence the questions). She also provides the students with evaluative feedback on their work (which accounts for most of her statements). The roles of the pupils are to answer the teacher's questions and comply with her directives. Hence their speech consists mainly of elliptical declarative mood clauses, contains no directives, and contains only one question (repeated three times) – asking the teacher for clarification of what they are to do.

10 Expressing judgments and attitudes: Modal auxiliaries and modality

Text 10a

. . . I think, um, the ferries go on till quite late, eleven thirty or something – and there must be some buses operating at um, in, the other end, for all the people coming off the ferry. I think what they probably do is just have, um, the one bus, not all the, y'know, not all the numbers.

In text 10a, the speaker is using declarative mood clauses to give information. However, he admits to some doubt about the information he is giving. In some cases, the doubt may be small, as in *there must be some buses operating*. In other cases, the doubt may be greater, as in *I think what they probably do is just have, um, the one bus*. Had the speaker been even less sure of his facts, he might have said something like *what they might do is just have, um, the one bus* or *what they possibly do is just have, um, the one bus*. In other words, the clauses in this text extract contain the speaker's judgments of the **likelihood** of the information in the clauses being true.

Text 10b

I'd like you and maybe Thani[1] and Susi and Tagata to go . . . excuse me I'd like some manners thank you William. I'd like you to go and you must know your address and say it clearly. It has to be said in English because the fire department only has a person who can speak English on the other end of the phone . . .
   Those people who I have told their address is correct, I'm going to give you a partner and you may quietly go and sit by my maths books over there and practice.
                                        (From Thilani Nissanga, University of Auckland)

In text 10b, a teacher is giving directives to her class. However, the directives are in declarative mood not imperative mood, and the students are, at least ostensibly, given varying degrees of freedom as to whether or not to

1 The names in this extract have all been changed.

carry out the directives. The degree of freedom may be relatively great, as in *you may quietly go and sit,* or it may be relatively small, as in *you must know your address and say it clearly.* We can say that these clauses contain degrees of **requirement** for the students to perform certain actions.

Given the authority role of the teacher in this context, all the directives would no doubt be interpreted by the students as instructions intended to be obeyed. However, by expressing degrees of requirement in this way, she is making the instructions less direct and more friendly.This can be compared with another section of the lesson (already looked at in Chapter 8), in which the teacher uses imperative mood for direct orders that she expects to be immediately obeyed.

Sit beautifully. Fold your arms everyone please. Now be patient and button up those lips, tightly. Sit on your bottom Tagata. Sit on your bottom. I didn't say move I said sit still, cross your legs, fold your arms and button up your lips, thank you.

Both likelihood and requirement belong to the area of interpersonal meaning called *modality.* It is possible to define modality both broadly and narrowly. A broad definition would encompass *all* expressions of interpersonal meanings that lie between *it is so* and *it is not so* or between *do it* and *don't do it.* A narrow definition of modality encompasses only the *modal auxiliaries* (see Section 4.1.2) and their uses, and sometimes also adverbs functioning as *Modal Adjuncts,* such as *possibly, probably,* and *certainly.* This chapter will take a fairly broad view of modality. However, the area is one that is very rich in English. Consider, for example, the following (invented) examples, which are just a few of the ways in which a speaker could indicate that he or she considers that the information in the clause has a high likelihood of being true.

This must be true.
This has to be true.
This is definitely true.
This is obviously true.
I'm quite sure that this is true.
It is certain that this is true.
There can be no doubt that this is true.
I am convinced that this is true.
It is my strong belief that this is true.
How could this not be true?
How could anyone in their right mind doubt that this is true?
If this isn't true I'll eat my hat.

It would, of course, be impossible to cover the whole variety of such expressions in this chapter.

2. The closest I came to death has to be the day we went swimming at Piha.
3. Fourish, I should arrive.
4. The Dutch, on current form, will take it lying down.
5. It couldn't have been him. He doesn't even know her.
6. Security checks for such things as weapons, pornography, or drugs might still be made.
7. Some of the new capitalist economies of Central and Eastern Europe could be coming into the Community before too long.
8. They won't be open yet. It's much too early.
9. You've gotta be joking.

The fact that a number of different modals may be grouped together as expressing more or less the same level of likelihood does not, of course, mean that their meanings are identical or that they can freely be exchanged for one another in all contexts. It is not possible in this chapter to consider all the possible nuances of meaning of every one of the modals. However, a useful distinction for teaching purposes is that between *predictions* and *deductions,* even though there is a certain amount of overlap between the two categories.

10.1.2   *Deductions and predictions*

Predictions are based on a certain premise, which may be a given situation, a general principle, or even a hypothetical condition. Predictions are typically about the future but *can* also be about the present or the past. Typical instances of prediction are found in the following example, which was looked at in Chapter 8 (example 63):

(1) Mass marketing computing systems will continue to be silicon-based, the major change being in the machine architectures used, with a very rapid take-up of parallel computing techniques. This should benefit the users of information systems . . . Hardware-based approaches to text retrieval may require a move away from inverted files . . .

In such predictions about the future, the use of *will* to express high likelihood shades into its use as a future tense marker (see Sections 8.2.2.3 and 8.3).

   Deductions are based on direct or indirect evidence. They are typically about the present or past but *can* be about the future. Typical instances of deductions occur in the following example.

(2) The results do not give the expected 50/50 ratio. So there must be more to the problem. It could well be that some factors affect each other while other factors remain independent.

Table 10.1   *Deductions and predictions*

Deductions	Predictions
They must be arriving at about five because coffee has been laid on for five thirty.	Unless anything unforeseen happens, they will arrive at about five.
There must have been someone in during the weekend. The lights have been left on.	Someone will* have been in over the weekend. The office is never left empty.
He must be in the cupboard. I can hear scratching noises.	He will be in the cupboard. He always goes in there when he is afraid.
	Unless anything unforeseen happens, the motion should get through unopposed.
	They should be there already. It only takes a couple of hours.
They may be there already. I can see smoke coming out of the chimney.	They may be there already. It only takes a couple of hours.
They could be there already. I think I can see smoke coming out of the chimney.	They could be there already. It only takes a couple of hours.
They can't have left yet. The lights are still on.	They won't have left yet. They never leave before 8.

*Some speakers tend to use *would* rather than *will* in this context.

Even when predictions are about the present or past and when deductions are about the future, it is still normally possible to distinguish between the two, as Table 10.1 may help to make clear. Note that *must* and *can't* are typically used for deductions, while *will, should* and *won't* are typically used for predictions. *May, might,* and *could* are freely used for both.

In some contexts, however, the distinction between predictions and deductions can be blurred. For example, in

(3) Ah! That must be Aunt Agatha. Only relatives and creditors ring in that Wagnerian manner.

it would be possible to replace *must* with *will*. However, in such contexts a discernible difference in meaning usually remains, with *will* implying that the situation can be assumed to follow inevitably from a premise and *must* implying that the situation has been deduced by the speaker from the evidence.

Substituting *should* for *will* in a prediction such as *he will be in the cupboard* weakens it from a confident prediction to what we might call a reasonable assumption. However, *should* is not normally used in this way for deductions. The following example, in which *should* is used to express mid likelihood in a deduction about a present situation, is decidedly odd.

(4) Someone's left their wallet on the table. Oh, it's got a "P" on it. It should be Peter's. (compare: *It's probably Peter's* and *It must be Peter's*) [*inv.*]

And no native speaker would accept this use by a learner of *should* for a deduction about a past situation:

(5) The solution should have been contaminated by dirt in the test tube. (*compare:* The solution was probably contaminated . . . *and* The solution must have been contaminated . . .)

Should is in fact used much more commonly to express requirement than likelihood (see Section 10.2). When it is used in clauses referring to past situations, such as number 5 and clauses such as *she should have come yesterday,* a requirement rather than likelihood interpretation is usual. When modals of likelihood are taught, *should* therefore needs to be carefully contextualized to ensure that learners do not try to use it in contexts in which it would be inappropriate or ambiguous.

10.1.3   Expressing past likelihood

Modals of likelihood can be combined with relative past tense to express deductions and predictions about past situations. For example:

(6) Someone must have taken the message.

Learners sometimes have trouble with this and may omit *have* and/or attempt to mark the modal for past tense.

The modal (or semimodal; see Section 4.1.2) *have to* does have a past tense form of its own — *had to.* This makes possible a distinction between clauses such as

(7) The butler must have been the murderer.   [*inv.*]

in which a conclusion about the past is deduced in the present, and:

(8) The butler had to be the murderer.   [*inv.*]

in which a conclusion about the past was deduced in the past.

10.1.4   Likelihood based on conditions

It was noted earlier that predictions can be based upon conditions. Such conditions are often expressed in the form of an *if* clause, for example:

(9) . . . their future will be affected if they have a criminal record.

(10) If they do not trust the government, they may be afraid to invest their capital in the country.

In sentences 9 and 10, the conditions (*they have a criminal record* and *they do not trust the government*) are presented as possible situations. Such conditions are sometimes referred to as **real conditions.**

However, sometimes predictions are based on hypothetical situations, or **unreal conditions.** In other words, the speaker or writer predicts a situation that would result from different conditions from those which actually exist, existed in the past, or are likely to exist in the future, for example:

(11) . . . believe that evil deeds are performed by persons who, if they got the proper therapy, would not do them again . . .
(12) If we could buy truffles as cheaply as turnips, would they have the same allure?
(13) . . . they concede that Dutch might be less offensive to them if it were not so closely related to their own tongue.
(14) But where would America be if the Dutch, who once colonized Manhattan, hadn't shown folks how to "husselen"?
(15) Expansion of the use of computer technology throughout the territory would certainly not have reached its current proportions if Hong Kong had not developed its own facilities . . .

In all of the above, the implication is that the conditions are *not* the case. In other words, *they do not get the proper therapy, we can't buy truffles as cheaply as turnips, Dutch is related to their own tongue, the Dutch did show folks how to "husselen,"* and *Hong Kong did develop its own facilities.*

The general rule is that a condition is marked as unreal by the tense of the finite verb group being one step back in the past relative to its tense in the expression of a real condition, as shown in the following:

Real condition	*Unreal condition*
Simple present	Simple past
Present continuous (present in present)	Past continuous (present in past)
Simple past	Past perfect (past in past)
Past continuous (present in past)	Past perfect continuous (present in past in past)

Numbers 11, 12, and 13 refer to unreal conditions in the present. Therefore the tense is past (*got, could,*[2] *were*). Note that in number 13, *were* is used rather than *was*. This usage tends to be restricted to formal, usually written, contexts as well as a number of common expressions such as *if I were you*. However, some people still consider it incorrect to use *was* in unreal conditions, although it is commonly heard.

2 Note that *could* is not a modal of likelihood here. It is the simple past tense of *can* expressing ability.

Numbers 14 and 15 refer to unreal conditions in the past. Therefore the past perfect (past in past) is the tense choice (*hadn't shown, had not developed*).

There is one modal of likelihood not yet considered – *would*. *Would* properly belongs alongside *will* as a modal expressing high likelihood in predictions. However, unlike the other modals of likelihood, *would* is used *only* in predictions based upon unreal conditions. This means that whenever *would* is used, an unreal condition is implied. Thus, in

(16) If you put an antenna there, it wouldn't necessarily change it.

despite the fact that *put* could be either present tense or past tense, the condition would normally be interpreted as unreal (i.e., *you are not about to put an antenna there*), because of *wouldn't* in the main clause.

In fact, the majority of occurrences of *would* are not with *if* conditional structures such as those exemplified above, despite the fact that this is the context in which *would* is usually taught to learners. The unreal condition may take any number of different forms. For example, in the following sentence the unreal condition is not represented by a clause but by a prepositional phrase:

(17) What would U.S. National Security be without the "spook" (ghost) that the Dutch sent Washington's way?

Here the unreal condition could be unpacked into a clause such as *if they didn't have the "spook"* . . . etc.

In many other cases, the unreal condition may not be explicitly stated at all but has to be inferred from the context, for example:

(18) . . . they wouldn't want to look through the phone book. Your house would be burnt down, wouldn't it?

In this example, a primary school teacher is working with her students on how to report a fire at home. The implied condition is something like: *if you were really reporting a fire at home and if you forgot to tell them your address.*

Task 10c

1. As far as possible, reconstruct the implied unreal conditions associated with the following instances of *would*.
   a. Today it would be difficult to find an office that does not have at least one computer . . .
   b. . . . nuclear energy is very polluting and dangerous. Even a slight error would lead to tremendous damage to the environment and destruction of human life.

   c. B: . . . transformers are very useful and expensive
     A: Oh?
     B: Those, um, they would cost about eight dollars each.
   d. Now is the time to make justice a reality for all of God's chil-
     dren. It would be fatal for the nation to overlook the urgency of
     the moment.
2. Explain the uses of *would* in Extract 8.

Implied unreal conditions can present problems for learners. In reading or listening, they may fail to pick up on the fact that a particular instance of *would* signals that the situation in question is hypothetical or unreal.

Some learners avoid *would* in their own production and tend to overuse *will*. For example:

(19) ?Without this atmosphere, everything on the earth will die.

Other learners greatly overuse *would*. Sometimes this seems to be because they identify it simply as a marker of mid or low likelihood. In other cases, it may be an overgeneralization from the use of *would* as a politeness marker (see Section 10.5). For example:

(20) *After graduating from this course, I think I would become an English teacher or work in the government.
(21) *On Wednesday 3 June the electricity supply to your premises would be disrupted from 2 p.m. to 5 p.m.

10.1.5   Teaching conditionals

Traditionally, conditional meaning and the related tense and modal auxiliary usages are taught in terms of three types of *if*-clause conditional structures:

Type 1 (real conditions):	If it rains, they'll get wet.
Type 2 (unreal conditions – present):	If it rained, they would get wet.
Type 3 (unreal conditions – past):	If it had rained, they would have got wet.

There are some potential problems with this approach. First, if the second and third type are presented as transformations of the first, then it may be very hard for learners to grasp the essential meaning differences between them. The difficulty is compounded if, as in the examples given, the same experiential meaning is used to present all three structures. To avoid this, each of these structures needs to be fully (and separately) contextualized so that their different meanings become clear, in particular the distinction between real and unreal conditions.

Second, if the structures are represented as fixed formulas (i.e., present tense in *if* clause + *will* in main clause; past tense in *if* clause + *would* in main clause; past perfect in *if* clause + *would* + perfect in main clause), then learners are likely to become puzzled when they come across sentences such as:

(22) If it is wrong, then we are in big trouble.
(23) If I wanted something, I just took it.
(24) If it had rained, the streets would still be wet.

The point is that each clause selects for tense independently, depending upon the time reference and the reality of the condition. (Note that in example 23 the condition is *real* – both clauses refer to situations in the past, the meaning of *if* is, in fact, close to *whenever* in this sentence.) Even sentences such as the following are not uncommon, particularly in speech:

(25) I would be very surprised if he does turn up here again.

In such sentences, the use of present tense in the main clause points to a real condition, while the use of *would* in the main clause points to an unreal condition. Such sentences do in fact seem to suggest that the situation is very unlikely without ruling it out altogether.

Learners need not, of course, be explicitly taught every possible permutation of conditional structures. However, the basic forms need to be presented in such a way that learners can appreciate the contribution of each tense and modal selection to the meaning of the structure in context, rather than seeing the structure as an arbitrary formula.

Third, it has already been noted that *would* commonly occurs where the unreal condition is unstated or in a form other than an *if* clause. The *if*-clause construction may still be a good place to introduce the concept of unreal condition. However, further work may well need to be done on *would* in different contexts.

Finally, it may be worth noting that some teachers and grammar books talk of a further type of conditional using *should* in the condition clause, either with *if* or with Subject Finite inversion, for example:

(26) If you should see him, please give him my regards.
(27) Please feel free to contact me should you have any inquiries regarding the above.

The use of *should* presents the condition as slightly more unlikely than an ordinary real condition. However, this usage is not very common and tends to be restricted to very formal contents. It is probably not worth spending time on this with beginning or intermediate learners.

Questions for discussion

- Suggest some contexts for the introduction and practice of unreal conditionals that would clearly distinguish them from real conditions.
- Suggest some activities for helping advanced learners who tend to overuse *would* (producing errors such as numbers 20 and 21).

10.1.6 Modal Adjuncts of likelihood

Modal Adjuncts are the second system of the grammar dedicated to the expression of modality. They are usually realized by adverbs such as *certainly* and *possibly,* but may also be realized by prepositional phrases such as *without doubt* and *in all probability.* Like the modal auxiliaries of likelihood, Modal Adjuncts can be ranked from high likelihood to low likelihood.

Task 10d

Identify the Modal Adjuncts of likelihood in the following sentences and rank each according to likelihood: high, mid, or low.

1. Why am I so devoted to teaching? It's definitely not for money.
2. Maybe my whole family should jump off the balcony, one by one.
3. . . . the territory would certainly not have reached its current proportions if Hong Kong had not developed . . .
4. . . . her programmed life work could conceivably be carried on indefinitely by successors applying the expert system.
5. It was probably the Dutch who taught the Americans to hustle . . .
6. Perhaps I should have allowed him this privacy, but I ran after him and caught him.

10.1.7 Personal judgments of likelihood

When modals of likelihood are used, there is normally an implication that it is the speaker or writer who is making the judgment of likelihood. However, it is possible to make it explicit that a personal judgment of the speaker or writer is involved by using certain mental process clauses (of the cognition type) or attributive clauses with adjectives of likelihood functioning as Attributes, for example:

(28)   I doubt if anyone who knew Meng in school ever visited him at home.
(29)   I don't think anyone is going to shut down the newspapers or shut off the television networks in the foreseeable future.

(30)   And it's I think made of carbon . . .
(31)   I am sure I am on the right track.
(32)   . . . discrimination as a child in Oakland or being consciously aware of
       prejudice, but I am certain both were present, directed not only at
       African-Americans but also Asian-Americans.

A sign that expressions such as *I doubt, I think,* and *I am certain* function
more like Adjuncts of modality than like full mental or attributive clauses is
that if a tag is added it is normally formed from the Finite of the clause
which they precede. For example:

(28) a. I doubt if anyone . . . ever visited him, did they?   (not *do I?*)
(32) a. I am certain both were present, weren't they?   (not *aren't I?*)

Such expressions can be combined with modals, as in:

(33)   I think most of you should have at least a rough idea of the advantages
       of the computer system.

Such explicitly personal assessments of likelihood are more common in
contexts such as face-to-face conversation, although they are by no means
restricted to spoken language.

10.1.8   Impersonal judgments of likelihood

The use of adjectives of likelihood functioning as Attributes in clauses with
postponed Carriers (see Section 7.1.4) has the effect of making the judgment of likelihood explicitly *impersonal;* that is, it removes the speaker or
writer's personal responsibility for the judgment, for example:

(34)   It is inevitable that within the next few decades computers will substan-
       tially replace the use of pen and paper . . .
(35)   It is probable that the earth is just as old as the moon.

Such impersonal expressions of likelihood are more common in formal
written language, although they are by no means restricted to written
language.

10.2   Requirement

As noted earlier, requirement in the broad sense concerns the area of
meaning between *do it* and *don't do it.* In other words, the speaker or writer
expresses varying degrees of requirement that a certain action should be
carried out (or not carried out).

Task 10e

Identify the expressions of requirement in the following examples:

1. You are not permitted to bring any books or papers into the examination hall, other than those specified on the cover of the question paper.
2. You have to be quiet while I talk to each person, because you might be the person who gets left out and doesn't know your address properly.
3. The police have been told that they may search newsrooms without warning and with nothing more than a judicial warrant.
4. You are required to submit a formal proposal first.
5. Animal lovers who think that hunting is cruel but do not subscribe to the extremist view should first ensure that they know all the facts.
6. It is advisable to make a backup copy immediately.
7. It soon became necessary to link these individual PCs so they could work together in groups.

As the examples in task 10e illustrate, requirement can be expressed using:

Modal auxiliaries such as *have to, may,* and *should*
Clauses with verbs such as *permit* and *require*
Clauses with Attributes such as *necessary* and *advisable*

The modal auxiliaries will be looked at first, followed by other expressions of requirement.

10.2.1   Modal auxiliaries of requirement

Like the modal auxiliaries of likelihood, the modal auxiliaries used to express requirement can be ranked according to the strength of the requirement. High requirement can be glossed as *obligation* or *necessity,* mid requirement can be glossed as *advice,* and low requirement can be glossed as *permission.* For example:

Requirement	Example with modal auxiliary
High positive:	. . . but there is something I <u>must</u> say to my people who stand on the warm threshold which leads to the palace of justice.
High negative:	In the process of gaining our rightful place, we <u>must not</u> be guilty of wrongful deeds.

Mid positive:	Animal lovers who think that hunting is cruel but do not subscribe to the extremist view <u>should</u> first ensure that they know all the facts.
Mid negative:	We <u>should not</u> spend too much time watching television.
Low positive:	J_____, you <u>can</u> copy yours on to a piece of paper too now.
Low negative:	. . . you <u>don't have to</u> do it right now but . . .

Within high requirement, it may be useful for teaching purposes to make a distinction between obligation and necessity, although as with the distinction between deduction and prediction, there are areas of overlap. The distinction is essentially between requirement which derives from the authority of the speaker or writer and requirement that is presented as arising from circumstances. Table 10.2 should make this clearer. As the table suggests, *must* (and *must not*) can be used for both obligation and necessity, although the obligation interpretation is probably more common when the subject is *you.*

Will is normally used only for obligation. The use of *will* implies sufficiently strong authority on the part of the speaker to ensure that there is almost no doubt that the obligation will be complied with. *Need,* on the other hand, is normally used only for necessity. Note also that normally only the lexical verb (i.e., formally not modal; see Section 4.1.2) *need* is used as the positive form, whereas the negative form used for low requirement may be *need not* (*needn't*) or *do not need to* (*does not need to, did not need to*).

Have (got) to, like *must,* can be used for both obligation and necessity. In all three examples in Table 10.2 listed under obligation, the speaker (the

Table 10.2   *Obligation and necessity*

Obligation	Necessity
. . . you <u>will</u> carefully and clearly give <u>your</u> address and cross street.	
You <u>must</u> go and apologize to her immediately.	Highly perishable, the truffle <u>must</u> be transported quickly to the market.
. . . but look, you boys <u>have to</u> go over and color it in.	You may <u>have to</u> cut the earth wire to slip <u>sleeves</u> over the halves.
	Now and again where it gets steep I <u>have to</u> stand up on the pedals and really tread hard.
	Nowadays, most parents <u>need to</u> go to work in order to earn a <u>living.</u>

same primary school teacher as in the example just discussed) is clearly the source of authority for the requirement, whereas in the two *have to* examples listed under necessity, external circumstances are clearly the source of the requirement and *need* could replace *have to* with little difference in meaning.

Note that *have got to* is regarded as more informal than *have to* and tends to be avoided in formal written contexts. In British English *got* can also be used in interrogatives, for example:

(36)   Have we got to go now?

The variant without *got* (e.g., *have we to go now?*) is very rare and is generally considered archaic. However, the question form using the auxiliary *do* and treating *have* as a lexical verb, for example,

(36) a. Do we have to go now?

is becoming more and more common in British English and is the only form generally used in U.S. English.

Task 10f

How would you rank the modals of requirement in the following examples?

1. I cried a lot when we had to leave our house.
2. We need to criticize false understandings of utopia.
3. When you set up your network, you do not need to throw your old computers away.
4. . . . and you will carefully and clearly give your address and cross street. When you've done that you will say what kind of fire . . .
5. You may quietly go and sit by my maths books over there and practice.
6. You may not leave the hall during the last fifteen minutes of the examination.
7. Now and again where it gets a bit steep I have to stand up on the pedals and really tread hard.
8. You ought to have waited just a little longer.
9. You needn't be so aggressive about it . . .
10. Any complaint concerning the conduct of this poll shall be lodged with the Acting Academic Secretary no later than noon, 17 July, 1993.

As with the modals of likelihood, there is a potential problem with the relationship between positive and negative modals of requirement in that the negative sometimes negates the modality and sometimes the rest of the clause. Thus, both *must* and *mustn't* express high requirement (*obliged to* and *obliged not to*). However, *need* expresses high requirement (*necessary to*), whereas *needn't* expresses low requirement (*not necessary to*). Similarly, *have (got) to* expresses high requirement (*obliged to*), whereas *do not have to* or *haven't got to* expresses low requirement (*not obliged to*). Conversely, *may* expresses low requirement (*permitted to*), whereas *may not* expresses high requirement (*obliged not to*).

10.2.2   Modal auxiliaries and past requirement

Of the modals of requirement, only *should/should not, ought to/ought not to,* and *need not* (negative form only) can combine with relative past tense to express past requirement, for example:

(37) You ought to have waited until you were better prepared.
(38) The plane he should have taken to Saigon . . .
(39) We needn't have worried.

Note that in examples 37, 38, and 39 the implication is that the requirement was not fulfilled: *you didn't wait until you were better prepared; he didn't take the plane to Saigon; we did worry about it.*
On the other hand, the past of *have to* is used to express a past requirement with the implication that it was fulfilled, for example:

(40) Yesterday I had to go into town to sort a few things out.   [*inv.*]

10.2.3   Personal and impersonal judgments of requirement

In order to be explicit about the source of authority for the requirement, that is, to make the judgment of requirement explicitly *personal,* clauses with verbs such as *advise, require, expect, allow, forbid,* and *permit* can be used, for example:

(41)   I would advise you not to start any large scale data gathering yet.
(42)   We require you to submit a formal proposal first.   [*inv.*]
(43)   I forbid you to even talk to her again.   [*inv.*]

The requirement can be made *impersonal* by using the same verbs in passive voice, for example:

(41) a. You are advised not to start any large scale data gathering yet.
(42) a. You are required to submit a formal proposal first.
(44)   All citizens between the ages of 18 and 30 are permitted to apply for the course.

Included in this category are structures such as

(45)   We are supposed to arrive before nine.   [*inv.*]

which are not, strictly speaking, passive clauses (*supposed* is best interpreted as an Attribute).

An even more impersonal effect can be achieved by the use of adjectives
of requirement in attributive clauses with postponed Carriers (see Section
7.1.4), for example:

(46)   It soon became necessary to link these individual PCs so they could
        work together in groups.
(47)   It is compulsory for students to attend all tutorials.

Learners sometimes produce forms "between" these different structures,
for example:

(48)   *Secondary school students are compulsory to attend all lessons.

10.3   Other areas of modality

In addition to likelihood and requirement, the areas of **frequency, inclination, potentiality,** and **ability** can be regarded as kinds of modality.

10.3.1   Frequency

Frequency can be compared to likelihood. Where likelihood expresses
judgments about how probable a state of affairs is, frequency expresses
judgments about how usual a state of affairs is.

(49)   He'll walk past you without even saying "Hi."   (meaning *often walks
        past you*)
(50)   . . . but long journeys like that can be very uncomfortable.   (meaning
        are sometimes)

However, modal auxiliaries are not so widely used for frequency as for
likelihood. More commonly used are Adjuncts of frequency, such as *always, usually,* and *seldom,* which in Section 8.5 are treated as a subtype of
Circumstantial Adjuncts of time.

The use of *will* (*'ll*) in sentences such as number 49 could be interpreted
as an extension of its use for prediction, and the use of *can* in sentences
such as number 50 could be interpreted as an extension of its use for
potentiality (Section 10.3.3). In most teaching contexts, the explicit teaching of the use of modal auxiliaries to express frequency will probably not be
a high priority.

10.3.2   *Inclination*

Inclination can be compared to requirement. Where requirement is concerned with the strength of a *directive* to do something, inclination is concerned with the strength of an *offer* to do something.

As with requirement, three levels of inclination can be recognized: high, which can be glossed as *determination;* mid, which can be glossed as *intention;* and low, which can be glossed as *willingness.* However, only a few modal auxiliaries are used for inclination: *will* (stressed and unstressed), *won't, would* (past), and, less commonly, *shall.* Very often context and intonation make it clear which level is intended. For example:

Inclination	*Example*
Low	I'll take some of the scripts so long as you're not expecting anything in before next week.
Mid	Now. I will tell you right now what the activity is.
High	I *will* go and you can't stop me. (Italic type indicates that will is stressed)

Other ways of expressing inclination include the following:

(51) They are willing to forget all about it . . .   (Low – willingness)
(52) I'm going to put that up on the wall.   (Mid – intention)
(53) I was determined to get a proper education.   (High – determination)

Note that there is a subtle distinction between *will* and *be willing.* The former leaves little doubt that the action will be carried out, whereas the latter leaves open the possibility that the action will not be carried out. Thus, it would be strange to replace *am willing* with *will* in the following example:

(54)   I'm willing to help but I just don't have the time.   [*inv.*]

There is also a distinction between *will* and *be going to. Going to* usually implies that the intention already exists, that is, that the speaker has already made up his or her mind to carry out the action. The use of *will,* on the other hand, often implies that the decision is made more or less at the moment of speaking, for example:

(55)   A: Don't give up. Everybody fails the first time.
         B: I know. I'm going to try again later. I've already put my name down.   [*inv.*]
(55) a. A: Don't give up. Everybody fails the first time.
         B: You're right. I'll try again later. Where do I put my name down?

10.3.3 Ability and potentiality

Ability and potentiality are not really concerned with judgments and attitudes in the same way as the other areas of modality. However, because they can be expressed by modal auxiliaries, they are usually regarded as a kind of modality. The modal *can* expresses both ability and potentiality, for example:

(56)   I am someone who <u>can</u> make friends easily.   (ability)
(57)   . . . this situation <u>can</u> and will be changed.   (potentiality)

The essential difference between *ability* and *potentiality* is that with the former it is internal abilities and skills that make it possible for a certain action to be performed or situation to come about whereas for the latter it is external circumstances that make it possible.

Can referring to ability can often be replaced by *be able to* with little or no difference in meaning, for example:

(58) a. I am someone who <u>is able to</u> make friends easily.

The negative *cannot* (*can't*) expresses negative potentiality and ability, for example:

(59)   When you get old, you <u>can't</u> talk to people because people snap at you.
(60)   I just <u>can't</u> talk fluently in English.

Past potentiality and ability are expressed by *could,* for example:

(61)   I was fascinated by the prospect that sociologists <u>could</u> be paid to study what interested me about human life.
(62)   . . . those few who <u>could</u> type did so with two fingers and great difficulty.

Could also combines with relative past tense, as in

(63)   It <u>could have been</u> a lot funnier.

This expresses a situation which had the potentiality to come about but did not.

Like other areas of modality, potentiality can be expressed impersonally, for example:

(64)   It is possible to design an artificial intelligence "expert system" . . .

Sometimes, potentiality is called *possibility.* This label has been avoided here because it might be confused with low likelihood. The following examples illustrate the difference between the two types of modality.

Low likelihood (possibility):   I may be there in an hour
                                   It is possible that I will be there
                                   in an hour

Potentiality: I can be there in an hour
                                                 It is possible for me to be there in
                                                 an hour.

10.4   Summary of modal auxiliaries and their meanings

Table 10.3 provides a summary of the meanings of the modal auxiliaries that have been looked at. As the table makes clear, the same modals may be used to express different kinds of modal meanings, leading to the possibility of ambiguity. Although the meanings will (nearly) always be disambiguated by the context, this does present learners with an additional complication in developing control over modality.

10.5   Modality, context, and speech act

Not only are many of the same modals used for likelihood, requirement, and, to a lesser extent, other areas of modal meaning, but within the same area of modal meaning the precise meaning of a particular modal expression will vary considerably from context to context. For example, the modality in a clause such as

(65) you may go

would normally be classified as low requirement (permission). However, in a context such as a teacher giving instructions to students (as in text 10b at the beginning of this chapter) the clause is likely to be interpreted by the student as an order which is to be obeyed.

In addition, modals are used with different moods to express a range of speech acts. For example, interrogatives involving potentiality or ability can function as both offers and requests, for example:

(66) Can I give you a hand with that?
(67) Could you explain to me about these parts of this radio?

Note the use of the past tense form *could* in number 67. This is not a reference to past ability. Rather it suggests a kind of unspoken unreal condition (see Section 10.1.6) along the lines of *if I were to ask you . . .* This has the effect of making the request less direct and more polite. The answer *Yes, I could* would, of course, be inappropriate as it implies *but I won't.*

Similarly, *would* is frequently used in polite requests in a similar way to make the request seem less direct and therefore more polite:

(68) . . . would you go off and finish coloring yours please.

(69) Would you please send me an application form. . .

Interestingly, if *will* is substituted for *would* in these clauses, although on the surface they are still questions about willingness, they are likely to be interpreted as impatient requests or even commands.

Could and *would* are also used to make the expression of opinions seem more tentative, for example:

(70) It could always be argued, of course, that not enough money was made available by the government.

Table 10.3 *Modal auxiliaries and their meanings*

Modal Meaning	Modal Auxiliaries
Likelihood	
Positive	
High (certainly)	must, have (got) to, will, shall, would
Mid (probably)	should, ought to
Low (possibly)	may, might, could
Negative	
High (certainly not)	cannot (can't), could not (couldn't), will not (won't) (shan't), wouldn't
Mid (probably not)	should not (shouldn't)
Low (possibly not)	may not, might not
Requirement	
Positive	
High (obliged/necessary)	must, have (got) to, will, shall, need*
Mid (advised)	should, ought to
Low (permitted)	can, may
Negative	
High (obliged/necessary not to)	must not (mustn't), may not, cannot
Mid (advised not to)	should not (shouldn't), ought not to (oughtn't)
Low (permitted not to)	need not, don't have to, haven't got to
Frequency	will, can, could, may
Inclination	will, will not (won't), shall, shall not (shan't)
Potentiality/ability	can, could

*Strictly speaking, not formally a modal auxiliary.

(71) . . . this would seem to indicate that education has failed to keep pace with technological needs.

It has already been noted how some learners tend to overuse *would*.

10.6   Learning and teaching modality

The modal auxiliaries potentially present problems in that (1) the same modal may be used to express quite different types of modal meanings, (2) different modals may express very close or overlapping modal meanings, and (3) the precise meaning or force of a modal may vary from context to context.

Some learners may speak a first language which has forms roughly comparable to English modal auxiliaries. However, this does not mean that they are used in precisely the same ways in precisely the same contexts. For example, although French does have modal auxiliaries, it uses Adjuncts much more often than English, and the appropriate translation in the context of *he may come tomorrow* will often be:

(72) Il vient demain peut-être.
    He comes tomorrow perhaps.

(Jackson 1985: 95)

Similarly, while Cantonese has verb group auxiliaries that are roughly comparable to English modal auxiliaries, it also has a range of modal sentence final particles; where English might use a modal auxiliary or Adjunct, Cantonese might use one of these particles, as in the following example, where the modal particle *gwa* is used:

```
          He   come not  come  A   (A is a particle used with questions.)
(73) A: Keuih leih  m  leih   a?
        "Is he coming?"

          come  GWA
     B:  leih  gwa
        "I think so."
            or
        "Probably."
```

The various uses of a modal such as *will* or *must* across different areas of modality clearly have something in common, and it is often possible to articulate a single "underlying" meaning for a particular modal, from which its more specific meanings can be derived. It is tempting to believe that making this explicit to learners could reduce the learning burden. However, it is this writer's experience that an abstract characterization of the meaning of a particular modal is of little use to most learners, whose difficulties have to do with nuances of modal meaning in specific contexts. Nor is it very useful to present the most important meanings or uses of each modal one by one, as this generally serves simply to confuse the learners. In most teaching contexts, the most effective way of dealing with modals is to take each area of *modal meaning* separately (deduction, prediction, obligation, necessity, etc.) and present and practice appropriate modals embedded within a rich context so that learners can develop a feel for how they are used.

Questions for discussion

- Which modals of likelihood might you introduce to learners first? Suggest contexts for introducing and practicing them.
- Suggest some activities for sensitizing intermediate or advanced learners to the varying degrees of directness and politeness conveyed by using different modals in directives.
- Suggest some activities for sensitizing advanced learners to the different contexts in which personal and impersonal expressions of likelihood and requirement are used.

Summary

1. The expression of degrees of likelihood and requirement are two areas of modality.
2. Likelihood is expressed by modals and Modal Adjuncts and by certain kinds of attributive and mental process clauses.
3. Expressions of likelihood can be grouped according to the level of likelihood they express – high (certainly), mid (probably), and low (possibly).
4. A distinction can be made between the use of modals of likelihood in predictions, which present a state of affairs as following from a certain premise, and in deductions, which present a state of affairs as having been deduced from available evidence.
5. Predictions can be based upon real or unreal conditions. Such conditions are most typically realized by *if* clauses. A condition is marked as unreal by a tense form one step back in time than in the expression of the same state of affairs as a real condition. The modal *would* expresses high likelihood based upon an unreal condition.
6. Judgments of likelihood can be made explicitly personal by using mental-cognition process clauses such as *I think that* and attributive clauses such as *I'm sure that*. They can be made impersonal by postponed Carrier attributive clauses such as *it is probable that.*

7. Requirement is similarly expressed by modals and by various kinds of clauses. Expressions of requirement can also be grouped into high (obligation and necessity), mid (advice), and low (permission).
8. A judgment of requirement can be made explicitly personal by using clauses such as *I require you to* and *I forbid you to.* The judgment can be made impersonal by using passive versions of such clauses or postponed Carrier attributive clauses such as *it is necessary for you to.*
9. Other areas of meaning which can be included under modality include frequency, inclination (the degree of willingness to do something), ability, and potentiality.

Key terms introduced

This text	*Alternatives used in the field*
ability	
frequency	usuality
inclination	willingness
likelihood	probability; epistemic modality
potentiality	possibility
real conditions	type 1 conditional
requirement	obligation; necessity; deontic modality
unreal conditions	type 2 and 3 conditionals; counterfactuals (normally type 3 only)

Discussion of tasks

Task 10a

1. I am certain
2. It is not likely that, may
3. I am sure
4. might
5. should
6. must
7. definitely
8. I think
9. probably
10. I doubt if
11. It is probable that

Note that in numbers 1, 3, and 5, the modal auxiliary *will* is probably best regarded as marking future tense, although there is not a clear line between this usage and its use to express high likelihood.

Task 10b

1. might, low
2. has to, high
3. should, mid
4. will, high
5. couldn't, high negative
6. might, low
7. could, low
8. won't, high negative
9. gotta, high

Task 10c

1. Possible reconstructions of the unreal conditions are:
   a. If one were to look (for such an office) . . .
   b. If there were such an error . . .
   c. If you were to buy one . . .
   d. If it were to do so . . .
2. From Extract 8:
   Line 4: If one were to call him simply a "Thai novelist" . . .
   Line 5: If one were to ask him . . .
   Last paragraph: If I had not left my village . . . (explicitly stated)

Task 10d

1. definitely, high
2. maybe, low
3. certainly, high
4. conceivably, low
5. probably, mid
6. perhaps, low

Task 10e

1. are not permitted to
2. have to
3. may
4. are required to
5. should
6. It is advisable
7. It . . . became necessary

Task 10f

1. had to, high
2. need to, high
3. do not need to, low negative
4. will, high
5. may, low
6. may not, high negative
7. have to, high
8. ought to, mid
9. needn't, low negative
10. shall, high

11 Organizing messages: Theme and focus

In previous chapters, we have looked at some of the resources of English grammar for talking about processes, participants, and circumstances, in other words for representing experiential meaning. Resources for expressing various kinds of interpersonal meaning have also been examined. In this chapter, we will be investigating one system for organizing these two kinds of meaning to produce clauses and sentences which are appropriate and coherent in their context, in other words a system for realizing **textual meaning.**

Many teachers have had the experience of seemingly correcting every grammatical mistake in a piece of written work, yet finding that the text still seems muddled or incoherent. Teachers often find it difficult to put into words either for themselves or for the learner exactly what is wrong.

One source of incoherence is inappropriate word order. There are many ways in which sentences and clauses can be rearranged without changing their experiential or interpersonal meanings. To illustrate this, we can again take the clause first looked at in Chapter 1.

With a quick movement of its tail, the sea-serpent would overturn fishing boats
. . .

The following are some of the ways in which the clause could be rearranged:

The sea-serpent would overturn fishing boats with a quick movement of its tail.
Fishing boats the sea-serpent would overturn with a quick movement of its tail.
As for fishing boats, the sea-serpent would overturn them with a quick movement of its tail.
Fishing boats would be overturned by the sea-serpent with a quick movement of its tail.
It was fishing boats that the serpent would overturn with a quick movement of its tail.
What the sea-serpent would do was to overturn fishing boats with a quick movement of its tail.

Each of these six versions is grammatical, and one can suggest contexts in which each would be appropriate. They differ from one another and from the original clause in their *textual meaning,* that is, the ways in which the same experiential and interpersonal meanings have been organized as a message. If a learner selects a form of organization for a particular message inappropriate for its context, then at the very least it will sound odd and the coherence of the text may be affected.

Task 11a

The following three versions of a text are identical in their experiential and interpersonal meanings. Which version reads best? Can you suggest why?

Version A

Michelangelo was another outstanding man of the Renaissance. He was one of the last great Renaissance artists, for it was Italy that by the time of his death in 1584 was falling into decline.

Sculpture he concentrated on initially. A figure of David began to be carved by him from a huge block of marble at Florence in 1501. This he finished in 1504 when he was 29. David he showed with a sling on his shoulder, going to fight Goliath. Fourteen feet high was the statue.

He was asked by Pope Julius II when in Rome to paint the ceiling of the Sistine Chapel. This task was worked upon by Michelangelo lying on his back on the top of high scaffolding, his neck stiff, paint trickling onto his face for four years from 1508 till 1512. What the Pope was impatient about was to see the decoration of the Sistine Chapel completed and numerous enquiries about progress were made by him.

Version B

Michelangelo was another outstanding man of the Renaissance. He was one of the last great Renaissance artists, for by the time of his death in 1564 Italy was falling into decline.

Initially he concentrated on sculpture. At Florence in 1501 he began to carve a figure of David from a huge block of marble. This was finished in 1504 when he was 29. David was shown with a sling on his shoulder, going to fight Goliath. The statue was fourteen feet high.

When in Rome he was asked by Pope Julius II to paint the ceiling of the Sistine Chapel. For four years from 1508 till 1512 Michelangelo worked on this task, lying on his back at the top of high scaffolding, his neck stiff, paint trickling onto his face. The Pope was impatient to see the decoration of the Sistine Chapel completed and made numerous enquiries about progress.

Version C

Michelangelo was another outstanding man of the Renaissance. He was one of the last great Renaissance artists, for Italy was falling into decline by the time of his death in 1564.

He concentrated initially on sculpture. He began to carve a figure of David from a huge block of marble at Florence in 1501. He finished this in 1504 when he was 29. He showed David with a sling on his shoulder, going to fight Goliath. The statue was fourteen feet high.

Pope Julius II asked Michelangelo when in Rome to paint the ceiling of the Sistine Chapel. Michelangelo worked on this task for four years from 1508 till 1512, lying on his back at the top of high scaffolding, his neck stiff, paint trickling onto his face. The Pope was impatient to see the decoration of the Sistine Chapel completed and made numerous enquiries about progress.

The published version of this extract is from Barcan, Blunden, and Stories (1972: 163).

11.1 Marked and unmarked word order

Some of the differences in textual meaning among the three versions of the above text can be explored by first considering what is the most usual word order (or, more strictly, *order of constituents*) in English and what are less usual word orders.

Task 11b

1. How would you rank the following clauses on a scale from "most usual, basic word order" to "most unusual, least basic word order"?
   a. Michelangelo showed David with a sling on his shoulder.
   b. At around 5000 B.C., man learned to smelt and shape copper.
   c. Michelangelo was another outstanding man of the Renaissance.
   d. David was shown with a sling on his shoulder.
   e. Him I really can't bear.
   f. This example I invented.
   g. Painfully, she dragged herself to her feet.
   h. Man learned to smelt and shape copper at around 5000 B.C..
   i. This example was invented.
   j. She dragged herself painfully to her feet.
   k. I really can't bear him.

    l. I invented this example.

    m. David he showed with a sling on his shoulder.

2. What generalizations can you make about word order in English declarative clauses?

As task 11b illustrates, we feel instinctively that there is a kind of default word order for declarative clauses, that is, a word order which we use unless there is some good reason in the context for using a different word order. This is known as the *unmarked word order.*

11.2   Theme and Rheme

To understand the effects of different textual organizations of a clause, at least two questions need to be asked. First, what is the jumping-off point, or point of departure (Halliday 1994: 737), of the message in the clause? Second, which part of the message is presented as most important, or most *newsworthy?* The first question is considered in the next few sections; the second question is covered in Section 11.8.

Each of the following three clauses has a different point of departure.

(1) a. Michelangelo finished the statue of David in 1504.

(1) b. The statue of David was finished by Michelangelo in 1504.

(1) c. In 1504 Michelangelo finished the statue of David.

In 1a, *Michelangelo* is the point of departure; in 1b, it is *The statue of David,* and in 1c, it is *In 1504.* The technical term for this point of departure function is **Theme.** Everything else in the clause is known as the **Rheme.**

As Examples 1a through 1c show, the Theme can be identified as the first constituent in the clause. However, the Theme is more than just the constituent that happens to come at the beginning of the clause. As that part of the clause's message that the speaker or writer has selected as the jumping-off point, it provides a kind of frame for the interpretation of the rest of the message. It is, in a sense, what the clause is "about." For example, 1a above could be glossed as something like *now I am going to tell you something (else) about Michelangelo – he finished the statue of David in 1504.* 1b could be glossed as something like *now I am going to tell you something about the Statue of David – it was finished by Michelangelo in 1504.* 1c could be glossed as something like *now I am going to tell you about something that happened in 1504, Michelangelo finished the statue of David.*

11.3 Marked and unmarked Themes

In 1a and 1b the word order is unmarked and the Theme is the Subject. In other words, *Michelangelo* in 1a and *The statue of David* in 1b function simultaneously as Subjects and as Themes. Such Themes are referred to as *unmarked Themes.* Any Themes other than the Subject, for example *in 1504* in 1c, are therefore referred to as *marked Themes,* although there are, of course, degrees of markedness.

It is only in declarative mood clauses that the unmarked Theme is the Subject. In *yes-no* interrogative mood the unmarked Theme is the Finite, and in *wh-* interrogative mood, the unmarked theme is the *wh* word (whether or not this represents the Subject; see Section 9.3.1), for example:

(2) Do I look insane to you now?
(3) When will you be satisfied?

In imperative mood, the unmarked Theme is the Predicator, for example:

(4) . . . button up those lips, tightly.

unless it is preceded by a Subject, as in:

(5) You wait and see . . .

Note that version A of the Michelangelo text consists of many marked Themes, while version C consists of all unmarked Themes. Version B (the original) is quite typical of written texts in having mainly unmarked Themes with some marked Themes. A complete thematic analysis of this text can be found in Eggins, Wignell, and Martin (1993).

11.4 Selection of marked Themes

As has already been noted, when any constituent other than the Subject functions as Theme, it is regarded as a marked Theme. Such a constituent may be thought of as in some way having been moved from its unmarked position to the front of the clause. Technically, we can say that it has been **thematized.** Thus, in sentence b in this clause from task 11b:

(6) At around 5000 B.C., man learned to smelt and shape copper

we can say that the Circumstantial Adjunct *at around 5000 B.C.* has been thematized. Similarly in the clause

(7) This example I invented. [*inv.*]

we can say that the Object *this example* has been thematized.

To understand the possible motivations for selecting a constituent other than the Subject to begin a clause, that is, to understand why thematization occurs, it is necessary to look at the relationship between a clause and its context.

11.4.1 Thematized Objects and Complements

Objects in the initial position of a clause are highly marked, as has already been observed (in task 11b). They are not common in English, particularly in written English. However, they do occur in certain contexts.

If we try to reconstruct a context in which the thematized Objects in clauses such as *this example I invented* and *him I really cannot bear* (both from task 11b) would seem natural and appropriate, we might come up with something like:

(8) Most of the examples come from the texts, but this example I invented, as I couldn't find an authentic one.

and

(9) I find I get on with her very well, but him I really cannot bear.

In these examples, the marked Themes highlight a *contrast* between *most of the examples* and *this example* in number 8 and between *her* and *him* in number 9. As thematized Objects are highly marked, they often have this kind of *contrastive* effect.

Even where thematized Objects are not contrastive, they normally carry a strong emphasis, as in the following example.

(10) . . . we launched into a study of the elements of architecture, which in the Beaux-Arts system meant walls, porticos, arcades, doorways, corniches and balustrades. Dealing with these elements required the use of one of five orders. These we studied, first from Vignola, later from the classic documents . . .
(from *MicroConcord: Corpus Collection B.* Oxford University Press, 1993)

Attribute Complements as Themes are similarly highly marked, for example:

(11) A socialist I am and a socialist I shall always be.
(12) Strange indeed was the sound that came from within.

Task 11c

Identify the thematized Objects in the following extracts. Can you explain the use of these marked Themes?

1

The slogan of the US Army Corps of Engineers was: "The difficult we do immediately. The impossible takes a little longer."

2

. . . they claim that such restrictions on individual liberty are an inevitable consequence of moves towards greater social equality and social justice.

This argument I simply do not accept. There is no evidence that the removal of some of the most glaring instances of inequality in our society has led to any curtailment of individual rights.

11.4.2 *Thematized Circumstantial Adjuncts*

Thematized Circumstantial Adjuncts are far more common than thematized Objects and Complements, and they are not normally so marked. In the following example, the thematized Circumstantial Adjunct signals a shift in perspective from *economic* integration of Western Europe, which has been the topic of the text to this point, to *physical* integration.

(13) Even physically, Europe's neighborhoods are drawing closer, with road and rail lines bridging the Baltic countries, a new waterway joining the North Sea with the Black Sea, the Channel Tunnel linking Britain and France scheduled to open at the end of this year, and the rapid growth of high-speed trains.

(Dyson 1993: 17)

It is common for two or more thematized Circumstantial Adjuncts to be used in succession to signal stages in the organization of a text. For example, the first paragraph of this chapter (not written with exemplification in mind) is organized around two Circumstantial Adjuncts of place.

(14) In previous chapters, we have looked at some of the resources of English grammar for talking about processes, participants, and circumstances, in other words for representing experiential meaning. Resources for expressing various kinds of interpersonal meaning have also been examined. In this chapter, we will be investigating one system for organizing these two kinds of meaning to produce clauses and sentences which are appropriate and coherent in their context, in other words a system for realizing **textual meaning.**

The choice of Themes is related to what Fries (1983) calls the **method of development** of a text. In the following extract from an article about the consumption of olive oil in the United States, the method of development is chronological and the thematized Circumstantial Adjuncts are all of time.

(15) In 1983, Americans consumed almost 9 million gallons of olive oil, both imported and domestic, which represents a 30% increase over consumption in 1980, just three years earlier. In the early 1980s, per capita yearly consumption in the United States was about 5 ounces (a little more than half a cup), which was minimal compared to French per capita annual consumption of 1.5 gallons, 3 gallons for Spain, and 5 gallons for Greece.

In 1984, the total American consumption of olive oil increased by 10% over the year before, and a large part of that growth was due to the exploding popularity of expensive, extra virgin olive oil.

(Lang 1986: 101)

(23) La pastasciutte Franco la prende sempre qui.
      The pasta Franco it orders always here
      "Franco always orders the pasta here."

(MacWhinney and Bates 1984)

and

(24) No, la lasagna l'ha consigliata Elizabeth.
      No, the lasagna it recommended Elizabeth.
      "No, Elizabeth recommended the lasagna."

(MacWhinney and Bates 1984)

In both of these, the Theme is the Object, which is picked up later by a pronoun. The point is not that a clause like *The pasta Franco always orders it here* would be impossible or ungrammatical in English. It is a possible clause, especially in spoken English. The point is that the thematized Object would be more marked in English and more restricted in its use than in Italian. Italian learners of English may therefore overuse such a marked thematic structure.

Chinese and Japanese (among other languages) are well known for their widespread use of absolute Themes, for example:

      plant vegetables, still is   this   field good
(25) zhong   cai   hai shi zheikuai tian hao   (Mandarin Chinese)
      "As for planting vegetables, this field is better."

(Courtesy David Li Chor Shing, City University of Hong Kong)

      Fish   THEME red snapper SUBJECT good
(26) Sakana   wa   tai   ga   ii.   (Japanese)
      "As for fish, red snappers are good."

(Shibatani 1987)

In example 26 *wa* marks the Theme and *ga* marks the Subject.

Again, while comparable absolute Themes do occur in English, as has been noted above, they are much less common and they serve to strongly highlight the Theme. Chinese and Japanese speakers tend to overuse such structures in English.

First priority for all learners will, of course, be to master unmarked word order for declarative, interrogative, and imperative moods. However, a text which consists entirely of unmarked Themes, particularly if the Theme is the same participant over a long stretch, can seem flat, monotonous, and sometimes rather childish, as in this example in which every Theme except one is *I*:

(27) I wake up at half past seven. I wash my face and brush my teeth, and I have my breakfast. My father always takes me to school about eight o'clock. I arrive school. I start my lesson after morning assembly. I have

eight lessons in one day. I go home at about five o'clock because I stay at school to do my homework, therefore later.

(Courtesy D. Mahoney, City University of Hong Kong)

Questions for discussion

- Suggest some activities for use with intermediate learners to raise their awareness of the role of thematized Circumstantial Adjuncts in text organization.
- How might you help learners who overuse absolute Themes?

11.6 Nonexperiential Themes

All the Themes that have been considered so far are either participants (as in *Michelangelo carved the statue of David*) or circumstances (as in *For four years from 1508 to 1512 Michelangelo worked . . .*). In other words, they all function to represent aspects of *experiential meaning*. However, a problem for analysis is when such experiential constituents are preceded by other elements, as in the following example:

(28) . . . but you shouldn't actually mention their names . . .

The first experiential constituent in this clause is the participant *you* and it can still be regarded as the Theme, or, more accurately, as the **Experiential Theme.** *Conjunctions,* such as *and, but, so, if,* and *when,* must always come at the beginning of the clause. In other words, the speaker or writer has no choice of whether to thematize them or not to thematize them (a clause such as *you but shouldn't actually mention their names* is not acceptable). Learners simply have to learn that their position is fixed at the beginning of the clause, and they can be ignored in an analysis of the thematic structure of a clause.

The analysis is not quite so straightforward with the constituents underlined in the following examples.

(29) The original has, unfortunately, long since disappeared.
(30) Not surprisingly, the grapevine is another favourite design.
(31) In my view, the results do suggest a clear preference for some kind of bilingual program.

Modal Adjuncts, such as those looked at in the previous chapter (*probably, definitely,* etc.), and adverbs and prepositional phrases such as *unfortunately, in my opinion, frankly, hopefully,* and *fortunately,* express the speaker or writer's attitude toward the message in the clause. Unlike conjunctions, they may be thematic or nonthematic. In other words, they may occur in front of the Experiential Theme (as in numbers 30 and 31) or somewhere after the Experiential Theme (as in number 29). When they are thematic, they provide the frame for the interpretation of the interpersonal meaning of the clause, analogously to the way in which Experiential Themes provide a frame for the interpretation of the experiential meaning. The Themes of number 31 can be glossed as something like *now I'm going to tell you something that is my own opinion and it is something about the results.* Modal Adjuncts as Themes can be referred to simply as **Interpersonal Themes.**

Similarly, **Conjunctive Adjuncts,** such as *however, thus, in fact, thus, furthermore, moreover, first, then,* and *for example,* can be thematic or nonthematic, as the following examples illustrate.

(32)   However, we should not forget that it has only been in the last few decades that . . .
(33)   The biggest shake up of all, however, is that money and financial services can move across borders . . .
(34)   Thus, for many reasons, the truffle harvester is more of a gambler . . .
(35)   Dutch truckers can thus run against German trucks on the Berlin-Munich route . . .

Such Conjunctive Adjuncts, when thematic, provide the frame for the interpretation of the textual meaning of the clause by relating the clause logically with what has gone before. They are therefore called **Textual Themes.** The Themes of a clause such as

(31) a. On the other hand, in my view, the results do suggest a clear preference for continuing some kind of bilingual program.

can be glossed as *now I'm going to tell you something that in some way contrasts with what has gone before* (Textual Theme), *is my own opinion* (Interpersonal Theme), *and is something about the results* (Experiential Theme).

Thus, the identification of Themes is a little more complicated than simply equating them with the first constituent of the clause. The Themes of a clause in fact extend up to the end of the first *experiential* constituent of the clause and they may also include one or more Interpersonal Themes and Textual Themes. According to Halliday (1994), the sequence in such multiple Themes is typically *Textual Theme^Interpersonal Theme^Experiential Theme,* as in number 31a.

For advanced learners, mastery of a range of Interpersonal Themes will be important for the expression of arguments and opinions in both spoken and written English. It is a difficult area for learners because of the often quite subtle nuances of attitude that can be conveyed by Modal Adjuncts.

For students of writing in particular, some attention may also need to be given to Textual Themes. Learners often have a repertoire of a few such Adjuncts which they overuse. It in fact takes much sensitivity to context to know whether to explicitly mark a logical relationship with a Conjunctive Adjunct, which Adjunct to choose, and whether or not to thematize it. This is complicated by the fact that some Conjunctive Adjuncts are less "naturally" thematic than others. For example, *however* is more likely to be thematic than *also,* and *too* is rarely thematic, especially in writing. Sometimes, learners tend to thematize *all* Conjunctive Adjuncts. However, a text with too many thematized Conjunctive Adjuncts can seem pedantic and ponderous, for example:

(36)   R_____ proposes to construct a golf course in S_____ village. This will bring many advantages to the area, including job opportunities and increased tourism. However, the project has been objected to by environmental groups. Therefore, R_____ has hired a consultancy firm to investigate the project. In addition, a committee will be formed to keep control of the construction costs. Also, an important task of the committee will be to minimize the impact of the construction on the surrounding area.

(Courtesy J. Flowerdew, City University of Hong Kong)

11.7   Focus of information

Earlier it was stated that in order to investigate the textual organization of a clause, two questions need to be asked. First, What is the jumping-off point, or point of departure (i.e., the Theme)? Second, What part of the message is presented as the most important, or most newsworthy? The first question has been considered in some detail. To answer the second question, it is necessary to digress very briefly into the area of phonology.

Speech can be divided into **tone groups,** which represent the basic units of information into which a speaker "packages" what he or she has to say. Each tone group contains one syllable that is more prominent than other syllables in the tone group. In the following example, the double slash indicates the tone group boundary and capital letters identify the most prominent syllables.

| TONE GROUP 1 | TONE GROUP 2 |

(37) You just press f SEven // and it goes OFF

The syllables *sev(en)* and *off* are made more prominent by the fact that they carry a major pitch movement. Such syllables are known as *tonic syllables* or simply **tonics.** A tonic syllable functions to draw the attention of the listener to the part of the message in the tone group which the speaker wants the listener to pay most attention to. In other words, it marks the **Focus** of information in the tone group. The Focus is in fact the constituent which contains the tonic syllable – in example 37, *f seven* and *goes off.* The Focus is the culmination of the **new** (i.e. presented as "newsworthy") **information.** Other information in the tone group may be backgrounded because it is something that has been previously mentioned or that can be taken for granted, or is in some way less newsworthy. This is usually called **given information.**

It is very common for the tonic to be near the end of the tone group – usually the last stressed syllable, as in both tone groups in example 37. Where the boundaries of a tone group coincide with those of a clause, as they often (though not always) do, the unmarked Focus will therefore be in the Rheme, while the Theme will typically consist of given information. A common pattern of development in texts, particularly written texts, is for new information to be introduced first in the Rheme of one clause and then to be picked up as given information in the Theme (or Themes) of a subsequent clause (or clauses), for example:

> (38) At Florence in 1501, he began to carve a figure of David from a huge block of marble. This was finished in 1504, when he was 29. David was shown with a sling on his shoulder, going to fight Goliath. The statue was fourteen feet high.

Here new information, *a figure of David,* is introduced in the Rheme of the first clause. It then becomes the Themes (although in different wording) of the clauses beginning each subsequent sentence in the paragraph.

It has been noted that the tonic is typically the final stressed syllable of a tone group and that given information typically precedes new. However, this by no means has to be the case, particularly in spoken language. A speaker can in fact choose to put the tonic on a syllable of almost any word in a tone group (although function words like prepositions and pronouns usually do not take the tonic). For example, in a typical reading of the following sentence, the tonic (and therefore the Focus) would fall on *Laur(ence):*

> (39)   We promised to go to lunch with LAUrence

However, in a certain context the speaker might want to put the tonic elsewhere, for example:

> (39) a. We promised to go to LUNCH with Laurence.

Here the Focus is on *lunch,* and *Laurence* is backgrounded given information.

The Focus can even be mapped on to the theme, for example:

> (39) b. WE promised to go to lunch with Laurence.

Such a marked placement of Focus, like a highly marked theme, is typically contrastive.

In written English, marked tonic placement can be indicated by special orthographic conventions such as capital letters or underlining. However, in general, written English does not have quite the freedom of tonic placement that spoken English has.

11.8 Other ways of organizing the message

Two important parts of the organization of the message of a clause – the departure point or Theme (realized by initial position) and the Focus (realized by tonic placement) – have been identified. In the unmarked case, Theme is mapped on to Subject and Focus occurs at the end of a tone group, typically in the Rheme of a clause. It has also been noted how the unmarked patterns can be changed by thematizing constituents other than the Subject and by shifting the tonic backward. However, there are other options in the grammar for organizing the message in a clause. These include *voice selection,* use of *existential clauses,* and *clefting.* Each of these will be looked at in turn.

11.8.1 Voice selection

In the first of the following two clauses *active voice* has been selected. In the second, *passive voice* has been selected.

(40)   Michelangelo finished the statue of David in 1504.
(40) a. The statue of David was finished (by Michelangelo) in 1504.

In the active voice clause the noun group functioning as Actor (*Michelangelo*) also functions as Subject and as Theme. However, in the passive voice clause, the Actor is either not expressed at all or occurs in the Rheme as the Object of the preposition *by.* The Theme and Subject of the passive version is the Goal, which in the active voice version is mapped on to the Direct Object. In other words, the two clauses have the same experiential meanings but they differ in their textual meanings, having two different points of departure.

The selection of passive voice allows the speaker or writer to thematize participants such as Goals, Recipients, and Phenomena (i.e., participants mapped on to Direct and Indirect Objects in active voice clauses) without producing marked Themes. Thus in number 40a, the Goal (*the statue of David*) is thematized, but as it is also the Subject, the Theme is unmarked.

The usefulness of this can be seen by returning to an extract from the Michelangelo text looked at earlier.

(41)   At Florence in 1501, he began to carve a figure of David from a huge
        block of marble. This was finished in 1504, when he was 29. David was
        shown with a sling on his shoulder, going to fight Goliath.

In this section of the text, the writers wish to shift to talking about the statue of David. As has already been noted, they do this by introducing *a figure of David* as new information in the Rheme and then picking it up as the Theme of subsequent clauses. They could have done this simply by thematizing the Objects:

(41) a. At Florence in 1501, he began to carve a figure from a huge block of marble. This he finished in 1504, when he was 29. David he showed with a sling on his shoulder, going to fight Goliath.

However, thematized Objects are highly marked and tend to be contrastive. The selection of passive voice in the original version allows the writers to thematize *This* and *David* without producing an inappropriate marked Theme.

The selection of passive voice can also be motivated by the desire not to switch Theme, for example:

(42)   She put her head out of the window and was struck full in the face by a snowball.

Here the Theme of the second clause is still *she* (although it is ellipsed). The selection of passive voice allows *she* to remain the Theme without producing what would be a very marked thematic structure (. . . *her a snowball struck full in the face*).

The fact that participants which are mapped onto Subjects in active clauses can appear as Adjuncts in the Rhemes of passive voice clauses means that they can naturally take the tonic and therefore be the Focus of information. For example, in all the following examples the Actors are new information, and the use of passive voice allows them to be placed in the unmarked position for new information near the end of the clause.

(43) Extended courses are normally provided by universities.
(44) . . . the food of a region is shaped by the fat it is cooked in.
(45) The castle was built by Guichard d'Oingt.

As number 39b shows, to put the Focus on the Actor in an active voice clause involves shifting the tonic to the beginning of the clause, which results in very marked intonation.

Passive voice gives us the option not only of focusing on the Actor, but also of not expressing the Actor at all, as in both of the passive voice clauses in the Michelangelo text extract cited in number 41. The Actors are *understood,* and it would be very odd to add *by Michelangelo* to each clause. In other cases, Actors may be omitted not because they are understood but because they are unimportant or irrelevant information in the context, for example:

(46) The 17 commissioners may speak any of the nine official languages at their weekly meetings. Simultaneous translation is provided for all, with small limitations.

(47) Today, about 6 tons of truffles are imported annually into the United States from both France and Italy.

In these extracts, it is irrelevant who provides the translations or who imports the truffles.

Such so-called **Agentless** (Actorless, Senserless etc., depending on process type) passives are very common. Indeed, grammar books for ESL learners often explain the use of the passive voice in terms such as "we use the passive when the person or thing that performs the action is unimportant or unknown." Although this is partially true, it is not a helpful guide for learners. For example, in one version of the well-known story *The Three Bears,* Baby Bear says, *"Someone has been eating my porridge and has eaten it all up."* Here the person or thing that performs the action is certainly unknown. However, this does not mean that Baby Bear ought to have used passive voice.

Conversely, in numbers 43 through 45, the Actors are far from being unimportant or unknown. In fact, as stated earlier, one motivation for selecting passive voice may be precisely to focus upon the Actor.

The point is, of course, that the choice between active and passive is not simply a question of whether the Actor is known or important but is also a question of which participant it would be most appropriate to thematize in the context and what information is to be treated as most newsworthy.

Task 11e

Identify the passive voice clauses in the following examples and try to explain why passive rather than active voice is used and why there is or is not an explicit Actor.

1. Despite this system-gridlock tendency, technological innovations do occur. Raymond Nelson's National Research Council Workshop suggests that the explanation is both obvious and paradoxical: technological innovation is produced not by technology but by design.
2. There will be neither rest nor tranquility in America until the Negro is granted his citizenship rights.
3. That my four little children will one day live in a nation where they will not be judged by the color of their skin but by the content of their character; I have a dream today.
4. Monsoon Asia includes those countries which are affected by the MONSOON RAINS. (from Extract 2)

11.8.1.1 LEARNING AND TEACHING PASSIVE VOICE

It has already been noted that some languages thematize constituents more freely than English. Sometimes, such thematization is combined with a much greater freedom of Subject ellipsis, for example:

	RHEME	
THEME		
(48) cơm	thổi rồi	(Vietnamese)
rice	cook already	

"The rice has already been cooked."

(Ngyuen 1987)

The thematic structure of this clause can be roughly glossed as *as for the rice [somebody] has cooked [it]*. In other words, *com* is a thematized Object/Goal, and the Subject/Actor has been omitted. This can be compared with the following example from the same source, in which a Subject/Actor is present:

	Tag		
THEME			
(49) cơm	mẹ	thổi	rồi
rice	mother	cook	already

"The rice mother has already cooked."

(Ngyuen 1987)

The point is that while clauses like *cơm thổi rồi* can be glossed as *as for the rice, [someone] has cooked [it]*, this exaggerates the markedness of the thematic structure within Vietnamese. In fact, in context the functional equivalents in English of such clauses are often unmarked passive clauses, such as *the rice has been cooked*. Such languages typically do not have a regular distinction in the verb group comparable to the English active-passive distinction, and learners with language backgrounds of this type may have particular difficulty in mastering this distinction.

Languages also have different ways of shifting the Actor to the focus position, without involving a change in voice. In Spanish the Actor can be shifted to the end of the sentence without any change in the voice of the verb, particularly where contrast is involved, for example:

(50) compro el coche Elena
      bought the car Elena
      "The car was bought by Elena"
              or
      "It was Elena who bought the car."

(Green 1987)

Moreover, languages which have a passive voice form do not necessarily use it in contexts in which English might use the passive. Sometimes active voice with a generalized pronoun is preferred, for example:

(51) On dit que . . . (*French*)
　　 One says that . . .
　　 It is said that . . .

In other cases, a reflexive construction may be used where English might use a passive, for example:

(52) Des fleurs se vendent ici tous les matins. (*French*)
　　 Some flowers themselves sell here all the mornings.
　　 "Flowers are sold here every morning."

The traditional way of teaching passive voice is to present it simply as a transformation of active voice, with little or no attention to context, for example:

Active:　　 The teacher punished the student.
Passive:　　 The student *was* punished *by* the teacher.

Clearly, with such an approach, students are unlikely to learn much about how passive clauses are used in context to maintain thematic development, to achieve appropriate patterns of given and new information, and so on. Learners who do not have a comparable form in their own language with similar functions in similar context are likely to see the passive simply as an arbitrary mechanical transformation.

Questions for discussion

- Think of some contexts in which a large number of passive voice clauses typically occur. How can such contexts be exploited for teaching purposes?
- Suggest a game or task exploiting the use of passive voice clauses to focus on Actors in *by* phrases.
- Suggest some activities for intermediate or advanced learners to raise their awareness about choices between active and passive voice in maintaining text coherence.

11.8.2 *Existential clauses*

In Chapter 7, the experiential structure of existential process clauses was considered. From the point of view of textual meaning, the Theme is typically *there* or a Circumstantial Adjunct, while the Existent occurs in the Rheme and is typically the unmarked Focus of information, for example:

<pre>
                                 EXISTENT/FOCUS
(54)   Once upon a time there were   three bears.   They lived . . .
</pre>

Existential clauses are often used to introduce new participants into a text, where they may subsequently be picked up as Themes, as in the example just given.

Clauses such as

(55)   There are a lot of foreign students living in this building.

can be compared to:

(55) a. A lot of foreign students live in this building.

The existential structure in number 55 serves in a sense to push the participants *a lot of foreign students* away from the Theme, which as we have seen is typically associated with given information, and into a position more appropriate for new information. The second process must then be realized by an embedded clause, typically a V*ing* clause as in number 55.

Different languages have different ways of achieving this kind of organization of information. In Spanish the Subject can simply be moved into the Rheme, leaving the verb at the head of the clause, for example:

(56)   Viven gitanos en las cuevas.
        live gypsies in the caves
        "There are gypies living in the caves."

(Green 1987)

Different kinds of learners tend to overuse or to underuse existential structures in English. Some learners may simply append *there is* (*are,* etc.) to the front of a clause without changing it to an embedded clause, for example:

(57)   *There are a lot of foreign students live in this building.

Such structures even occur in the informal speech of native speakers. However, they are considered incorrect in formal, particularly written, contexts.

11.8.3   Clefting

Clefting involves the division and repackaging of the information in a clause into two parts, for example:

(58)   We are now going to look at clefting.   [*inv.*]
(58) a. It is clefting that we are going to look at now.
(58) b. What we are going to look at now is clefting.

Versions 58a and 58b are known as *cleft sentences.* The type represented by 58a will be referred to as an *it* **cleft,** and the type represented by 58b will be referred to as a *wh-* **cleft.**

11.8.3.1 *IT* CLEFTS

The following are examples of *it* clefts.

(59) However, it is in the realm of high technology that computer disciplines have really began to make themselves felt.

(60) ... though it is the connection between my education and my personal experience that has helped me see the significance of these social categories ...

(61) It was in this introductory sociology course that my political and sociological imagination was born.

As these examples show, an *it* cleft has *it* in the Subject position and a linking verb (usually a form of *be*) followed by a *that* clause (or sometimes a *wh-* clause). The cleft clauses in numbers 59 through 61 can be related to the following noncleft clauses:

(59) a. However, computer disciplines have begun to make themselves felt in the realm of high technology.

(60) a. The connection between my education and my personal experience has helped me to see the significance of these social categories.

(61) a. My political and sociological imagination was born in this introductory sociology course.

In the cleft versions, the tonic naturally falls on a syllable within the constituent immediately following the linking verb, and therefore this constituent becomes the Focus. Thus in number 59 the Focus is *in the realm of high technology,* in number 60 the Focus is *the connection between my education and my personal experience,* and in number 61 it is *in this introductory sociology course.* The cleft also backgrounds other information by putting it in an embedded clause (*that computer disciplines have really began to make themselves felt; that has helped me to see the significance of these social categories; that my political and sociological imagination was born*).

In the preceding examples, the Foci of information are Circumstantial Adjuncts or the Subject. However, other constituents can also be focused on, for example, Objects:

Noncleft: We saw the uncensored version last week.
Cleft: It was the uncensored version that we saw last week.

Clefts allow a speaker or writer to assert something strongly, often in contrast to something else that has been said. They are particularly useful in written English, where there is not the freedom to put the Focus on different parts of a message by moving the tonic. They can be used to highlight a piece of information central to a particular stage in the development of a text. For example, the context that precedes number 59 is as follows:

(62) Another sign that the computer age is with us can be found in many executive offices where a computer terminal is becoming increasingly common. Previously, managers were generally loath to touch a keyboard and
those few who could type did so with two fingers and great difficulty.
Now, though, times are changing and it is not inconceivable that the next
generation of executives will have their own terminals plus the skills and
knowledge necessary to use them to maximum effect.

However, it is in the realm of high technology that computer disciplines
have really begun to make themselves felt.

(Murdoch 1992)

The first paragraph is about computer use by business executives. At the
beginning of the second paragraph the cleft introduces the important new
information *in the realm of high technology,* which will be the topic of the
following part of the text. The use of the cleft also suggests that the
computer disciplines have not really made themselves felt yet among business executives, but they have in the area of high technology.

A similar pattern can be seen with number 63:

(63) My education has been critical to realizing the significance of these social
categories, though it is the connection between my education and my personal experience that has helped me see their sociological importance.
    I grew up the oldest child in a white, upwardly mobile middle-class
family with working-class origins.

(Anderson 1991: 384)

Again, the cleft introduces important new information which will be the
topic of the following section of text. It also again implies contrast: *it was
not just education, but the connection between my education and my personal experience.*

11.8.3.2 WH-CLEFTS

The *wh-* cleft is the last of the structures motivated by the requirements of
textual meaning that will be examined. In *wh-* clefts, the message is presented as an identifying clause (see Section 7.2), with the Identified realized by a *wh-* clause. The two examples of *wh-* clefts below can be compared to the noncleft versions which follow them.

	IDENTIFIED	IDENTIFIER
(64)	What I want to talk about today	is the organization of clauses as messages.

	IDENTIFIED	IDENTIFIER
(65)	And what they do	is they get a current and they divide it.

(64) a. I want to talk today about the organization of clauses as messages.
(65) a. They get a current and they divide it.

The *wh-* cleft functions like the *it* cleft in that it focuses on one part of the information, normally the Identifier. It is common for the Identified/*wh-* clause to come first, that is, to be the Theme, as in the preceding examples. However, as with any identifying clause the order *can* be reversed, for example:

(64) a. The organization of clauses as messages is what I want to talk about today.

wh- clefts can be used to focus on a Subject, an Object, or an Adjunct, as in the following:

(66)   But where I worked for the first few months was on the factory floor itself.

A *wh-* cleft can also focus on a Complement:

(67)   What we are is lost, if you ask me.

In context, *wh-* clefts often announce what is going to be the main topic of the whole text or the next part of a text, as in number 64 and in the following example:

(68)   Those people who I have told their address is correct, I'm going to give you a partner and you may quietly go and sit by my maths books over there and practice. This is what you're going to practice. So listen carefully.

Like *it-* clefts, *wh-* clefts often involve contrast, for example:

(69)   George V's last words have been incorrectly recorded. What he actually said was "Book at Bognor."

Often the contrast takes the form of *wh- not X but Y,* for example:

(69) a. What George V actually said was not "Bugger Bognor" but "Book at Bognor."

The following example is similar, except that the second half of the contrast is in a separate sentence.

(70)   What seems to me objectionable about these phrases is not that they are in some sense "wrong." . . . Rather, I think they are misleading.

11.8.3.3 LEARNING AND TEACHING CLEFTS

The ways to assign focus vary greatly between languages. As has been seen, sometimes the element to be focused on can simply be shifted to the end of the clause, as in example 50, from Spanish. In Mandarin Chinese, the verb *shi* (meaning *be – is, was,* etc.), usually plus the particle *de* at the end of the clause, can be used to assign Focus, for example:

	is	Chen	Madame	tell	me	DE
(73)	Shi	Chen	nushi	gaosu	wo	de.

"It was Madam Chen who told me."

Learners have a tendency either to avoid clefts entirely or to overuse them.

Questions for discussion

- Clefts tend not to get taught. Do you think they should be explicitly focused on in a teaching program? If so, at which proficiency level would you introduce them?
- Suggest ways of introducing and practicing *it* clefts that do not involve explicit transformations from noncleft clauses.

Summary

1. The Theme of a clause is its point of departure as a message. Theme in English is realized by initial position. The rest of the clause is known as the Rheme.
2. In declarative clauses the unmarked Theme is the Subject, in *yes-no* interrogatives it is the Finite, in *wh-* interrogatives it is the *wh-* element, and in imperatives it is the Predicator.
3. Thematized Objects and Complements are highly marked and are often contrastive. Thematized Circumstantial Adjuncts are less marked.
4. Selection of Themes is related to the method of development of a text.
5. Speech may be divided into tone groups, each with one most prominent syllable known as the tonic. The tonic marks the Focus, which is the culmination of new (newsworthy) information in the clause. Other back-grounded information is known as given information. There is a strong tendency for given information to precede new information, especially in writing.
6. Selection of passive voice may be motivated by the need to thematize a Goal (or other participants that would be mapped onto the Object in an active voice clause) without producing a marked Theme. Passive voice also allows Actors (or other participants that would be mapped onto the Subject in an active voice clause) to be in the Focus of information, without the use of marked intonation. It also allows such participants to be omitted entirely.
7. *It* clefts and *wh-* clefts are both structural devices for placing Focus on different constituents of the clause.

Key terms introduced

This text	*Alternatives used in the field*
Absolute Theme	
Agentless passive	
Experiential Theme	Topical Theme
Focus	
given information	presupposed/shared/old information
Interpersonal Theme	
it cleft	predicated Theme; cleft sentence
method of development	
new information	
Rheme	Comment
Textual theme	
thematize	front; topicalize
Theme	Topic
tone group	
tonic	nucleus
wh- cleft	thematic equative; pseudo-cleft sentence

Discussion of tasks

Task 11a

Version A is clearly very odd. The word order of many of its clauses is completely inappropriate. It is much harder to choose between versions B and C. The original text is in fact version B, which does read a little better, particularly in paragraph two.

Task 11b

1. Most teachers I have done this task with group the clauses in the following way:

Very unusual, least basic:	a – pronoun Object in initial position
↑	f and m – (nonpronoun) Object in initial position
	b and g – Circumstantial Adjuncts in initial position
↓	
Most unusual, most basic:	a, c, d, h, i, j, k, and l – Subject in initial position

2. Some teachers feel that passive clauses are slightly less usual or less basic than active clauses and therefore d and i should be regarded as slightly more unusual or basic than b, h, j, k, and l.

We can generalize that word order in which the Subject comes at the beginning of the clause is the most usual and basic. Where an Object (especially a pronoun Object) begins the clause, the word order is very unusual (least basic). Clauses beginning with Circumstantial Adjuncts lie somewhere between these extremes.

Task 11c

1. *The difficult* contrasts with the following (unmarked) Theme *the impossible.*
2. *This argument* refers back to the previous portion of text and provides a major "jumping-off point" for the next section – a refutation of the argument. It is therefore strongly highlighted.

Task 11d

The thematized Adjuncts of place at the beginning of paragraph one (*In China*) and paragraph two (*In India*) mark the basic organization of the text into two narratives from two different countries. The second marked Theme in both paragraphs (*One summer's day* in paragraph one and *Long, long ago* in paragraph two) is an Adjunct of time, which sets the basic temporal frame for each narrative.

The second narrative is much more temporally extended than the first, and a succession of thematized Adjuncts of time mark stages in the chronological organization of the story: *After a wild youth; For years; (but) one day; on waking; Years later; After his first mouthful; Ever since.*

Note that *on waking* could be interpreted as either a dependent clause or a prepositional phrase functioning as Circumstantial Adjunct (see next chapter). Whatever analysis is preferred, this constituent serves to frame a stage in the narrative.

Task 11e

1. The passive voice clause is *technological innovation is produced not by technology but by design. Technological innovation* is given information in this clause and it is what the whole sentence is about. It is therefore appropriately selected as Subject/unmarked Theme. The new important information is *not by technology but by design,* which is appropriately placed at the end of the clause.
2. The passive voice clause is *until the Negro is granted his citizenship rights. The Negro* is given information in this clause. There is no explicit Actor (the person or persons who will do the granting of rights), as it is not important or relevant information in this context.

3. The passive voice clause is *where they will not be judged by the color of their skin but by the content of their character. They* is given information, what the whole sentence is about. There is no explicit Actor (or Senser), as the implication is that "*everyone* will not judge them."

   Note that the prepositional phrases *by the color of their skin* and *by the content of their character* do not contain participants (i.e., they are not the entities doing the judging). These phrases realize Circumstantial Adjuncts of manner (i.e., *how* they are judged).

4. The passive voice clause is *which are affected by the MONSOON RAINS.* The important new information is *MONSOON RAINS,* which is appropriately placed at the end of the clause.

12 *Combining messages: Complex sentences*

Example 1 is a sentence from the speech of a primary school teacher (the same teacher as in Extract 6). Sentence 2 is from Extract 7.

(1) The things will be here and you will know what to do, as you will be able to carry on by yourself if you've finished your other work, so long as you tidy up at the end.
(2) The payoff for the rigours and longueurs of scientific research is the consequent gain in understanding of the way the world is constructed.

Even without knowing the source of these two sentences, it would be clear that they are from very different contexts. At the very least, most readers would probably identify number 1 as spoken language and number 2 as written language.

One of the ways in which these two extracts differ from each other is that number 2 has very long noun groups (*the payoff for the rigours and longueurs of scientific research* and *the consequent gain in the way the world is constructed*) and a great deal of nominalization (this was explored in Section 3.5). Number 1, on the other hand, has relatively short noun groups (*the things, you, your other work,*) and little or no nominalization (*work* is the only word that might be considered a nominalization).[1]

A second way in which these two extracts differ is that number 1 consists of a number of structurally related clauses:

The things will be here
and you will know
what to do
as you will be able to carry on by yourself
if you've finished your other work
so long as you tidy up at the end.

Number 2, on the other hand, consists of just one clause (excluding embedded clauses). Number 2 is in fact an identifying clause consisting of two

---

1 In some analyses, *what to do* would be treated as a nominal clause and therefore also as a kind of nominalization. However, following Halliday 1994, it is here analyzed as a ranking clause (see Section 6.1.2).

noun groups (functioning as the Identified and the Identifier) joined by the linking verb *is*.

A sentence which consists of only one ranking (i.e., nonembedded) clause, such as number 2, is known as a **simple sentence,** while a sentence which consists of more than one ranking clause, such as number 1, is known as a **complex sentence.**[2] The word *sentence* is actually somewhat problematic. In written language, a sequence of structurally related clauses normally begins with a capital letter and ends with a full stop. In other words, the sequence is marked as being a *sentence.* In spoken language, however, one has to take intonation into account, as well as the presence of conjunctions such as *and, if,* and *so long as* to decide whether clauses are structurally related or not. In addition, a sequence of structurally related clauses in speech might not be acceptable as a sentence in written language. If number 1 were to be written, for example, it would probably be split up into two or more sentences. There is, in fact, a general tendency for such sequences to be longer and more complex in speech than in writing. For such reasons, the term *sentence* is sometimes used to refer only to written language, and a different term is used to refer to sequences of structurally related clauses in speech. In this book, the familiar term *sentence* is retained for both written and spoken language. However, it is important to bear in mind that a sentence of spoken language may look very different from a sentence of written language.

The first part of this chapter will consider the *structural* relationships between clauses in complex sentences. The second part will look at complex sentences from the point of view of the *logical* relationships between clauses.

12.1   Independent and dependent clauses

Clauses can be independent or dependent. **Independent clauses** can potentially stand alone and are not structurally dependent on other clauses. If a sentence has only one clause, that clause is, of course, normally an independent clause. The following sentence consists of two independent clauses.

(3) <u>You get off at the stop just before the beach</u> and <u>on the left you'll see Bellview Drive.</u>

A **dependent clause** is structurally dependent on another clause, as in the following example:

2 In traditional grammar, a distinction is made between *compound* sentences, which contain only linked independent clauses, and *complex* sentences, which contain dependent clauses. In this book, no such distinction is made. Any sentence containing more than one ranking clause will be called a *complex sentence.*

(4) While it was cooling, they went into the woods in search of sweet honey.

Dependent clauses cannot normally stand alone. A corollary of that is, of course, that every sentence must have at least one independent clause. Apparent exceptions are cases such as answers to questions, for example:

(5) a. A: Why did you switch it off?
       B: 'cause the picture was so bad.

The clause in the answer can be regarded as dependent on *I switched it off,* which has been omitted because it is understood from the question. In other words, it can be analyzed as a case of ellipsis of the independent clause.

12.2   Structural relationships between clauses

There are two basic kinds of structural relationships between clauses – **linking** and **binding.**

12.2.1   *Linking*

The following examples (as well as number 3 in Section 12.1) illustrate linking:

(6) Don't worry about it; Grandma doesn't know what she means.
(7) Put up or shut up!
(8) (I want it) because I need it and I was promised it.
(9) While soaking oneself in the hot water and letting the cares of the day dissolve away, one can contemplate the strangeness of a society which allows . . .

In linking, the clauses are in a relationship of equality. They must all be independent clauses (as in numbers 6 and 7) *or* all dependent clauses (as in numbers 8 and 9). The clauses are either simply juxtaposed (in writing, often with a comma, colon, semicolon, or dash between them) or they are joined by a *linking conjunction* (*and, but, or,* etc.).

A sequence of two linked clauses can occasionally be reversed with no significant change in the logical relationship between the two clauses. For example, the two linked clauses in number 8 could be reversed, as could the clauses in the following sentence:

(10) Dino wanted the supreme but I wanted the one with anchovies.
       I wanted the one with anchovies but Dino wanted the supreme.

Note that the linking conjunction *but* does not belong to either clause and therefore stays between them when the sequence is reversed.

Very often, however, the logical relationship between the messages in linked clauses depends upon the sequence. This is often the case even where the conjunction is *and,* for example:

(11) She came in, took her coat off, and went straight upstairs.

In this sentence, the sequence of the clauses represents the chronological sequence of the three actions.

Similarly, in the following sentence, the cause and effect implication depends upon the sequence:

(12) I felt very tired and decided to have an early night. [*inv.*] (*compare:* I decided to have an early night and felt very tired.)

A further characteristic of clauses linked by conjunctions is that if the subject of two or more linked clauses is the same, it can be omitted in the second and any subsequent clauses. This is illustrated in numbers 11 and 12 above. This is one of the few contexts in which *Subject ellipsis* is permissible in English.

12.2.2 Binding

Examples 13 through 19 illustrate binding:

(13) Although the sun is shining, it's raining in my heart.
(14) These are bony growths up to one and a half meters long, which are used as weapons in fights with other stags during the mating season (rut).
(15) Had it been left to me, I would have forgotten the whole thing.
(16) . . . thick columns of thunder cloud are formed, creating almost vertical walls . . .
(17) These books appealed to Eros while educating it.
(18) By ordering directly from the publisher, we can avoid all the delay.
(19) Although not entirely happy with it, we accepted the compromise agreement.

In **binding,** the clauses are in a relationship of inequality. In each of the preceding examples, the underlined clause is dependent on an independent clause. However, a clause may also be dependent on another dependent clause, as shown in the following example:

(20) Because we were unhappy about the initial results, which were frankly a bit of a mess, we rethought the whole thing.   [*inv.*]

In this sentence, *which were frankly a bit of a mess* is dependent on *Because we were unhappy about the initial results,* which in turn is dependent on the only independent clause in the sentence: *we rethought the entire thing.*

There are a number of ways in which a clause may be marked as a dependent clause:

- By a *binding conjunction* such as *although, if,* and *because* (e.g., number 13)
- By *wh-* words such as *who* and *which* (e.g., number 14)

tion. However, the possibility of ellipsis in the second and any subsequent clauses can lead to problems. Subject ellipsis has been noted above. Ellipsis can be extended to other constituents which are the same in both clauses; for example, there is ellipsis of both Subject and Finite (*he was*) in the following sentence:

(23) He was severely beaten and left for dead.

Learners sometimes overdo ellipsis, as in the following example, in which the whole verb group (presumably *have been*) has been omitted from the second clause:

(24) *Our parents forgive us even though we have done wrong or unfaithful to them.

(Crewe 1977)

Another problem that sometimes occurs with linking is that learners may use Conjunctive Adjuncts as if they were linking conjunctions, for example:

(25) ?Only four students came therefore the presentation was cancelled.
(26) *We were out looking for clients meanwhile they just sat in their offices.

This is not particularly surprising, as many such Adjuncts do commonly occur in the second of two linked clauses where they make explicit the logical meaning between two clauses linked by *and*. For example:

(27) The anticyclone is colder, drier and heavier than the ascending warm moist air and therefore flattens out the rising thunderstorm tops . . .
(28) They sat all night in front of the fire planning the next stage of the journey, and meanwhile the storm raged outside.

Some problems may be related to a learner's native language. For example, Swahili has the forms *juu ya hayo* and *kwa hivyo,* which can be translated as *in addition* and *because of this.* However, the two forms are linking conjunctions in Swahili, while in English *because of this* and *in addition* function only as Conjunctive Adjuncts. According to Grant (1987), this may mislead Swahili speaking learners of English into producing sentences such as:

(29) *He worked hard because of this he was made a prefect.

The binding relationship tends to cause more problems for learners. Learners sometimes write sentences consisting of only dependent clauses, for example:

(30) *Because it was very dark. The boys missed the road.
(31) *I did my homework. While my brothers just watched television.

Such mistakes may be due to confusion over the difference between Conjunctive Adjuncts and conjunctions. For example, compare number 31 with the following:

(32) I did my homework. Meanwhile my brothers just watched television.

However, the problem may simply be a failure to understand the rules of punctuation – using a full stop where a comma is required. It is possible to probe whether a learner's problem is with sentence structure or with punctuation by having the learner read aloud the clause sequences in question.

Some languages regularly mark twice the logical relationship between two clauses, once in the dependent clause and once in the independent clause. This can lead to learners producing sentences such as:

(33) *Although they lay fewer eggs but they look after them more carefully.

The use of conjunctions like *although* and *but* together like this does occasionally occur in English, particularly in instances of spoken English where there is a great distance between the beginning of the dependent clause and the independent clause. However, it is regarded as incorrect in written English.

The distinction between finite and nonfinite dependent clauses can also cause problems. A finite dependent clause must have both a Finite and a Subject. To form a nonfinite dependent clause both the Finite and the Subject must be omitted, for example:

(34)   While she was working in Zimbabwe, she developed a great love for the African landscape.

(34) a.   While working in Zimbabwe, she developed a great love for the African landscape.

Learners sometimes produce intermediate forms such as:

(35)   *While she working in Zimbabwe, she . . . .

(36)   *While was working in Zimbabwe, she . . .

A related problem concerns the use of conjunctions and prepositions with finite and nonfinite dependent clauses. Some binding conjunctions can only be used in finite clauses, for example, *as, wherever, because, in order that, so that,* and *as long as*. Other binding conjunctions can be used in both finite and nonfinite clauses, for example, *while, when, since, until, if, unless,* and *although*. Prepositions, such as *in, by, without, despite, in spite of, as a result of,* and *because of* can only be used in nonfinite clauses. Learners sometimes use the wrong combinations, for example:

(37)   *Because living far away from the college, I must get up very early every day.

(38)   *Despite I have studied English for so many years, I find it difficult to understand native speakers.

Nonfinite dependent clauses may have no Subjects, and there are often more restrictions on their positioning than with finite dependent clauses because it must be clear which participant in the independent clause the dependent clause relates to. Learners sometimes produce sentences such as:

(39)   ?While waiting for a bus, a beggar asked me for some money.
(compare: *While I was waiting for a bus, a beggar asked me for some money.*)

Perhaps one of the most difficult problems facing the learner is to develop the sense of when it is best to express two messages as two separate sentences, when to combine them through linking, and when to combine them through binding. As noted previously, the choice is highly context-dependent.

Learners are often given practice in linking and binding by being required to combine separate sentences into one sentence or to transform a linking relationship between two clauses into a binding relationship. Out of context, such exercises are likely to be very mechanical and may do little to enable learners to use the structures appropriately. Alternatively, clauses to be combined can be presented in complete texts, so that the learners have to pay attention to the flow of information to decide where and how to combine clauses. This allows learners to appreciate that the structures are not arbitrary but contribute to the coherence of a text. In general, the structural relationships are best learned along with the *logical* relationships (cause, purpose, time, place, etc.) between clauses. These will be explored in the next section.

Questions for discussion

- Identify any places in the following text where you think the text could be improved by (1) combining clauses which are in separate sentences; (2) separating clauses which are combined; (3) linking clauses instead of binding them; (4) binding clauses instead of linking them.

I have five brothers. My eldest brother is skinny and spunky. He's got a nice face. He is a doctor now but before he was at a Higher College. It is called T. High School. He is very smart at lessons, especially science. My second eldest brother is sometimes very funny. He is not like my biggest brother. He is not very smart but his favorite lesson is math. He is the brother that I love most because he is not smart at school but he is well behaved.

- Suggest some activities that might help the learner who produced this text to more appropriately choose when to link clauses, when to bind them, and when to present them as two separate sentences.

12.3 Logical relationships between clauses

A wide range of logical relationships can hold between structurally related clauses. Following Halliday (1994), these relationships can be classified into three broad types: **elaboration, extension,** and **enhancement.**[3]

12.3.1 Elaboration

One clause may elaborate the message in another clause by restating it in different words, giving more details, being more specific, giving an example, or otherwise clarifying it in some way. Elaboration can be combined with both linking and binding, as the following examples show.

Elaboration and linking

(40) Today we stand at the brink of the Thoughtware Revolution; we've only just begun to assimilate the lessons of the information revolution.
(41) I was surrounded by birds – they were tuis.
(42) Frogs are members of the amphibia group of animals, that is they live on land and water.
(43) It won't take long, actually it can be done in less than five minutes.
(44) There are many obstacles en route, they may for example encounter waterfalls, . . .

Elaboration and binding with finite dependent clause

(45) These are bony growths up to one and a half meters from base to tip, which are used as weapons in fights with other stags during the mating season.
(46) I managed to get two A's and a B, which is not too bad, I reckon.
(47) They also learn how to use a variety of software, which enables them to perform a wider range of tasks.

---

3 Halliday (1994) in fact makes a distinction between expansion – which includes the three categories of elaboration, extension, and enhancement – and projection. This latter term refers to dependent clauses following mental and verbal processes (Section 6.1.5).

Elaboration and binding with nonfinite dependent clause

(48) Heading dogs move sheep quietly, taking them where their master tells them.

(49) . . . thick columns of thunder cloud are formed, creating almost vertical walls.

As the preceding examples show, elaboration combined with linking takes the form of two juxtaposed clauses (sometimes referred to as *apposition*). In writing there may be a semicolon, comma, or dash between the linked clauses. In speech, it is intonation that indicates that two such juxtaposed clauses should be regarded as structurally combined rather than separate sentences, although it is not always clear-cut. In numbers 40 and 41 the precise logical meanings of the elaboration are not explicitly marked. In numbers 42, 43, and 44 the logical meanings are marked by *that is, actually,* and *for example.* Some other markers of elaboration are *in other words, for instance, in particular, in fact,* and *indeed.*

Elaboration combined with binding, where the dependent clause is finite, as in numbers 45, 46, and 47, gives the structure which in traditional grammar is referred to as a *nonrestrictive relative clause* or sometimes a *nondefining relative clause.* The elaboration is sometimes just of one noun group within the independent clause, as in number 45 , and sometimes of a larger part of the clause or of the whole clause, as in numbers 46 and 47. Note that such elaborating clauses are exceptions to the generalization that with binding the sequence of the independent and dependent clauses can be changed.

This kind of elaboration should be distinguished from the defining or restrictive relative clauses (i.e., embedded clauses) looked at in Chapter 3 (Section 3.4.2). The following examples should make this clear:

(50)   My brother, who lives in the U.K., is getting married in June.   [*inv.*]

(50) a. My brother who lives in the U.K. is getting married in June.

In number 50 the elaborating clause *who lives in the U.K.* provides some additional information about *my brother.* The implication is that I have only one brother. In number 50a, the embedded clause serves to identify which of my brothers is being referred to. The implication is that I have other brothers who do not live in the U.K. In speech, a defining relative clause is normally part of the same tone group as the noun group within which it is embedded and there is therefore no pause before it. An elaborating (nondefining relative) clause, however, normally has its own tone group and there may thus be a pause both before and after it. This is usually (but not invariably) reflected in writing by putting commas around the elaborating clause.

12.3.2 Extension

One clause may extend the meaning in another clause by **addition,** glossed as the *and* relationship; by **variation,** glossed as the *instead* relationship; or by **alternation,** glossed as the *or* relationship.

The following sentences exemplify the *addition* type of extension.

Addition and linking

(51) It had caught food on the way and shared it with the dog.
(52) He always preferred classical music but his wife was really into jazz.
(53) They have not learned to read, nor do they have the expectation of delight or improvement from reading.

Addition and binding with finite dependent clause

(54) A LAN is a network over a small geographical area, while a WAN is a number of LANs linked together . . .

Addition and binding with nonfinite dependent clause

(55) Input, storage, retrieval, processing and display (or redissemination) are archival functions, as well as being computer functions.
(56) . . . seeking for enlightenment wherever it is readily available, without being able to distinguish between the sublime and the trash.

Number 51 represents a simple additive relationship. In number 52 there is some contrast between the added information and the information in the first clause, and so the linker *but* is used (in fact, the logical relationship can be conceptualized as *and but*). This relationship is usually described as *adversative.* Number 53 represents a negative additive relationship.

Among the examples of binding, number 56 also represents an adversative relationship, marked by the preposition *without.* However, where the dependent clause is finite, it is hard to draw a line between a simple additive relationship and an adversative relationship (out of context, number 54 could be interpreted either way).

The following sentences are examples of the *variation* and *alternation* types of extension.

Variation and linking

(57) Don't cut the wire, but slice away just enough insulation on each to expose a section of bare wire.

Alternation and linking

(58) You either freeze to death or you burn up.

Variation and binding

(59) They also improve productivity by allowing people to focus on more creative work instead of having to spend lots of time doing the mundane work
. . .

Alternation and binding

(60) If it's not too cold it's too hot!

Note that *but* can be used to mark both an additive or adversative and a
variative relationship.

12.3.3   Enhancement

One clause may enhance the meaning of another clause by providing circumstantial information, including the basic categories of time, space,
means, comparison, cause or reason, purpose, condition, and concession.
Enhancement combined with binding gives what in traditional grammar are
called *adverbial clauses.*

   The following section gives two examples of each of the basic categories
of enhancement, the first as combined with linking and the second as
combined with binding. (There is only one example for purpose, which is
not normally combined with linking.)

Time

(61) It can become an expert in the thought ways of the individual students and
then propose learning levels appropriate to that student.   (*linking*)
(62) While it was cooling they went into the woods in search of sweet
honey.   (*binding*)

Space

(63) Somebody has been lying on my bed - and there she is!   (*linking*)
(64) However, where publishing does become electronic, it will seriously affect
conventional publishing.   (*binding*)

Means

(65) They crawled silently along on their bellies and in that way were able to
get very close to the animals.   (*linking*)
(66) He tells Bob which way to go by whistling and shouting.   (*binding*)

Comparison

(67) We looked to the East for adventure and opportunity and in the same way
they looked to the West.   (*linking*)

(68) It blots the liquid up as a paint brush holds paint. (*binding*)

Cause or reason

(69) How she found her way home we do not know, for she had been brought to our new house by car. (*linking*)
(70) As the air from the upper atmosphere is clear, the eye of the hurricane is typically cloudless and relatively calm. (*binding*)

Purpose

(71) She is studying English so that she can get a white collar job. (*binding*)[4]

Condition (positive)

(72) They may turn us down and in that case we'll just have to start again from scratch. [*inv.*] (*linking*)
(73) If you wish to fit a flush socket in a lath-and-plaster wall try to locate it over a stud or nogging. (*binding*)

Condition (negative)

(74) You'd better return it immediately, otherwise they're likely to accuse you of stealing it. [*inv.*] (*linking*)
(75) Unless they are given explicit instructions, they just sit around on their backsides all day long. (*binding*)

Concession

(76) He knows his stuff alright but doesn't seem to be able to get it across to the students. (*linking*)
(77) There are some attractive tree-lined streets, although most of the trees look pretty bare and scrawny. (*binding*)

Task 12c

Using the categories time, space, means, comparison, cause or reason, purpose, condition (positive and negative), and concession, how would you label the logical relationships between the clauses in the following examples of binding?

1. After they left, a little girl named Goldilocks passed by their house.
2. It doesn't matter whether a cat is black or white so long as it catches mice.

---

4 The logical relationship between two linked clauses such as *she wants to get a white collar job, so she is studying English* could be interpreted as purpose. However, strictly speaking, the logical relationship here is of reason.

3. There will be neither rest nor tranquility in America until the Negro is granted his citizenship rights.
4. Now, whenever I see a tui, I remember my holiday and all those tuis.
5. You can't talk to people because people snap at you.
6. . . . make good the surrounding plaster before you wire and fit the socket.
7. Despite having lived there for over twenty years, all the elderly will have to move away from their familiar home area.
8. A draft in German never gets beyond a superior's in-tray unless translated into English or French.
9. Without their being something essential to the viewer as a moral and religious being, the works lose their essence.
10. . . . the purchaser of our house phoned to ask whether we had lost a cat.
11. Seeing you've come so far, you'd better come in.
12. The Germans, Italians, and Spaniards do not mind playing second fiddle to French – provided English has to as well.

12.3.4   Nonfinite enhancement clauses and Circumstantial Adjuncts

The meanings in context of enhancement clauses and of Circumstantial Adjuncts can be very close. Structurally, too, the dividing line between nonfinite enhancement clauses and Circumstantial Adjuncts is not altogether clear, for example:

(78)   When we arrived at the wharf, we found that the boat had already left.
(78) a. Arriving at the wharf, we found that the boat had already left.
(78) b. On arriving at the wharf, we found that the boat had already left.
(78) c. On arrival at the wharf, we found that the boat had already left.

The underlined units in the preceding examples vary in the extent to which the process is nominalized. Most linguists would agree in regarding numbers 78 and 78a as finite and nonfinite dependent clauses and number 78c as a prepositional phrase (realizing a Circumstantial Adjunct), on the grounds that *arrival* is clearly a noun. Analysis of number 78b depends upon whether one regards it as more like 78a or more like 78c. Following Halliday (1994), structures like 78b have been treated in this chapter as nonfinite clauses, on the grounds that forms like *arriving* are still more verbal than nominal. However, some linguists would prefer to treat all such structures as prepositional phrases. For learners, it does not matter what labels one attaches to these structures, providing that their meanings are clear and that learners know when they can and when they cannot use them (see Section 12.2.4).

12.3.5 Learning and teaching logical relationships between clauses

The fact that the same conjunction or preposition may have different meanings, depending on context, can be a problem. For example:

(79) Goldilocks was hungry, so she decided to eat some of the porridge.
(80) I only went there so I could see what he looks like in the flesh.

In number 79 the logical relationship is of cause, while in number 80, it is of purpose (*that* could be added after *so*). Similarly, in number 81 the logical relationship is of time, in number 82 it is of reason, and in number 83 it is of comparison, although the same conjunction is used in all three sentences.

(81) As our standard of living improves, we may come to look upon more of our wants as needs.
(82) As this air from the upper atmosphere is clear, the eye of the hurricane is clear.
(83) It blots the liquid up as a paint brush holds paint.

It is not likely to be very useful for learners to go through a list of conjunctions one by one and illustrate all their possible meanings. It makes more sense to explore separately the major logical relationships, properly contextualized, establishing the most commonly used realizations for each.

Questions for discussion

- Suggest some activities for practicing finite elaborating clauses (defining relative clauses) that exploit their role in providing additional information.
- Suggest some contexts for practicing (1) enhancement clauses of cause and reason and (2) enhancement clauses of concession.

Summary

1. A complex sentence is a sentence which contains more than one ranking (i.e., nonembedded) clause.
2. Clauses can be independent, with the potential to stand alone, or dependent, normally unable to stand alone and dependent on another clause.
3. Clauses may be in a structural relationship of equality, called linking, or of inequality, called binding. In linking, the clauses must either all be independent clauses or all be dependent clauses. In binding, one clause must be dependent either on an independent clause or on another dependent clause.
4. In linking, clauses may be simply juxtaposed or may be joined by linking conjunctions (e.g., *and, but, or*). In binding, a clause may be

marked as dependent by (a) a binding conjunction (e.g., *if, although, because*), (b) a *wh-* word (e.g., *which, who*), (c) a different word order from an independent clause, or (d) being a nonfinite clause.

5. In binding it is generally easier to change the sequence of the clauses than in linking. The last clause in a complex sentence typically contains the most important information. Part of the motivation for selecting binding rather than linking can be the freedom it gives to arrange clauses in a sequence appropriate to the textual meaning.

6. Logical relationships between clauses can be classified as follows.
   a. *Elaboration.* One clause elaborates the information in another clause by restating it or by clarifying it in some way.
   b. *Extension.* One clause extends the information in another by addition (and), variation (instead), or alternation (or).
   c. *Enhancement.* One clause enhances the information in another by providing circumstantial information such as time, space, means, comparison, cause or reason, condition, and concession.

Key terms introduced

This text	*Alternatives used in the field*
addition	
alternation	
binding	hypotaxis; subordination – this term usually includes embedding
complex sentence	compound and complex sentences
dependent clause	subordinate clause – this term usually includes embedded clauses
elaboration (elaborating clause)	clause in apposition (if an independent clause); nondefining relative clause (if clause is dependent and finite)
enhancement (enhancing clause)	adverbial clause
extension (extending clause)	
independent clause	free clause
linking	parataxis; apposition and coordination
simple sentence	
variation	

Discussion of tasks

Task 12a

1. Linking (of three clauses).
2. Binding – *when she saw the three bears* is a dependent clause marked by the binding conjunction *when.*
3. Binding – *taking them where their master tells them* is marked by being a nonfinite clause.
4. Linking (linked by *but*). Note that the nonfinite clause *to expose a section of bare wire* is embedded within the noun group *enough insulation of each to expose a section of bare wire;* that is, it is not a ranking clause.
5. binding – *where publishing does become electronic* is marked by the *wh*-word *where.*
6. Binding – *although they live in a world in which the most terrible deeds are being performed and they see brutal crime in the streets* are dependent clauses marked by the binding conjunction *although;* these two clauses are themselves in a linking relationship.
7. Binding – *as well as being computer functions* is a dependent clause marked by being nonfinite and by the complex preposition *as well as.*

Task 12b

In this text, the main events of the narrative are represented by independent clauses, which are often linked together in sentences, with the sequence of clauses representing chronological sequences in the story, for example, *he embraced the way of asceticism, became a begging monk called Bodhi Dharma and went to China as a Buddhist missionary.* Dependent clauses in this paragraph contain information about events which take place at the same time as a main event, for example, *vowing never to sleep again in penance for his wild nights of debauchery* and *suddenly stimulated.* They also provide additional circumstantial information relevant to the main events, for example, *when he was meditating* (time), *on waking* (time), *overwhelmed by remorse* (cause), and *passing the place of his sacrifice once more* (time).

Task 12c

1. Time
2. Condition
3. Time (could be interpreted as negative condition)
4. Time
5. Reason

6. Time
7. Concession
8. Negative condition
9. Negative condition
10. Purpose
11. Reason
12. Condition

13 Issues in the learning and teaching of grammar

Grammar has had a bad press over the last couple of decades. This has not prevented language teachers in many parts of the world from continuing to teach grammar, either in ways hallowed by time or in new and interesting ways. And, judging from the number of recent publications dealing with the issue (see, e.g., Dirven 1990; Loschky and Bley-Vroman 1990; Celce-Murcia 1991; Ellis 1993; Odlin 1994; Bygate, Tonkyn, and Williams 1994), there is now a noticeable revival of interest in grammar teaching. However, there remains a widespread uneasiness in the profession about the place of grammar in second language teaching.

13.1 Grammar and communicative language teaching

Since the development of communicative language teaching (CLT) in the mid-1970s, grammar teaching has tended to be associated with a more or less discredited approach to second language teaching (often labeled the structural approach), in which syllabuses consisted of a progression of discrete grammatical items to be mastered one after another and methodology consisted largely of the presentation of rules and example sentences followed by extensive drilling of the grammatical patterns. (For an accessible account of language teaching methodologies before CLT see Richards and Rodgers, 1986.) Such an approach did not, it has been argued, enable learners to use the language to communicate appropriately in real contexts.

There is, of course, always a tendency for a new school to exaggerate the evils of the old school, and some of the criticisms of previous approaches ignored the extent to which many pre-CLT teachers (and some textbooks) did give learners opportunities to use in authentic contexts the structures they had learned. Nevertheless, much of the criticism is valid. The rules of grammar found in many textbooks of the period (and it must be admitted in some currently used textbooks) were often at best half-truths and did little to help learners see how the structures could be used meaningfully in context. This is hardly surprising. Language is an elusive, subtle thing, and as a reader of this book will be aware, any rule one may try to articulate about grammatical items and structures and about how and when they are used is likely to be far too complex to be of direct use to most learners. It is also fair to say that some of the rules of grammar found in textbooks are based on tradition rather than analysis of authentic samples of modern English.[1]

It is also true that the practice exercises in many textbooks of the 1950s, 1960s, and even 1970s typically involved manipulation of sentence-level structures, with little or no context. In some cases, the exercises could be successfully completed without the learners even understanding the meanings of the forms they were manipulating.

In rejecting structural language teaching, CLT drew its theoretical inspiration from linguists such as Halliday (e.g., Halliday 1973) and Hymes (e.g., Hymes 1972), as mediated through applied linguists such as Widdowson (e.g., Widdowson 1978) and Wilkins (e.g., Wilkins 1976). It stressed the development of what Hymes (1972) called *communicative competence,* that is, the ability not just to produce correct sentences, but to know when, where, and with whom to use them. Syllabuses were designed around semantic *notions,* such as time, place, and quantity, and *functions* (that is, communicative uses of language[2]) (see van Ek 1975; Wilkins 1976; and Munby 1978). Within this framework, a methodology was developed consisting of activities designed to maximize opportunities for communication. (See Brumfit 1984 and Nunan 1989 for overviews of such activities.)

For Hymes, grammatical competence was a part of communicative competence, and several scholars closely associated with the development of CLT have continued to stress the relationship between grammar and communication. For example, in an influential paper published in 1980, Canale and Swain included grammatical competence as one of the four types of competence they considered should be included in any definition of proficiency (the other three being sociolinguistic competence, discourse competence, and strategic competence). More recently, Littlewood has written that "communicative language use is only possible . . . by virtue of the grammatical system and its creative potential" (Littlewood 1985: 40); and Widdowson has written that "a proper understanding of the concept of communicative competence would have revealed that it gives no endorsement for the neglect of grammar" (Widdowson 1990: 40).

Nevertheless, for some teachers, the teaching of grammar has come to be seen as at best a minor part of the development of communicative compe-

---

1 This is beginning to change with information from corpus studies beginning to find its way into grammars intended for learners (see, e.g., the *COBUILD English Grammar* (Collins 1990).
2 See Chapter 1 for some discussion of the various meanings of this term.

tence and at worst downright inimical to it. This is no doubt partly due to the association of grammar teaching with the rule plus drilling methodology referred to above. It is also due to a rather odd but quite widespread view of grammar as simply a surface skill – something to do with mere accuracy – that can be polished up once learners have managed to communicate their meanings.[3] This view is bolstered by the persistence of a number of dichotomies in the ESL literature such as form vs. function, form vs. meaning, fluency vs. accuracy, meaning-based instruction vs. form-based instruction, and even communication vs. grammar, all of which suggest that linguistic form on the one hand and meaning, function, and communication on the other are somehow opposed to one other.

13.2 Grammar, meaning, and communication

It may be useful at this point to refer back to the characterization introduced in Chapter 1 of language as a resource for communication, or in Halliday's words, language as "meaning potential" (Halliday 1973). Within this perspective, grammar is seen as a network of interrelated systems. Each system contains a set of options from which the speaker selects according to the meaning he or she wishes to make. The selections the speaker makes from a number of systems are realized simultaneously by grammatical items organized into structures. Thus, for example, the clause *he distributed seeds of the miraculous tree* has selected two-participant (Actor + Goal) action process from the transitivity system, simple past from the tense system, declarative from the mood system, active from the voice system, and unmarked from the theme system.

In order to communicate, we need to be able to (1) represent what it is we want to talk about and to locate it in time, which means selecting appropriate process types, participants, circumstances, and tenses; (2) make the content interpersonally relevant and appropriate, which means selecting appropriate moods, modalities, and polarities; and (3) make the whole message relevant to what has been said previously and to the situational context, which means selecting appropriate thematic organization and appropriate reference. Seen from this perspective, grammar is not an optional add-on to communication. It lies at the very heart of communication.

13.3 Learning how to mean differently

What then of language learning? In his influential study of the early years of first language learning, Halliday coined the phrase *learning how to mean*

3 For an interesting discussion of this point see the introduction to Martha C. Pennington (ed.), *New Ways in Teaching Grammar,* Alexandria: TESOL (1995).

(Halliday 1975). Along similar lines we might characterize second language learning as *learning how to mean differently,* where *differently* is used in two senses – first in the sense of learning how to cast a large number of more or less familiar meanings into different wordings; and second, in the sense of learning to make new meanings in new cultural contexts.

Learning to communicate in a second language involves gaining progressive control over the systems of options in the new language; learning which options to select to make which meanings in which contexts; and mapping the configurations of grammatical functions realizing the options on to one another in structures (as in the example *he distributed seeds of the miraculous tree* given in Section 13.2).

Beginning second language learners may control a few structures, a limited number of lexical items, and perhaps some formulas or unanalyzed chunks, such as *je m'appelle X* ("my name is X"), *que es esto?* ("what is this?"), and *ni hao ma* ("how are you?"). In other words, they are likely to have very limited options for making meanings in particular contexts. A typical strategy such learners use is to generalize one structure for a range of meanings, for example:

Rising intonation for all questions (as in **you go now? *you from where?*)
Imperative mood with an all purpose politeness marker for all directives (as in **please give me book*)
ZERO Referrer for indefinite and definite reference with mass and count nouns (as in **put milk and nut in bowl*)
Simple present (often with a time Adjunct) for all time references (as in **last night I go to cinema with my friend*)
Simple fronting for all types of thematization (as in **my book somebody take*)

Note that the smaller the number of meaning distinctions a learner controls, the more dependent on context his or her language is likely to be, both in terms of understanding and being understood.

As a learner develops greater control over the systems of the grammar, he or she is able to make more delicate distinctions of meaning appropriate for different contexts, for example, to:

Use *wh-* questions and tag questions to request different kinds of information and also to presuppose certain answers
Use different moods and modalities to give directives varying with the speaker's relationship to the addressee, the strength of the request, and the nature of the service requested
Use Referrers to refer to entities not immediately obvious from the context
Use various forms of thematic organization (e.g., passive voice and clefts)

to foreground and background information and make longer stretches of text coherent

In short, learning a second language means gaining progressive control over a new potential for making meanings. This perspective has implications for the general approach we might take to the teaching of grammar, implications which are very consistent with the principles of CLT.

13.4 Grammar teaching and research into language learning

Empirical studies of the ways learners master the grammar of a second language would seem to be the place to look for insights that might inform teaching. And indeed, recent findings in the field of second language acquisition (SLA) are potentially very relevant to pedagogy.

One interesting possibility that has emerged is that learners with different backgrounds (including different mother tongues) all learn certain second language structures according to the same relatively fixed sequence. It has been further suggested that teaching a particular structure will only be of benefit if the learner has reached the stage when he or she is "ready" to learn the structure (Pienemann 1985). While such research is promising, it is difficult at the present stage to apply the findings widely in the classroom. Studies of second language learning sequences have as yet involved only a fairly small number of the possible structural configurations of English grammar. The most commonly cited studies are of the acquisition of morphemes (e.g., Dulay and Burt 1973; Bailey et al. 1974), of negation (e.g., Schumann 1979), of questions (e.g., Butterworth et al. 1979) and of relative (embedded) clauses (e.g., Eckman et al. 1988; Doughty 1991). Furthermore, most of the studies are based upon a notion of grammar as a set of discrete formal rules or grammatical operations that can be "acquired" one after another. Studies of second language learning based on a meaning-based or functional view of grammar are still in their infancy. Second language learning research unfortunately lags behind first language learning research in this respect.

Studies have also tried to determine whether *explicit* grammar teaching can lead to *implicit* knowledge of grammar – in other words, whether explicit grammatical knowledge can be converted through *practice* to the automatization (or routinization) necessary for a speaker to be able to produce an appropriate structure in an appropriate context without delay. In a review of the available evidence, Ellis (1993) concludes that explicit grammar instruction can help learners acquire implicit knowledge, provided that the instruction is directed at features that the learners are ready to acquire. Otherwise it will not succeed.

Once again, however, the research in this area cannot yet provide clear implications for teaching. Most of the relevant studies seem to assume that explicit teaching of grammar involves teaching formal rules at sentence level and often have a definition of "practice" that seems to exclude the use of structures in meaningful activities.[4]

13.5   Methodological options

It is doubtful whether anyone will ever come up with a perfect method for second language teaching, one that will ensure success with every kind of learner in every kind of context. The search for such a method has in fact more or less been abandoned (Richards 1990). Learners are too varied in their reasons for wanting to learn, the amount of time they have available, their levels of motivation, previous learning experiences, maturity, preferred learning styles and strategies, and cultural backgrounds. And learning and teaching contexts are too varied in terms of class size, available resources, opportunities to use the target language outside the classroom, officially prescribed syllabi, and so on.

What can be done is to consider a number of methodological options and their potential advantages and disadvantages in light of the perspective on grammar and grammar learning that has been developed throughout this book. One way of looking at some of the options is set out in Figure 13.1.

13.5.1   Input

Input refers to the samples of language to which learners are exposed and from which they are expected to learn the ways of meaning of the target language.[5]

Mode refers to the ways in which the samples may be presented. In many classrooms, input often comes from coursebooks from which students are asked to read aloud. This may not be an ideal form of input. Reading aloud is itself a skill, and one which would not be a high priority for most learners. It is common for the intended language focus to be obscured by a reader's difficulties with rhythm, intonation, and the pronunciation of individual words. Perhaps more importantly, reading aloud can obscure the differences between spoken and written language. More formal styles of written English are quite inappropriate read aloud. Concomitantly, authen-

---

4 For an accessible discussion of the research and its implications for teaching, see Pica (1992).

5 This is not meant to imply that every time grammar is taught there must be an input stage. For consolidation of features previously introduced, learners may, of course, require only practice.

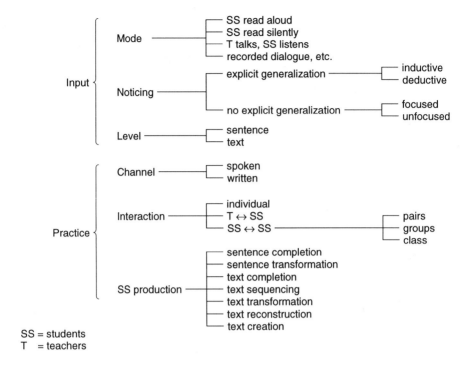

Figure 13.1   Some methodological options in grammar teaching.

tic dialogue is very hard to write, and many textbook dialogues represent a language which is typical neither of spoken language nor of written language. (One notable exception is Slade and Norris 1986.) On the whole it is probably preferable for learners to silently read written text and to listen (without reading) to spoken text in the form of recordings or, if these are not available, to presentations by the teacher. (Some teachers are very skilled at telling stories dramatically, acting out dialogues, and so on.) That said, it must be admitted that some learners greatly enjoy acting out dialogues and can become very good at it.

Level refers to whether the input language consists of isolated sentences or of one or more texts. It will already be apparent that input consisting of texts is generally favored by this author. As we have seen, it is extremely difficult if not impossible to adequately illustrate with just sentence level examples the usage of grammatical systems such as reference, voice, tense, mood, and modality. The texts used need not present lengthy, difficult input. For beginners, a text can be very simple. For example, a simple narrative can be constructed with just three or four sentences, and dialogue can consist of a short interactive exchange.

Noticing refers to activities designed to make learners' attend to grammatical features in the input. This may involve the formulation of *explicit generalizations*. It is still often assumed that such generalizations, or rules, should be given to learners first for them to apply. In other words a *deductive* approach is often used. An alternative to this is an *inductive* approach, in which learners work out the generalizations for themselves from data in the input. Such an approach is favored (although not exclusively) in recent approaches to explicit grammar teaching that have come to be known as *consciousness-raising activities* (see Rutherford 1987 and Fotos and Ellis 1991). Consciousness-raising activities differ from other types of explicit grammar teaching in that they make no claim that the knowledge gained from such activities can become automatized and available for immediate use.[6] A text-based consciousness-raising activity for ergativity (based on two texts looked at in Chapter 5) might proceed as follows.

How Olive Oil Is Made

The olives are first washed in water and then crushed under millstones. The resulting paste is spread on to mats. The mats are stacked up to fifty at a time and pressed under 300 to 400 tons of pressure. The resulting liquid contains oil and water. It is put into tanks and left to settle. The oil rises to the surface.

The Rain Cycle

Water evaporates from seas, rivers and lakes and rises into the air as vapor. As the vapor cools, it condenses into droplets around tiny particles of dust, smoke and salt. It then falls as rain.

1. Students read the two texts and the teacher checks their understanding of the two processes (perhaps using an information transfer technique).
2. The students are asked to compare and describe the finite verb groups in the two texts and, in groups, to try to come up with an explanation for the differences in verb groups between the two texts.
3. Students are given a list of verbs (such as given in Chapter 5, task 5a) and asked to discover which of them can be used in both types of verb group, using a dictionary if necessary.

A more detailed teaching activity using these texts is given in Lock (1995).

Text comparisons of this type can be very useful in consciousness-raising. Other possibilities include (1) comparing expressions of modality in two dialogues or two letters and having students try to reconstruct the likely identities and relationships between the speaker or writer and the addressee and (2) comparing a text consisting entirely of active voice clauses and unmarked themes with a text containing both passive and active

---

6 Some examples of consciousness-raising activities can be found in Pennington (1995).

voice clauses and some thematized Circumstantial Adjuncts and having students decide which text reads best and try to work out why, and so on.

Such activities do, of course, rely on a certain amount of existing knowledge on the part of the learners and a certain level of sophistication. They are generally best suited to relatively advanced learners for making explicit and systematizing their existing knowledge of the grammar and enhancing their ability to monitor and edit their language production.

Other kinds of activities can be designed to focus on features within the input without necessarily leading to the formulation of explicit generalizations by either teacher or students. Information transfer techniques have long been used (particularly in the area of English for specific purposes) for this purpose. The students can transfer information from spoken or written input on to pictures, maps, charts, tables, graphs, flowcharts, and so on in such a way as to focus their attention on specific grammatical features. An example of this from R. V. White's *Teaching Written English* (1980) is reproduced in Figure 13.2. The grammatical feature being focused on in the figure is, of course, passive voice in (manufacturing) process description.

A related technique often used for lower level learners is picture sequencing. For example, the students can be asked to sequence a series of pictures while listening to a narrative. They are then given a list of past tense verb forms and asked to match them with the pictures. The pictures and verbs can then become the scaffolding for the students' oral or written reconstructions of the story. A similar procedure can be used to focus on reference, with the students given a list not of verbs but of noun groups (some having indefinite Referrers, some definite Referrers, and some just pronouns) referring to participants in the story and asked to match them with the appropriate pictures. More examples of information transfer used to focus on grammatical features can be found in White (1980) and McEldowney (1982). Burgess (1994) provides a useful overview of such techniques.

13.5.2 Practice

Practice refers to the learners' use of specific grammatical features in production. Despite reservations about some of the more traditional forms of practice (e.g., decontextualized, sentence level drilling), few language learners or teachers would doubt that substantial practice of the structures of the language is essential for what was referred to earlier as the automatization of grammatical knowledge. Practice typically involves a great deal of repetition of the grammatical feature combined with feedback on performance. However, there is no reason why grammar practice activities should not be meaningful and exploit a range of communicative activities, such as information gap, games, simulations, role play, and so on. Useful collec-

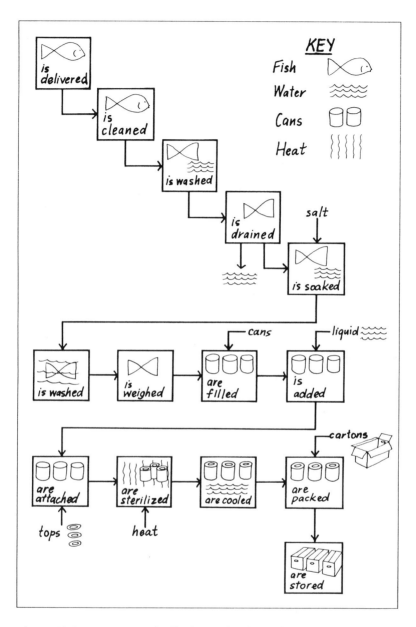

Figure 13.2   A grammatically focused information transfer task.
(White 1980:80.)

tions of grammar practice activities are Ur (1988), Rinvolucri (1984), Frank and Rinvolucri (1987), McKay (1987), and Celce-Murcia and Hilles (1988).

The *channel* for practice can of course be written or spoken (or a combination of the two), and the classroom *interaction* may be individual, teacher with student, or student with student. There is some evidence that the relatively uncontrolled conversation and negotiation of meaning involved in pair work and group work may be beneficial for learning (Long and Porter 1985).

One important variable is the extent of student language *production*. As already mentioned, traditionally, much practice was at the sentence level – sentence completion (e.g., gap-filling exercises and substitution drills), sentence transformation (e.g., changing active to passive voice, declarative mood to interrogative mood, etc.), and occasionally sentence creation (creating sentences from given specifications). Even before the critique of controlled sentence level practice sparked by proponents of communicative language teaching, teachers were aware that many students who learn to successfully complete such exercises remain unable to appropriately use the features practiced. With text level practice (both written and spoken), on the other hand, it is easier to build up strong associations between structures and their meanings in context, which makes it more likely that on later occasions the learners will be able to select appropriate structures in similar contexts.

In *text completion,* students have to pay attention to features of context in order to select appropriate items to complete a text. Some possibilities are:

Filling in short gaps (e.g., with Referrers, focusing on chains of reference)
Selecting between two or more structures at points in the text (e.g., selecting tense, focusing on temporal relationships or selecting voice, focusing on thematic progression)
Choosing between larger chunks of text (e.g., between two paragraphs with different thematic organizations or different Referrers)
Creating larger blocks of text (e.g., expanding a narrative with descriptive background, focusing on relational process clauses and past continuous tense with action processes, or reconstructing the missing half of a dialogue, focusing on mood and appropriate ellipsis).

In *text sequencing,* students have to pay attention to the relationships between grammar and context to sequence out-of-order units (e.g., clauses, sentences, or paragraphs) of a text. This may be particularly useful for focusing on reference and thematic organization, but it can also be used for focusing on sequence of tenses, and, with dialogues, on mood.

Text transformation involves recasting texts for different contexts and communicative purposes, for example:

Rewriting a set of rules or formal commands as friendly advice, focusing on mood and modality

Recasting a spoken explanation by someone about how he or she makes something (*first I strip off the bark,* etc.) as a semitechnical written text about how something is made (*first the bark is stripped off,* etc.), focusing on voice choice.

Text reconstruction is often combined with information transfer. For example, Figure 13.2 is intended to be used as a prompt for the students to reconstruct a text describing the process of fish canning. Similarly, a sequence of pictures matched with appropriate verb groups (as mentioned previously) can be used as prompts for the reconstruction of a narrative. In text reconstruction, grammatical features are the focus of the deconstruction and reconstruction of the text.

In *text creation,* the learners produce complete texts, either collaboratively or individually. An example of this in which the students' production is quite controlled is what is sometimes called *parallel writing.* This begins with work on an input text, focusing on the language features typical of the text type, and leads to the learners creating their own texts of the same type (Raimes 1983).

Questions for discussion

- If you are currently teaching, how would you characterize your usual approach to grammar teaching in terms of the options set out in Figure 13.1? Are there any alternative options that do not appear in the figure?
- If you are not currently teaching, examine a unit in an ESL coursebook. How can it be characterized in terms of the options in Figure 13.1?

13.6   The way forward

As indicated in the first paragraph of this chapter, grammar teaching is now very much on its way back into favor. However, it is important that there should not be a return to some of the practices of the past, which could lead to grammar teaching being again discredited. To avoid this, a number of things have to happen.

- First, teaching needs to be informed by descriptions of grammar which accurately reflect authentic language and show how grammar is a resource for making and exchanging meanings in context. This means that many of the rules of grammar still found in some of the textbooks used by teachers and learners will need to be jettisoned or radically revised, and that information from recent advances in text linguistics and functional linguistics needs to be more widely available and accessible to teachers.

- Second, grammar teaching needs to be integrated into the teaching of speaking, listening, writing, and reading skills. In other words, grammar should be seen as facilitating communication in all modes, not as an isolated area of study exemplified by "the grammar lesson."
- Third, grammar needs to be taught through engaging learners in meaningful and motivating activities.

This book has sought to make a contribution toward such an approach to grammar teaching. The message throughout has been that grammar is not a set of prescriptive rules for creating isolated sentences and therefore it should not be taught as if it were. The systems of grammar have evolved to allow us to talk and write coherently about our experience of the world and of our inner consciousness and to interact with one another as social beings. The teaching of grammar at all levels, therefore, needs to engage directly with the making of experiential, interpersonal, and textual meanings. Only thus can we truly meet the needs of learners of the language.

Appendix

Extract 1

1   The best known of New Zealand's birds is the kiwi, which has become the
symbol of New Zealanders. It's a small, tubby, flightless bird and, because
it is nocturnal, is not easy to observe. Kiwis may have no wings, feathers
that are more like hair than real feathers, short sight and a sleepy nature,
5   but the All Blacks have nothing on them when it comes to strength of leg!
For the kiwi has one thing in common with Australia's "cute" national
symbol, the koala – a shocking temper, which is usually manifested in
giving whatever or whoever it is upset with a thumping big kick. Despite
the fact that the night time is when they are most active, they are still fairly
10 lazy, sleeping for as many as 20 hours a day. The rest of the time they
spend poking around for worms which they sniff out with the nostrils on
the end of their long bill.

(From Wheeler, Tony, *New Zealand: A Travel Survival Kit.*
Victoria, Australia: Lonely Planet, 1985, pp. 14–15.)

Extract 2

1   Monsoon Asia includes those countries which are affected by the MON-
SOON RAINS such as Japan, China, SriLanka and India and South East
Asia including Thailand, Burma, Cambodia, Vietnam, Malaysia, Singapore and Indonesia. The POPULATION DENSITY which is expressed
5   as population over area is as high as 284 per square kilometre in Japan.

Within Monsoon Asia exist numerous MILLIONAIRE CITIES, i.e.
cities with a million people or more. Several exceed 10 million e.g. Shang-
hai and Tokyo.

The population of Monsoon Asia is distributed in ECOLOGICAL
10 NICHES or favoured growing areas, usually on river lowlands, and a large
number of Monsoon Asians live in the countryside.

Examples of these ecological niches include the North China Plain, the
Red River Delta of North Vietnam, the Ganges lowlands of India and the

Plains of Java in Indonesia where densities can reach as high as 100 per
15 km.

Accompanying the rapid rise in population is the process of UR-
BANISATION or city growth.

Monsoon Asia is going through a DEMOGRAPHIC TRANSITION or
population change.

(From Broad, A.E., *Form 5 Geography.*
Auckland: E.S.A. Books, 1986.)

Extract 3

1   In China there is a legend that the Emperor Chen-nung invented tea in the
year 2374 BC by accident. One summer's day he stopped in the shade of a
shrub and put water to boil to refresh himself (hot water is more refreshing
than iced water). A slight breeze plucked several leaves from the tree.
5   They fell into the boiling water. Chen-nung did not notice until he breathed
in the subtle aroma of the miraculous brew as he raised it to his mouth to
drink.

In India, however, a legend goes as follows:

Long, long ago there lived a prince called Darma. After a wild youth, he
10 embraced the way of asceticism, became a begging monk called Bodhi
Dharma and went to China as a Buddhist missionary, vowing never to
sleep again in penance for his wild nights of debauchery. For years his
faith helped him to keep his vow, but one day, when he was meditating on
the slopes of the Himalayas, the sleep so long postponed overcame him.
15 On waking, overwhelmed by remorse for breaking his word, he cut off his
eyelids, buried them and set off again, tears mingling with the blood on his
face. Years later, passing the place of his sacrifice once more, he saw an
unknown bush on the spot. He picked the leaves and steeped them in the
hot water which was his only nourishment. After the first mouthful, his
20 weariness was gone and his spirit, suddenly stimulated, attained the greatest heights of knowledge and beauty.

Continuing on his way, he distributed seeds of the miraculous tree as he
passed. Ever since, monks have drunk tea to aid their meditation.

(From Toussaint-Samat, Maguelonne. *History of Food.*
(Anthea Bell *trans.*) Blackwell: Cambridge, Mass., 1992.)

Extract 4

1   Yixing is a small town in Jiangnan to the south of the Yangzi River. The
town is set in beautiful surroundings. A branch of the Yangzi winds its way
peacefully through its centre and in spring, the green hills which ring the
town are covered with colourful flowers.

5   The story takes place in the middle of the third century A.D. during the early years of the Jin dynasty. For many years the people of Yixing had lived peaceful and happy lives. They worked hard to earn an honest living. Some fished in the waters of the river whilst others farmed the fertile lands along the banks.

10   However, the days of peace were now no more. People lived in daily fear of three evils.

The first evil was a man-eating tiger which lived in the mountains to the south of Yixing. It attacked wood-cutters and travellers through the mountains. Soon nobody dared to go into the mountains. The few wood-cutters

15   who did do so in order to earn their living never returned. At night the door of every house was shut tight and the small children were too frightened even to cry.

At about the same time, a huge sea-serpent over twenty feet long appeared at the bridge across the river. This was Yixing's second evil. With a

20   quick movement of its tail, the sea-serpent would overturn fishing boats and swallow alive everyone on board. Fishermen soon stopped fishing in the river and people living on opposite sides of the river lost contact with one another. This second evil was even worse than the first.

The third evil was a man named Zhou Chu. He was unusually strong

25   and he used his strength to bully the ordinary people of Yixing so that they came to regard him as the greatest of the three evils.

The beautiful town of Yixing had become a frightening place to live in. No one knew when one of the three evils might attack him.

(From Lock, G. (ed.), *The Three Evils of Yixing.*
Singapore: Singapore Book Emporium, 1979, p. 2.)

Extract 5

1   The tools with which a river excavates its valleys are the boulders and the sand that it sweeps along with it. The constant bumping and rubbing of these materials on the river bed wear it down and as the river surges from side to side, the walls become undermined, slabs of rock break off and fall

5   into the river, and the gorge is widened as well as deepened. The action is slow by human standards but it goes on year after year, century after century, aeon after aeon, and the result is the network of valleys that diversify the face of the earth and the stupendous quantity of waste that the rivers carry down to the sea. It is reckoned that the discharge of rock by the

10   Mississippi is equivalent to the lowering of the surface of its entire drainage basin by about a foot every 4,000 years.

(From Shand, S. J. 1938. *Earth Lore: Geology without Jargon.* As
adapted in L. D. Leet and F. Leet (eds.) 1961. *The World of Geology.*
New York: McGraw-Hill, pp. 200–201.)

Extract 6

1	Pupil:	Me, me.
	Teacher:	It's P_____'s. This looks to me as if it is a picture where someone is being kind and saying. . . . What is the person saying to this one, P_____?
5	Pupil:	He said go away.
	Teacher:	What's this one saying to this one, P_____? P_____, have you got your piece of paper to write it on?
	Pupil:	No.
	Teacher:	You have haven't you? Well you can finish that and when you've
10		written it on your piece of paper I'm going to write it on the special plastic stuff. Would you go off and finish colouring yours please. See these bits here? Make it really nice 'cos that's gonna be a lovely picture.
		Who's your partner P_____?
15	Pupil:	R_____
	Teacher:	This is going to go on the wall. This is a lovely one too. Whose is this?
	Pupil:	L_____.
	Teacher:	Beautiful L_____. There you are, L_____, go and finish it.
20		L_____, don't write on this. Leave that. Mrs S_____ will write on there. I'll give you your paper to write on to do a story about this. I will copy your story, L_____, on to here. OK? There you go. (Gives paper to pupil.) Who was your partner, L_____?
25	Pupil:	He hasn't got one.
	Teacher:	Well he doesn't seem to be . . . This is beautiful. S_____, who did it with you? This is lovely but look you boys have to go over and colour it in really nice, this is scribbly. You make it beautiful. Colour in very carefully, press hard. No writing there.
30		Finish your story and then I will write in here for you. Then you do your reading jobs. Off you go.
		That's lovely. This is beautiful. Whose is it?
	Pupil:	M_____.
	Pupil:	No.
35	Pupil:	K_____'s.
	Pupil:	Ours.
	Pupil:	And yours.
	Pupil:	No.
	Teacher:	That's . . .
40	Pupil:	Yes.
	Teacher:	That's beautiful. You two have finished. You've . . . all you've got to do is your story. Then reading jobs. Whose is this one?

Pupil: P_____.
Teacher: Yours, P_____?
45 Pupil: No.
Teacher: Who were you working with? Can you colour that sky in nicely?
         Colour these little birds beautifully and make some bigger peo-
         ple down here and then write your story on the paper because I
         want to . . . R_____, this is yours and M_____'s. I want
50   you to do another big person because you've done little wee
         people and I can't see them. So could you do a big person there
         (holds up another picture). Would you finish colouring them in?
Pupil: Yah.
Teacher: And finish your story.
55 Pupil: This is my story, this my story.
Pupil: What do we do? What do we do? What do we do?
Teacher: Who's your partner? Go and ask her.
Pupil: She doesn't know either.
Teacher: Yes she does. O_____, lovely work.
60 Pupil: That's M_____, M_____.
Teacher: You will wait. I'll find some paper for you.
(From Nissanga, Thilani. *A Study of Verbal Classroom Interaction at
Primary Level.*
Unpublished Diploma in ELT Project, English Department,
University of Auckland.)

Extract 7

1   The problems of interpretation cluster around two issues: the nature of
    reality and the nature of measurement. Philosophers of science have lat-
    terly been busy explaining that science is about correlating phenomena or
    acquiring the power to manipulate them. They stress the theory-laden
5   character of our pictures of the world and the extent to which scientists are
    said to be influenced in their thinking by the social factors of the spirit of
    the age. Such accounts cast doubt on whether an understanding of reality is
    to be conceived of as the primary goal of science or the actual nature of its
10 achievement. These comments from the touchline may well contain points
    of value about the scientific game. They should not, however, cause us to
    neglect the observations of those who are actually players. The over-
    whelming impression of the participants is that they are investigating the
    way things are. Discovery is the name of the game. The payoff for the
15 rigours and longeurs of scientific research is the consequent gain in under-
    standing of the way the world is constructed. Contemplating the sweep of
    the development of some field of science can only reinforce that feeling.
    (From Polkinghorne, John. *The Quantum World.* London and New
    York: Longman, 1984, pp. 1–2.)

Extract 8

1   Pira Sudham, in a remote village in Buriram Province, a part of Thailand's arid north-eastern region near the Kampuchean border, has become firmly established as one of Thailand's best known writers and novelists. Yet to call Pira simply a "Thai novelist" would be both misleading and an over-

5   simplification. It is true that Pira is indeed a Thai citizen, and he would be the last to deny his close relationship with, and affection for, his beautiful kingdom. Yet Pira is more than just a "Thai novelist" in that his first language, his formative experiences, and perhaps his first love, are Lao – the language of the great majority of Thailand's Esarn people, to whom

10 Pira owes his origins, inspiration, and to whom he now devotes much of his energies and time.

. . .

Pira Sudham was born to a rice-farming family in impoverished, rural Esarn, northeast Thailand. He made his way to Bangkok at the age of fourteen to serve the monks as a temple boy, an acolyte, in a Buddhist

15 temple. His departure from his village is similar to that of thousands of young boys from rural areas of Thailand to find lodging and food in order to be able to attain higher education.

"If I had not left my village then, I would have been another peasant. I would have been subject, like most villagers, to the mercy of nature:

20 floods, drought, disease, ignorance and scarcity. With endurance, I would have accepted them as my own fate, as something I cannot go against in this life," says Pira.

(From foreword to Sudham, Pira. *Monsoon Country,* 5th edition.
Bangkok: Shire Books, 1989: 7–8.)

References

Andersen, M. L. 1991. Education as a process of change. In B. B. Hess, E. W. Markson, and P. J. Stein (eds.), *Sociology.* New York: Macmillan.

Bailey, N., C. Madden, and S. Krashen. 1974. Is there a "natural sequence" in adult second language learning? *Language Learning* 24: 235–244.

Barcan, Alan, Dwight Blunden, and Stephen Stories. 1972. *Before Yesterday: Aspects of European History to 1789.* Melbourne: Macmillan.

Bateman, J., C. M. I. M. Mattiessen, K. Nanri, and L. Zeng. 1991. Mutilingual text generation: an architecture based on functional typology. *Proceedings of International Conference on Current Issues in Computational Linguistics,* Penang, Malaysia.

Bloom, Allan. 1987. *The Closing of the American Mind.* London: Penguin.

Brown, Jules. 1992. *Barcelona and Catalunya: The Rough Guide.* London: Brown, Harrap, Columbus.

Brumfit, C. 1984. *Communicative Methodology in Language Teaching.* Cambridge: Cambridge University Press.

Burgess, J. 1994. Ideational frameworks in integrated language learning. *System* 22, 3: 309–318.

Butterworth, G., and E. Hatch. 1978. A Spanish-speaking adolescent's acquisition of English syntax. In Hatch, E. (ed.), *Second Language Acquisition.* Rowley, Mass.: Newbury House, pp. 231–245.

Bygate, M., A. Tonkyn, and E. Williams (eds.). 1994. *Grammar and the Language Teacher.* Hemel Hempstead: Prentice Hall.

Campbell, G. L. 1991. *Compendium of the World's Languages.* London: Routledge.

Celce-Murcia, M. 1991. Grammar pedagogy in second and foreign language teaching. *TESOL Quarterly.* 25, 3: 459–479.

Celce-Murcia, M., and S. Hillies. 1988. *Techniques and Resources in Teaching Grammar.* Oxford: Oxford University Press.

Celce-Murcia, M., and D. Larsen-Freeman. 1983. *The Grammar Book: An ESL/EFL teacher's course.* Rowley, Mass.: Newbury House.

Christie, Francis, et al. 1992. *Language: A resource for meaning. Exploring explanations, Levels 1–4; Teachers' Book.* Marrickville, NSW, London, and Orlando, Fla.: Harcourt Brace Jovanovich.

Churchill, Caryl. 1990. Top Girls. In *Plays: Two.* London: Methuen.

Collins. 1990. *COBUILD English Grammar.* London and Glasgow: Collins.

Collins. 1987. *COBUILD English Language Dictionary.* London and Glasgow: Collins.

Comrie, B. (ed.). 1987. *The World's Major Languages.* London: Croom Helm.

Crewe, W. J. 1977. *Singapore English and Standard English: Exercise in Awareness.* Singapore: Eastern Universities Press.

Dirven, R. 1990. Pedagogical grammar (state of the art article). *Language Teaching 23:* 1–18.

Dolamore, Anne. 1989. *The Essential Olive Oil Companion.* Topsfield, Mass.: Salem House.

Doughty, C. 1991. Second language instruction does make a difference: Evidence from an empirical study of SL relativization. *Studies in Second Language Acquisition* 13, 3: 431–470.

Duguid, A. 1987. Italian speakers. In M. Swan and B. Smith (eds.), *Learner English: A Teacher's Guide to Interferences and Other Problems.* Cambridge: Cambridge University Press, pp. 58–71.

Dulay, H., and M. Burt. 1973. Should we teach children syntax? *Language Learning* 23: 245–258.

Dyson, John. 1993. A new Europe dawns. *Reader's Digest,* January 1993.

Eckman, F., L. Bell, and D. Nelson. 1988. On the generalization of relative clause construction in the acquisition of English as a second language. *Applied Linguistics* 9: 1–20.

Eggins, S., P. Wignell, and J. R. Martin. 1987. The discourse of history: Distancing the recoverable past. In *Working Papers in Linguistics 5: Writing Project – Report 1987.* Sydney: Department of Linguistics, University of Sydney. Republished in M. Ghadessy (ed.), *Register Analysis: Theory and Practice.* London: Pinter, 1993, pp. 75–109.

Ellis, R. 1993. The structural syllabus and second language acquisition. *TESOL Quarterly 27,* 1: 91–113.

Fotos, S., and R. Ellis. 1991. Communication about grammar: A task-based approach. *TESOL Quarterly 25,* 4:605–628.

Frank, C., and M. Rinvolucri. 1987. *Grammar in Action Again: Awareness Activities for Language Learning.* London: Prentice Hall.

Fries, C. 1981. On the status of theme in English: arguments from discourse. *Forum Linguisticum 6,* I: 1–38. Republished in J. S. Petofi and E. Sozer (eds.), *Micro and Macro Connectivity of Texts.* Hamburg: Helmut Buske Verlag, 1983, pp. 116–152.

Grant, N. 1987. Swahili speakers. In M. Swan and B. Smith (eds.), *Learner English: A Teacher's Guide to Interferences and Other Problems.* Cambridge: Cambridge University Press, pp. 194–211.

Green, J. H. 1987. Spanish. In B. Comrie (ed.), *The World's Major Languages.* London: Croom Helm, pp. 236–311.

Halliday, M. A. K. 1994. *An Introduction to Functional Grammar.* (2nd ed.). London: Edward Arnold.

Halliday, M. A. K. 1989. *Spoken and Written Language.* Oxford: Oxford University Press.

Halliday, M. A. K. 1978. *Language as Social Semiotic.* London: Edward Arnold.

Halliday, M. A. K. 1975. *Learning How to Mean: Explorations in the Development of Language.* London: Edward Arnold.

Halliday, M. A. K. 1973. *Explorations in the Functions of Language.* London: Edward Arnold.

Halliday, M. A. K., and J. R. Martin. 1993. *Writing Science: Literacy and Discursive Power.* London: The Falmer Press.

Hymes, D. H. 1972. On communicative competence. In J. B. Pride and J. Holmes (eds.), *Sociolinguistics.* Harmondsworth: Penguin, pp. 269–293.

Jackson, H. 1985. *Discovering Grammar.* Oxford: Pergamon.

Kaye, A. S. 1987. Arabic. In B. Comrie (ed.), *The World's Major Languages.* London: Croom Helm, pp. 664–685.

Lang, J. F. 1986. *Tastings: The Best from Ketchup to Caviar.* New York: Crown.

Littlewood, W. 1985. Learning grammar. *Institute of Language in Education Journal 1,* 1: 40–48.

Lock, G. 1995. Doers and causers. In M. C. Pennington (ed.), *New Ways in Teaching Grammar.* Alexandria, Va: TESOL, pp. 129–133.

Long, M. H., and P. Porter. 1985. Group work, interlanguage talk, and second language acquisition. *TESOL Quarterly* 19: 317–334.

Longman Dictionary of Contemporary English. 1978. London and New York: Longman.

Loschky, L., and R. Bley-Vroman. 1990. Creating structure-based communication tasks for second language development. *University of Hawai'i Working Papers in ESL 9,* 1: 161–212.

MacWhinney, B., E. Bates., and R. Kliegl. 1984. Cue validity and sentence interpretation. In *Journal of Verbal Learning and Verbal Behaviour 23:* 127–150.

Martin, J. R. 1993. Genre and literacy – modelling context in educational linguistics. *Annual Review of Applied Linguistics 13:* 141–172.

Martin, J. R. 1992. *English Text: System and Structure.* Amsterdam: Benjamins.

Martin, J. R. 1985. *Factual Writing: Exploring and Challenging Social Reality.* Geelong, Victoria: Deakin University Press.

Martyn, John, Peter Vickers, and Mary Feeney (eds.). 1990. *Information UK 2000.* London: British Library.

Matthiessen, Christian (in press). *Lexicogrammatical Cartography.* Tokyo, Taipei, and Dallas: International Language Science Publishers.

McEldowney, P. L. 1982. *English in Context.* Walton-on-Thames: Nelson.

McKay, S. L. 1987. *Teaching Grammar: Form, Function, and Technique.* London: Prentice Hall.

Monk, B., and A. Barak. 1987. Russian speakers. In M. Swan and B. Smith (eds.), *Learner English: A Teacher's Guide to Interference and Other Problems.* Cambridge: Cambridge University Press, pp. 117–128.

Munby, J. 1978. *Communicative Syllabus Design.* Cambridge: Cambridge University Press.

Murdoch, F. November 17, 1992. New VTC facilities widen study horizons. *South China Morning Post.*

Newman, J. n.d. *Workbook in Southeast Asian Linguistics.* Singapore: Regional Language Centre.

Nguyen, D. H. 1987. Vietnamese. In B. Comrie (ed.), *The World's Major Languages.* London: Croom Helm, pp. 777–796.

Nicholson, Louise. 1992. Rebirth in Beaujolais. *Condé Nast Traveler,* August 1992.

Nunan, D. 1989. *Designing Tasks for the Communicative Classroom.* Cambridge: Cambridge University Press.

Odlin, T. (ed.). 1994. *Perspectives on Pedagogical Grammar.* Cambridge: Cambridge University Press.

Pennington, M. C. (ed.). 1995. *New Ways in Teaching Grammar.* Alexandria, Va.: TESOL.

Pica, T. 1992. Language learning research and classroom concerns. *English Teaching Forum 30,* 2: 2–9.

Pienemann, M. 1985. Learnability and syllabus construction. In K. Hylstenstam and M. Pienemann (eds.), *Modelling and Assessing Second Language Acquisition.* Clevedon, England: Multilingual Matters.

Prentice, P. J. 1987. Malay (Indonesian and Malaysian). In B. Comrie (ed.), *The World's Major Languages.* London: Croom Helm, pp. 913–935.

Raimes, A. 1983. *Techniques in Teaching Writing.* Oxford: Oxford University Press.

Richards, J. C. 1990. Beyond Methods. chap. 3, *The Language Teaching Matrix.* Cambridge: Cambridge University Press.

Richards, J. C., and T. S. Rodgers. 1986. *Approaches and Methods in Language Teaching: Description and Analysis.* Cambridge: Cambridge University Press.

Rinvolucri, M. 1984. *Grammar Games: Cognitive, Affective and Drama Activities for EFL Students.* Cambridge: Cambridge University Press.

Rothery, J. 1993. *Literacy in School English.* Erskinville, NSW: Metropolitan East Region Disadvantaged Schools Program (Write It Right).

Rothery, J. 1986. Teaching writing in the primary school: A genre based approach to the development of writing abilities. In *Working Papers in Linguistics 4.* Sydney: Department of Linguistics, University of Sydney.

Rothery, J. 1984. The development of genres – Primary to junior secondary school. In F. Christie (ed.), *Children Writing* (ECT418 Language Studies). Geelong, Victoria: Deakin University Press.

Rutherford, W. E. 1987. *Second Language Grammar: Learning and Teaching.* London and New York: Longman.

Schumann, J. 1979. The acquisition of English negation by speakers of Spanish: A review of the literature. In R. W. Andersen (ed.), *The Acquisition and Use of Spanish and English as First and Second Languages.* Washington D.C.: TESOL.

Scott, F. S., C. C. Bowley, C. S. Brockett, J. G. Brown, and P. R. Goddard. 1968. *English Grammar: A Linguistic Study of Its Classes and Structures.* Auckland: Heinemann.

Sheehan, Neil. 1989. *A Bright Shining Lie: John Paul Vann and America in Vietnam.* New York: Vintage.

Shibatani, M. 1987. Japanese. In B. Comrie (ed.), *The World's Major Languages.* London: Croom Helm, pp. 855–870.

Slade, D. M., and L. Norris. 1986. *Teaching Casual Conversation.* Adelaide: National Curriculum Resources Centre.

Swan, M., and B. Smith (eds.). 1987. *Learner English: A Teacher's Guide to Interference and Other Problems.* Cambridge: Cambridge University Press.

Trimble, L. 1985. *English for Science and Technology: A Discourse Approach.* Cambridge: Cambridge University Press.

United States Travel and Tourism Administration. *U.S. Travel Information.*

Ur, P. 1988. *Grammar Practice Activities.* Cambridge: Cambridge University Press.

van Ek, J. 1975. *The Threshold Level in a European Unit/Credit System for Modern Language Learning by Adults.* Strasbourg: Council for Cultural Cooperation of the Council of Europe.

Vidal, Gore. 1993. *Creation.* London: Abacus.

White, R. V. 1980. *Teaching Written English.* London: Heinemann.

Whitlock, Ralph. 1992. Incredible journeys. *Guardian Weekly,* September 6.

Widdowson, H. G. 1990. *Aspects of Language Teaching.* Oxford: Oxford University Press.

Widdowson, H. G. 1978. *Teaching Language as Communication.* Oxford: Oxford University Press.

Wilkins, D. A. 1976. *Notional Syllabuses.* Oxford: Oxford University Press.

Acknowledgments

The author and publisher would like to thank the following for permission to reproduce copyrighted material:

Page 103, from *Top Girls* by Caryl Churchill. Copyright 1990. Reprinted by permission of Methuen Drama. Page 226, from Rebirth in Beaujolais by Louise Nicholson. In *Condé Nast Traveler,* August 1992. Copyright Louise Nicholson. Reprinted by permission. Page 274, Figure 13.2, from *Teaching Written English* by R. V. White. Copyright 1980. Reprinted by permission of Heinemann Publishers (Oxford), Ltd. Page 278, from *New Zealand: A Travel Survival Kit* by Tony Wheeler. Copyright 1985. Reprinted by permission of Lonely Planet Publications Pty. Ltd. Pages 278–279, from *Form 5 Geography* by A. E. Broad. Copyright 1986. Reprinted by permission of E.S.A. Publications. Page 279, from *History of Food* by M. Touissaint-Samat (trans. Anthea Bell). Copyright 1992. Reprinted by permission of Blackwell Publishers. Page 282, from *The Quantum World* by John Polkinghorne. Copyright 1984. Reprinted by permission of the Longman Group. Page 283, from foreword to *Monsoon Country,* 5th ed., by Pira Sudham. Copyright 1989. Reprinted by permission of Shire Books.

Every effort has been made to trace the owners of copyrighted material in this book. We would be grateful to hear from anyone who recognizes their copyrighted material and who is unacknowledged. We will be pleased to make the necessary corrections in future editions of this book.

Index